The Wisdom of Money

The Wisdom of Money

Pascal Bruckner

TRANSLATED FROM THE FRENCH
BY STEVEN RENDALL

Harvard University Press
CAMBRIDGE, MASSACHUSETTS
LONDON, ENGLAND
2017

First printing

First published as *La Sagesse de l'Argent*
© Éditions Grasset & Fasquelle, 2016.

Book design by Dean Bornstein

Library of Congress Cataloging-in-Publication Data
Names: Bruckner, Pascal, author.
Title: The wisdom of money / Pascal Bruckner ; translated from the French
by Steven Rendall.
Other titles: Sagesse de l'argent. English
Description: Cambridge, Massachusetts : Harvard University Press, 2017. |
"First published as La Sagesse de l'Argent © Éditions Grasset & Fasquelle,
2016."—Title page verso | Includes bibliographical references and index.
Identifiers: LCCN 2016044101 | ISBN 9780674972278 (alk. paper)
Subjects: LCSH: Money—Philosophy. | Money—Social aspects. |
Money—Moral and ethical aspects.
Classification: LCC HG220.3 .B7813 2017 | DDC 306.3—dc23
LC record available at https://lccn.loc.gov/2016044101

To my Tutsie

No one has condemned wisdom to poverty. . . .
I will scorn the entire domain of fortune,
but I shall select the better part of it,
if a choice be given me.

SENECA

Contents

Translator's Note

Quotations of works that first appeared in English are given, so far as possible, in their original form. Unless otherwise noted, all translations into English of quotations originating in other languages are my own. Quotations from the Bible cite the Revised Standard Version of the Bible, copyright © 1946, 1952, and 1971 the Division of Christian Education of the National Council of the Churches of Christ in the United States of America. Used by permission. All rights reserved.

I would like thank Lisa Neal for her careful reading and many suggestions for the improvement of this translation.

The Wisdom of Money

Introduction: Lenin's Wishes

In 1921, in a rare moment of lyricism, Vladimir Ilyich Lenin made the following promise to proletarians: he would have golden toilets made for everyone as soon as communism achieved world domination, once this metal had been deprived of all value. This was a twofold symbol. The most trivial places of communist society would henceforth be as luxurious as the palaces of the bourgeoisie. But above all, the working class would be relieved of the very incarnation of human rapacity—that accursed money, whose connections with anality had been underlined by Freud. Socialism would outdo capitalism at the same time that it disqualified it. A piquant detail: in 2013, the American celebrity Kim Kardashian and her husband, the rapper Kanye West, had gold-plated toilets installed in their house in Los Angeles at the modest cost of just over half a million dollars. $550,000. Lenin had been heard, though not necessarily by those whom he had addressed.

Money is one of those things that seem obvious but aren't. It is truly the commoner of life, as crude as it is burdensome. It seems to go without saying but remains a mystery in broad daylight. The French word for money ("argent") is marvelously ambiguous: it also stands for the silver long used to make coins. Nothing can be said about money without asserting the contrary: that it is vulgar and noble, fiction and reality. It separates and connects people; it frightens us when there is a lot of it and frightens us when there is a lack of it. It's a good that does evil, an evil that does good. The first coins, historians tell us, date from the third millennium

BCE in Ur, and were struck with the image of Ishtar, the goddess of fertility and death, a curious duality.[1] Money is the universal pidgin par excellence, comprehensible everywhere; anyone can manipulate it, no matter what his language or religion; everyone can convert it instantaneously, in the depths of the desert as well as in the most remote islands.

Money implies, first of all, confidence. In Rome, the first coins were connected with their owners and the credit they enjoyed. Today, disconnected from the gold standard, their value varies with the economic health of the nations that issue them. They are imbued with an aura of sacredness, because they incarnate a people or a precise community. Money features in two kinds of stories: those of the oppressors who crush the forsaken by financial means, and those of the oppressed who free themselves thanks to financial independence. In one case, it is a power that enslaves; in the other, a force that liberates. That is its ambiguity: when it is condemned, we want to defend it; when it is defended we want to attack it. Like sex, it is overflowing with meaning, giving rise to countless synonyms that never really designate what it is: bread, lettuce, gravy, jack, loot, moola, scratch, portraits of dead presidents. And this is true in all languages.

It is not only a unit of exchange and a receptacle of value, but above all a barometer of our desires. The measure of all passions, it has become the absolute passion in which all the others are reflected. Contrary to the commonplace about its making the world uniform, we have colored it with our many affects. The vices with which it is associated—cupidity, envy, avarice—existed before it, but in each case it seems to amplify them. The enthusiasms as well as repulsions that it arouses are themselves symptomatic. What is fascinating about it is its status as a creation that has escaped its creator's grasp and turned on him, a discreet offshoot turned into a mad tyrant.

To talk about money is always to talk about oneself. I was spared the injury of poverty; after a difficult youth my parents achieved a degree of affluence before sinking into debt. They began to count their pennies, and endured the bitterness of losing their social status. Death came to them when they were in a state of near destitution. So far as I was concerned, I moved from a careless indigence while I was a student to an intermittent prosperity. For a long time, I didn't worry about money, certain that luck would always be generous to me, and that the royalties derived from my writing were not a salary but a gift. Money offers the only truly precious value in this world: time, its inexhaustible abundance. In this respect it is liberating. When money is lacking, life is reduced to an eternal present that incarcerates us. I have always distinguished between my job and the reasons for existing. The two have sometimes coincided, but for all that without relieving me of the necessity of earning a living.

I recall with nostalgia that period; it was a time, lasting until I was in my forties, in which I considered money negligible. If there was some, that was good; if there was none, one got along. A marvelous nonchalance allowed me to consider material problems unimportant so long as I could explore the world, broaden my horizons, escape platitudes. It was a happy youth that lasted a long time, when the dividing line ran not between the necessary and the superfluous, but between the necessary and the essential. Among the essentials: the mysticism of the book, travel to Asia and India, feverish discussions, political commitments, demanding friendships, unusual experiences, multiple love affairs, and especially the opportunity to live my passion for writing. I like to think that money became a concern only with age, with the fear of not having enough of it in a society that has made it its center, with the end of the lyrical years and the Cold War, in the wake of the Thatcher and Reagan conservative revolution that forced Western culture to sober up and shift to more materialistic celebrations of tangible reality. It is a shift that is fading as we see once again different worldviews coming into violent confrontation.

Getting old means slipping into the order of calculation, into the order of the account balance. Everything becomes limited for us, days number fewer. Time is no longer a profusion, it becomes a reprimand. For me, however, the supreme luxury, even today, is not to own beautiful cars, big apartments, or vacation homes, but rather to be able to prolong the student life into an advanced age. A student's life is one of daily improvisation, a taste for wandering the streets, long hours in a cafe, a flaunted detachment, indifference to honors and emoluments, and the symbolic trinkets with which people like to deck themselves to ward off the passing years. In sum, it is the absurd but necessary illusion of beginning a new life every morning. In such a life, if I feel privileged, it's because I have invented that privilege for myself. Being neither the heir to a fortune nor a financier, I have never been rich enough to forget money or poor enough to neglect it.

Money is therefore a promise in search of wisdom. This should be understood in two senses: it is wise to have money, and wise to reflect critically on it. Money forces us constantly to arbitrate between our desires, our assets, and our debts. It makes everyone a philosopher in spite of himself: thinking well is also learning to spend well, for oneself and for others. Money is revealing: it exposes the tightwad and the profligate, the miserly and the envious, all betrayed by how they reach into their pockets. No one is at ease with money. Those who believe they detest it secretly worship it. Those who worship it overestimate it. Those who pretend to despise it are lying to themselves. A problematic passion, an impossible condemnation. That is the difficulty. But if wisdom does not consist in attacking the very thing we all recognize as the height of folly, what good is philosophy?

PART I

The Worshippers and the Despisers

ONE

The Devil's Dung

No one can serve two masters; for either he will hate the one and love the other, or he will be devoted to the one and despise the other. You cannot serve God and mammon.

MATTHEW 6:24

MONEY begins with the fearful and astonishing range of its invention. Anything serves as a vehicle for it: metals, shells, salt (whence the word "salary"), livestock ("pecuniary" comes from the Latin *pecus,* ox, just as "rupee" goes back to a Sanskrit root that also means livestock).[1] But this plasticity is full of dangers. The story of the Golden Calf, a symbol of materialism shared by all three monotheistic faiths, illustrates its power to mislead. When Moses had been gone for forty days to receive the Tablets of the Law on Mount Sinai, his people, who had just fled Egypt, began to doubt. They said to Moses's brother Aaron: "Up, make us gods, who shall go before us." All the gold rings that were in the ears of their wives, sons, and daughters were collected and melted down to make a statue of a calf. Then the Hebrews bowed down before it and offered sacrifices. When Moses came down from the mountain and saw his people dancing around the beast, he grew very angry and threw the tablets from his hands and broke them (Exodus 32:1–19). Thus the golden idol arises from impatience with the absence of the divine; humans, feeling abandoned, create a substitute for God that turns them away from him. Ironically, when the British artist Damien Hirst made a sculpture in 2008 called *The Golden Calf,* it was sold at auction for 10.3 million pounds sterling. A fine example of postmodernist rebellion: the denunciation of the Golden Calf becomes a new way of getting rich and amassing millions!

The Nuptials of Abundance and Poverty

In Greek mythology, Plutus is the god of wealth who, having offended Zeus, was blinded and left to distribute his favors arbitrarily. In Aristophanes's comedy *Plutus,* a man and his servant who chance to meet him see the opportunity to change this. They propose to have his eyes healed so that he can see all the worthy folk who have been deprived of bread. If he is able to reward those who are just and shun the perverse and ungodly, all mankind will become honest, rich, and pious. Plutus agrees when he is persuaded that his powers will thus be greater than Zeus's. Then a woman in rags appears; it is Penia, goddess of poverty. She is outraged at the plan to banish her, claiming herself to be the source of all good that comes to humanity. It is her presence among them that causes people to labor to produce the goods all need and desire. When Plutus is cured of his blindness by the special ministrations the men arrange, he is acclaimed by the gathering crowd. The surprising conclusion comes with the arrival of Hermes, messenger of the gods. Not only is Zeus indignant, he reports, but all the gods are suffering. As wealthy as people have become, they no longer make offerings to deities.[2]

Plato is the first puritan of money: in his ideal republic, he leaves trade to noncitizens—the *metics,* or "foreigners"—because this activity corrupts souls. He dreams of establishing a cordon sanitaire between merchants and the rest of the population to avoid the contagion of their "complete abandonment and baseness." The introduction of money into the city would be, all things considered, "the worst calamity" and would make it "distrustful and inimical to itself."[3] In the *Sophist* and the *Theaetetus,* he denounces the rhetoricians who speak in exchange for compensation and who weigh each of their words in relation to its worth in gold. These vile merchants, "salaried hunters of distinguished young men," mass-produce arguments, whereas the philosopher, according to Socrates, should speak without requiring payment. The sophists prostitute truth, selling their talents to the highest bidder and becoming "merchants of spiritual things."

Curiously, in today's France this reproach is repeated in certain media that rebuke intellectuals for taking money for their speeches through specialized agencies; rather they should refuse even royalties and live in the ethereal heavens of "intellectual values."[4] This argument is also made by the European Commission that seeks, under the influence of American multinationals, to do away with authors' royalties, which have allegedly become "reactionary" in the digital era. Everyone ought to have access to works free of charge, on the condition that they pay, of course, the service providers.[5] Intellectual creation would thus be subject to the pipeline industry (Google, Apple, Amazon, etc.), which could blithely pillage literary or artistic content. In short, they would have us return to the Old Regime's patronage system, with the monarchs of old being replaced by private conglomerates. We might retort, in the spirit of Beaumarchais, that to be able to create, one first has to eat. Any man out to make money would be better to give up the trades of reflection and writing: they provide meager fare for those who adopt them and favor instead a cultural proletariat whose fate is anything but enviable (even if literary careers are not without other satisfactions). The sophists—and this is their merit—may have invented royalties, or payments for writing and speaking, as a way of thinking in complete freedom. "Today, an author is a worker like any other, who earns his living by his work," Émile Zola wrote in 1880, adding: "Money has freed the writer, money has created modern letters."[6]

It is with Aristotle, the first great economic theorist, that money first achieved theoretical dignity. It is a convention that makes it possible to buy and evaluate dissimilar objects. Take a shoemaker, a fisherman, and a physician: they seek to exchange their services. They can resort to bartering; the shoemaker can pay the physician with a pair of shoes, or the fisherman can exchange a fish for a pair of sandals. This method presupposes the coincidence and simultaneity of each person's needs, which is improbable. Offering disparate goods, these three traders can fairly engage in commerce only through the mediation of money. Artificial and arbitrary—in Greek it has the same name as the law, *nomisma*, which is the etymon of the English "numismatics"— money reflects humans' bonds of mutual dependency. It is defined as the fair proportion between heterogeneous kinds of merchandise. For Aristotle, who intermingles justice and correctness, money can be nothing other than the compensation for labor that harms neither party: "the man who acts unjustly has too much of what is good, and the man who is unjustly treated, too little. Equality is a balance between more and less in which some is taken away from the person who has too much and given to the person who does not have enough."[7] And elsewhere: "The just is intermediate between a sort of gain and a sort of loss."[8]

At the outset, Aristotle distinguishes between two kinds of wealth management: the legitimate economics of the household, *oikonomia,* which seeks to make life pleasant for everyone, and the problematic chrematistics, which involves accumulation with no bounds.[9] The former is the reasonable management of material life in the realm of the family and servants. The latter refers to the speculative acquisition of the merchant whose concern is with turning profits, regardless of what he sells—a concern that divorces a thing's worth in use from its exchange value. (Marx would later adopt this same distinction.) How does money, which should be a simple measure of all things, succumb to the immoderation that the ancients considered the worst of all faults? By becoming its own goal, endlessly reproducing itself and no longer recognizing any limits to its expansion.

In Aristotle's thinking, it is not shameful to seek profit or glory as long as that is not done immoderately.[10] Aristotle holds the more sympathetic view of wealth that the Christians were later to develop: it is a necessity for the good life, provided it is coupled with virtue and kindness. The most virtuous of men take particular pleasure in improving their friends' fortunes. Aristotle maintains that life is by its nature essentially good and pleasant; what proves this is that everyone desires it. The best life is therefore the most desirable life, which is incontestably enjoyed by the people with sufficient virtue and means to live happily.[11] Later on, Seneca and Cicero, who were themselves immensely rich, saw higher levels of life, health, and riches as always preferable and noted we would be mad to deprive ourselves when they are available to us. None of these can replace either reason or wisdom, but they do constitute preliminaries or complements to those. Even for the Stoics, striving to be healthy and rich rather than ill and destitute was complying with the will of Providence. If by Providence our lot was to be sick and poor, we would conform to that. Providence does things well. Into the closed system of the Greek *cosmos,* money thus introduced a potentially destructive breach. It ruptured the virtuous circle of living well and having the means to live well, by dangling the temptation of unlimited gains.

God Is Mammon

From the beginning, Christianity has presented itself as a condemnation of profit. Jesus's famous metaphor is repeated over and over: "Truly, I say to you, it will be hard for a rich man to enter the kingdom of heaven. Again I tell you, it is easier for a camel to go through the eye of a needle than for a rich man to enter the kingdom of God" (Matthew 19:23–24). This seems unequivocal, and it marks a clear distinction from Judaism and, later, Islam.[12] In both of those faiths, wealth is cast as a gift of God that one can enjoy without shame, on the conditions that it was acquired honestly and that one gives alms. (The prophet Muhammad was himself a merchant).[13] The first bishops accused the Jews of worshipping money, and of having sold the Messiah, through the mediation of Judas, for a few pieces of silver. But it was the denunciation of usury that the Roman Church was to emphasize. Dante put usurers in the third ring of the seventh circle of hell, a place even worse than that of blasphemers and sodomites.[14] Time being God's property alone, it was forbidden to make money productive; it had to remain sterile. Aristotle had already condemned lending money at interest, describing the birth of money from money (in Greek, the word for interest, *tokoi*, also meant "offspring") as a monstrous pregnancy, contrary to nature.[15] Saint Augustine used the same metaphor in accusing usury of "spiritual fornication." This expression is symptomatic: fornication is the carnal act undertaken without procreative intent, driven only by concupiscence. This copulation, already guilty in itself, is worst when put in the service of a diabolical project: the self-engenderment of money, producing bastards.[16]

Therein lies the scandal: usury is oxymoronic, a *fertile onanism* that produces gain without effort, day and night, even on Sundays, while its owner sleeps, as it extorts immoderate interest from the borrower.[17] In the feudal period, didn't a noble from the Limousin go so far as to sow his fields with pieces of silver to gain prestige, hoping to reap some sort of magical harvest?[18] The condemnation arises from stupefaction with regard to the generation of the sterile, as if sperm could begin engendering without an egg. Usury? A sin that led those who engaged in it into eternal servitude to Satan, with the result that the lender's body will be transformed into an infernal moneybox (he will be refused burial in Christian ground) and will be seen in certain reliefs defecating ducats.[19] In Europe, it was the Jews who, being forbidden to engage in most occupations, turned to this activity, so that the word "Jew" became synonymous with "usurer," as was confirmed, for example, by the Fourth Lateran Council in 1215.[20] For that reason, Jews suffered persecution and humiliation, whereas Christian lenders, who were landowners and merchants, were dealt with more clemently.[21] In Judaism itself, lending at interest is forbidden within the community but authorized with outsiders.[22] What is a usurer? Someone who steals time, appropriating what the Creator gave to all men to share. The swindler must give back the fruit of his larceny or perish in hell.

Thus money is God's main rival. However, Catholic intransigence collides with two contradictions. The first resides in the parable of the talents: the argument developed in Matthew and Luke is well known.[23] Before leaving on a journey, a master entrusts three of his servants with a certain sum of money: five talents to the first, two to the second, and one to the third, in accord with the abilities of each. On his return, the one who received five talents gives him five more, the one who had two gives him four. The master congratulates them. As for the last servant, who had buried his talent in the ground, he is harshly reprimanded by his master and sent away. Matthew draws this stupefying conclusion: "For to every one who has will more be given, and he will have abundance; but from him who has not, even what he has will be taken away" (Matthew 25:29). This parable can be interpreted in at least two ways: as an exhortation not to waste the gifts received from God and to make them fruitful, with the two meanings of the word "talent," a coin and an ability to improve. The task of a free person is to cultivate his faculties, no matter how modest they may be, to engage in work and training. His value is no longer what he is by nature but what he does with what nature has given him.

In this fable we also find speculation praised by a master who pitilessly punishes the most destitute and favors those who are most capable of "putting money to work." (It is thought that they lent it at interest.) A strange morality that congratulates the skillful and deprives the disadvantaged relegates them to the shadows, where "men will weep and gnash their teeth." Isn't this the view of Gary Becker (1930–2014), who won the Nobel Prize for economics and for whom every individual is human capital acquired at the cost of various investments (training, education, health) and must produce a profit? He was himself preceded by Joseph Stalin, who spoke in 1935 of "The human being, the most precious capital," a formula previously uttered by the French minister of public education, Victor Duruy, in 1860.[24] Here we find all the ambiguity of the Catholic tradition, which generated both the condemnation of the Golden Calf and the quantifiable worldview. It depreciates money as much as it exalts it.

Another ambivalence: when it is written that God keeps the great account book, punishing the evil and rewarding the good in accord with their acts, this already uses a financial metaphor for retribution and sanction. When Fénelon, a bishop of Cambrai in the seventeenth century, wrote that eternity must be bought by making good use of time—God grants us each instant only by depriving us of the preceding one—he adopted a vocabulary that was later to be that of capitalism: time is money, accumulated merits or faults that will doom us. It introduces an element of calculation into the preoccupation with salvation, monetizing both sin and grace. Life is a debt that we pay back with death, the wages of sin. *From the outset, religious language is an economic language.* The Church translated this by explaining to believers that they had to redeem their sins and offer gifts to God to calm his wrath. The powerful gave lands and silver objects and paid fees to priests. The peasants were obliged to pay a tax to the clergy, the *dime* or tithe, one-tenth of their harvests.[25] Even penitence was liable to fees depending on the nature of the "sinful acts" committed.

Religion is a kind of commerce, and God is the treasurer-general of souls. He is the arch-banker who subjects the whole of creation to an implacable calculus. Saint Augustine sought to establish man's absolute debt to the Lord, "to whom none can repay the price which he paid for us, though the debt was not his to pay."[26] This was confirmed by John Bunyan (1628–1688), an English Baptist preacher and the author of *Pilgrim's Progress* (1678), an allegory of the Christian who travels from the earthly city to the celestial city, by comparing the relation between man and God with that between a shopkeeper and a customer who, no matter what his merits might be, is incapable of paying back the principal. What is the Christian paradise if not the place where we are definitively beyond the weighing of our faults and our merits, where we can give ourselves up to the innocence of our being? God is a mathematician, but he is also an accountant who demands his due and whom we try to appease by making offerings. The priceless is a retrospective invention: everything has always had a price, including God the Almighty and salvation.

Pascal himself, when he wants to convince atheists of God's existence, resorts to game theory and probability theory: "Let us assess the two cases: if you win, you win everything; if you lose, you lose nothing. Do not hesitate then; wager that he does exist."[27] Speculating on beatitude, Pascal gives priority to self-interest over faith; in evaluating the pros and cons, the prospect of an eternity of delights must win out over the small pleasures of life: the triumph of calculating thought. A loss today for a hundredfold yield later, that is the plan. In the meantime, we must have without possessing, use things without enjoying them. It is on the model of debt and repayment that Christianity founded its theological edifice; and it is that model that paved the way for the triumph of the market in the Western world, even if this triumph later turned against it. The ancient Greeks put an obole in the mouths of the deceased who were on their way to the kingdom of the dead, presided over by Hades, Zeus's brother. The dead had to pay their share. As for the host, specialists tell us that it was initially made like a coin, on the numismatic model—like the saint's halo, which brings to mind gold pieces, but only the better to exorcise them.[28] The believer's whole language is a language of waiting for a return on investment. Didn't Huysmans explain that pain is an advance on purgatory, a down payment made to the All Powerful?[29]

The Salvation Market

Another symbol of this connection between belief and business: the practice of indulgences. It really got going with the creation of purgatory in the twelfth century, a third place between hell and paradise that authorized those whose lives were neither good nor bad to liquidate their arrears. This posthumous makeup class allowed the living to enter into dialogue with the dead and to shorten their punishment; it opened up within Christian space a veritable stock market for salvation, whose rates constantly varied.[30] In the strict sense of the term, an indulgence is the remission of sins through an act of piety (a pilgrimage, gifts in hard cash, mortifications of the flesh) whose scale of value is determined by the Apostolic Penitentiary. The latter sets a fee for each sin and hastens the exit from purgatory by making offerings. The German Dominican Johann Tetzel, who sold indulgences in the name of the archbishop of Brandenburg (and who had a special interest in the sale because he received a commission of 50 percent promised by the Curia), is credited with the following statement: "As soon as a coin in the coffer rings, the soul from purgatory springs." And since purgatory established a whole system of "mitigating the suffering," it introduced into religion the notion of bargaining, with all its excesses.[31] Indulgences aroused fury among the Lutherans, who were outraged to see a human institution, the Vatican, drawing drafts on eternity, forcing God's hand.

As early as the twelfth century, the system of penitence at a price was being systematically set up. For example, people bought masses by the unit, as so many viatica for the hereafter. With the development of piety connected with indulgences, the wildest mercantile transactions flourished: by going on pilgrimages, giving to the orders of the Hospitallers, or reciting psalms, people hoped to shave years off their stay in purgatory. "For example, one sanctuary promised to acquire, in exchange for a confession, gifts, and prayers, seven years and seven quarantines [periods of forty days], while another promised forty times forty years. A pilgrims' guide in the Holy Land tells us that a systematic visit of the holy sites yielded, so to speak, forty-three times seven years and seven quarantines."[32] These remissions of punishment foreshadow the contemporary penitentiary system with its complex additions and subtractions. In the domain of extravagant accumulations, villagers, bourgeoisie, and nobles paid shares to have masses celebrated for the repose of their souls according to a plan that greatly resembles our real estate loans, in which the proportion of interest paid decreases over time: a maximum during the first years, slowly declining along an asymptotic curve: "A rich widow in the Dauphiné . . . demanded that in exchange for her gift 1,450 masses be celebrated over eighteen years (120 the first year, 110 for three years, 100 for four years, 75 for four years, 50 for the last six years.)"[33] The obsession with accounting was contemporary with the appearance of clocks in cities and the growing importance of mathematics in everyday life from the thirteenth century on: that was in fact when symbolic numerology gave way to the quantification of the world.[34] The Church also sold dispensations: the Rouen Cathedral's famous "Butter Tower" was financed by selling residents authorizations allowing them to eat fats during Lent. Thus to Luther's great dismay, Rome established a "soul market." The papacy that preached poverty and humility sank into luxury, orgies, ostentatious pomp, simony, the sale of sacramental offices and sacred objects—a remarkable return of the repressed. Luther revolted against Rome, which Thomas Müntzer called in 1521 "the Whore of Babylon," the Great Prostitute of the Apocalypse. To this day, the Catholic Church continues to issue indulgences, plenary or partial: stopping smoking, for example, or not contributing to the pollution of the environment can win the believer a remission of punishment provided that he is in a state of grace. In exchange for a modest sum one can have masses said for the dead, and thus maintain a solidarity between the living and the deceased. Trying to save itself from money, Rome has saved itself with it, in spite of itself, in order to remain afloat. How true is Kierkegaard's remark accusing the churches of being merely "a lucrative business of transportation to eternity that avoids discredit only because we have no news from the travelers."

At the same time that the Gospels celebrated asceticism and the grandeur of the poor, the churches covered themselves with brilliant gilding and sumptuous ornaments, especially after the Council of Trent, reacting against Lutheranism, had reaffirmed that images were licit (1563). The Church, protected by its status as the Bride of Christ, could amass treasures and manage the gifts of money, ornaments, and jewels that were presented to it and that soon amounted to fortunes. It even granted itself the right to practice lending at interest, without, however, imposing exorbitant rates.[35] The French Church's patrimonial strategy, which forbade levirate (the practice of a man marrying his brother's widow) and adoption by sterile couples, had as part of its goal to appropriate the capital of both these groups; by the end of the seventh century, it owned a third of the arable land in France.[36] To express and announce the splendor of heaven, the best the clergy could do was to resort to the talent of artists, to precious materials, a profusion of jewels, and reliquaries covered with rubies and emeralds.[37] Ravishing colors, lofty painted ceilings, soft and luxuriant fabrics gave the faithful a foretaste of the marvels that awaited them in the hereafter. The Kingdom was on earth, in the cathedral or the basilica. The Roman Church's praise of poverty contrasted with the pomp of an institution that was collapsing under the weight of its gold and multiplying the number of its richly brocaded priests (in the three religions of the book, rabbis, priests, pastors, popes, imams, and ulemas are often rotund, with a very ecclesial plumpness; the service of God feeds its men well). Doctrinaire rigor long went hand in hand with an indulgent attitude toward the rich, who were threatened with punishments in the hereafter but whose privileges in this world were left intact. As for bishops, cardinals, and popes, they lived amid unprecedented magnificence, with rare foods and various wines and beverages, not to mention sexual relations with courtesans, young people, or favorites, which earned them the hostility of the faithful. Elsewhere, in Byzantine Orthodoxy, we find a similar ceremonial debauchery, golden icons, ivory divans, rich ex-votos, and liturgical ornaments whose splendor is now found again in Russia, Romania, and Greece. The Orient of the Ottomans or the India of the Mughals deployed a similarly unprecedented splendor with a refinement that surpassed anything the sovereigns of the West had been able to imagine. The royal courts, the great mosques, the temples, the mausoleums (including the famous Taj Mahal) became oases of beauty and grandeur in which people perceived the first gleams of the hereafter.[38] Islam represents Eden as a magnificent garden filled with abundant springs, with luxuriant vegetation and all the fruits of the earth, a profane inkling of paradise.[39] The invisible is suggested by using the weapons of the visible. Whereas Confucianism sees wealth as an ally of virtue and the direct path toward self-improvement, Hinduism personifies it in the elephant-god Ganesh, an amiable figure and a promise of prosperity. But it also opposes the king to the renouncer, the rajah to the yogi—the one addicted to the illusory sumptuousness of the world, the other devoted to emancipation from this life and from the cycle of rebirths.

In the same way that religious music gave rise to the opera and that the mass, with its liturgy, its cardinals, and its choirboys, suggests a royal court or a theater stage, the churches, at least the most sumptuous of them, seem to be palaces devoted to the delights of the body and the senses. In them the idea of a revolutionary luxury for all is developed, a foretaste of the promise of redemption addressed to humanity as a whole. Only monasticism counterbalanced this indulgence in luxury and reminded people of the importance of the vow of poverty and spiritual asceticism. The Calvinists, horrified by these paintings and stained-glass windows, hastened, in their iconoclasm, to destroy the statues and whitewash the frescoes, particularly in Switzerland. In reaction, the Counter-Reformation gambled on beauty put in the service of the people, transfiguring the rigidities of dogma into works of art, giving rise to the extraordinary efflorescence of the Baroque. In return, Protestantism, which was opposed to the worship of images, put all its sensuality into music, and the genius of a Bach cannot be understood without Luther's intransigence with regard to representation.

Rome still has not emerged from these contradictions, despite Pope Francis's cosmetic attacks on "the new invisible tyranny of finance" and private property.[40] When he asserts, for example, "I do not like money, but I need it to help the poor and I need it to propagate the faith,"[41] he bears witness to an extraordinary schizophrenia (which we may all share), since the Vatican has a banking system that has been stained by a number of scandals over the past thirty years. (The "Vatileaks" of 2012 and 2013 revealed vast networks of nepotism and embezzlement within the Curia, not to mention the expensive way of life led by cardinals—by Msgr. Bertone, for instance, or by Msgr. Nunzio Scarano, who is suspected of having laundered the Mafia's money on behalf of the Vatican Bank.[42]) A great antinomy of the Church, which can tolerate money only while condemning it and which finds itself torn between its flaunted virtue and the pomp it displays, even if most priests are destitute.[43] For Rome, the arms of the sensible have to be used to glorify divine perfection. Didn't Stendhal himself praise the Jesuit and Catholic corruption that produced masterpieces and oppose the dreary Lutheran reason that engendered, in America, nothing but dollars?[44] Protestant aridity prefers to take refuge in abstraction and the idea, whereas Roman emotionalism bursts out in images, statues, paintings. The courts of the popes, who became veritable Italian princes, and their unrestrained manners scandalize us but also continue to fascinate us. The battle between sensualism and rigor must not end in either a victory or a defeat. But why see a contradiction where there can be cohabitation? We find the same tension in the Orthodox world, aggravated by Caeseropapism, that is, the close interweaving of the spiritual and temporal powers, especially because the Russian, Romanian, Bulgarian, Serbian, and Greek churches, courted by the established political powers and subject to low taxes, have enormous wealth and immense holdings.

Catholicism could preach fervent indifference to earthly goods all it wanted; it was unable to forestall the great movement of appetite for life and pleasures that overcame the mass of believers in the Middle Ages. Inversely, Lutheranism and Calvinism, with their insistence on faith in place of works, were to end up rehabilitating labor and prosperity. The Reformation, according to a paradox that has already been stressed by many people, was to take the form of a double movement: the obsessive quest for salvation along with the concern to improve the temporal sojourn. In the name of the hereafter, people were henceforth going to invest in and embellish this world. Contrary to Max Weber's often-refuted but still stimulating thesis, a revolution in the Church resulted from the economic success of certain regions (Germany, for example), and not from the religious beliefs that favored the birth of capitalism, which appeared in the city-states of Italy and even, Fernand Braudel was to say, as early as the Muslim revolution of the seventh century, which had "proto-capitalist" characteristics.[45] The famous idea popularized by Benjamin Franklin, according to which time is money, comes in reality from the end of the Middle Ages, from the fifteenth-century painter and cryptographer Leon Battista Alberti, and before him from monks who lived according to a rigorous division of hours and tasks marked by the bells.[46]

How did money, which according to Rome was an instrument of perdition, become an instrument of redemption according to the Protestants? That was Luther's fundamental revolution, carried out with his scatological metaphors and his deceptive quietism: the Christian's duty consisted first of all in faith and not in works. "Good works do not make a good man, but a good man does good works." There was no question of buying redemption by making donations or going on pilgrimages. The tree must be healthy if it is to bear good fruit. But piety also demands that the believer find fulfillment in profane business and help his neighbor in poverty. Catholicism relies on the distinction between those who pray and those who labor, charity and prayer being seen as more valuable than useful work.[47] After Luther, Calvin was to reverse this proposition and reformulate it as follows: "Working is praying." Work dissipates doubt regarding divine election and offers "certainty of salvation," it becomes *the great tranquilizer of the modern soul*. [48] It is not mere drudgery; it exploits this earth and obliges each person to enter into contact with others through the complementarity of competencies. One's occupation becomes a vocation, both a calling and a profession, as is indicated by the German term *Beruf* and the English term "vocation." This revalorization of profane need was to have a capital importance for the future: working in order to eat, formerly reserved for serfs and for base merchants, was thus ennobled.

As for the Calvinist doctrine of predestination (already present in Saint Augustine), it leaves our fate in the hands of God alone: some will be saved at the Lord's will, while others will not, no matter what they do. One can be a good person to whom grace is not granted, just as one can be a sinner to whom grace is granted in spite of everything. However, those who are doomed to perdition must behave as if they were going to be redeemed, on pain of sinking into despair. The sanctification of labor and the acquisition of riches (on the condition that modest use is made of them): that is the unforeseen consequence of a doctrine that seemed to preach fatalism and was finally to lead to embellishing this world for the greater glory of God while waiting for him to issue his judgments. There are no longer any tangible proofs of an individual's saintliness: neither fasts nor prayers, neither masses nor gifts to monasteries are Christian in themselves.[49] The condition of salvation was to remain a question without an answer, left in suspense right to the end. Only work and accumulation calm the sinner's anguish as he awaits the Last Judgment. Money remains more than ever a theological problem: it is a consolation that soothes the believer's wounds. To which is added the amazing ability of the most austere sects to build up gigantic fortunes—the Mormons in the United States, the Jains and the Parsees in

The Thirst for Gold

In his novel *Gold,* Blaise Cendrars recounts the amazing story of a Swiss adventurer, Johann August Sutter, who left in 1820 for California without a penny in his pocket, hoping to escape poverty.[50] After numerous tribulations, he acquired from the Mexican government vast tracts of land (at the time, much of the American West was still Mexican). He developed them, irrigated them, and supplemented the cultivation of fruits and vegetables by raising livestock. He soon employed thousands of men and was about to become the richest individual in the world. It was then that gold was discovered on his lands; the news attracted crowds of plunderers, unscrupulous freebooters who destroyed everything. Sutter was ruined and spent the rest of his life involved in numerous lawsuits, trying to recover his property.

Cendrars's novel, which is a metaphysical fable, tells us this: capitalism is not the ancient *auri sacra fames* (the accursed thirst for gold, according to Virgil) but rationalized greed, a process of creating wealth more than of capturing it. To confuse them is to confuse two orders of value: the one offered by nature in the form of lodes and nuggets, and the one created by human labor. Gold, that old "barbarous relic," as Keynes called it, has never lost its mythic power; it is still to this safe haven that we turn in crises. This is the metal's revenge on dematerialization. But it is no longer the mainspring of our economies, only that of our fantasies or our admiration. It is not an ordinary stone, it symbolizes the imprisoned sun, the primordial energy, even though jewelers and clockmakers couple it with pink, white, and gray. Didn't Saint Bonaventure proclaim that "God is light in the most literal sense"? But in gold, divine light is condensed to the point of opacity, so brilliant that it blinds us, producing what Ficino called "the shadow of God."[51]

There is a comic book character who combines the two systems of wealth, those of labor and extraction: Scrooge McDuck, the greedy figure created by Carl Barks in 1947. Scottish in origin, he belongs to a bankrupt clan. He begins by selling firewood and shining shoes. The first coin he earns, an American penny, becomes his fetish: he is nomadic, an emigrant. For him, destiny is American. Turning up in Louisville, Kentucky, the night of a festival, he exclaims: "What a country! The very air tastes of fortunes being made and lost."[52] A philosophical rancher born to a rich family (who turns out to be a young Theodore Roosevelt) tells him: "To *make* yourself rich through the glory of hard work, with the beat of a hardy life in your veins—by Godfrey, *that's* an accomplishment." Unlike the character in Molière's *Miser*, he was born at a time when the desire to enrich oneself was legitimate. A misanthropic complainer, he works hard—as a copper prospector, a gold prospector in the Klondike and in Transvaal, a traveler in Australia, an adventurer ready to take risks—and his avarice is already legendary: he pays his employees a pittance, exploits his family, and refuses to shoot a grizzly bear because bullets are expensive. Even if he operates at the limits of legality, he remains "honest" toward and against everything. Once he has become a multimillionaire, despite the bad example set by Flintheart Glomgold, his wicked double, and John D. Rockerduck, another rival, Scrooge McDuck likes to wallow in his gold swimming pool—a lake, or even an ocean—of coins, ingots, and bills in which he paddles, dives, and digs passageways. For him, money is a womb of inexhaustible fecundity that achieves the beauty of the colossal. He regenerates himself in it, and is never satisfied, especially since his treasure is regularly threatened by the Beagle Boys, a gang of dog-faced characters who play Robin Hood. Scrooge is unique in that he shamelessly romps about in gold, experiencing the ecstasy of saints imbued with transcendence. He does not recognize Seneca's distinction between the brilliance that dazzles and the luminescence that softly radiates.[53] In his view, everything that shines is magical. His grin is that of a voluptuary whose transports cannot be calmed. Scrooge McDuck is orgasmic.

India, the Mourides in Senegal—as if there were a profound relationship between the two universes of mysticism and monetary abstraction.

Whence the two different attitudes that we find today in northern and southern Europe regarding debt: for the Catholics (and in part members of the Orthodox Church), an account is opened as soon as one is born, but the deadlines can be modified, a flexibility that leads to a certain casualness in repayment. The sacrament of penance has the ability to liquidate sins. Catholicism makes allowances for human fallibility and shows an inexhaustible leniency when it comes to our shortcomings. For Protestants, on the other hand, a debt remains a debt (in German, one and the same word is used to designate fault and debt: *Schuld*), and earnestness and thriftiness require us not to tolerate excessive debt in the management of business affairs, whether private or national (Germany is the proof of this). The Catholic enters the Church as he would enter a benevolent bank that practices, through prayers and confession, the remission of penalties while awaiting the Last Judgment. The Protestant, on the other hand, does not benefit from any ecclesiastical clemency, because he faces his God alone. He himself has to provide the proofs of his piety, the only justification ultimately being earthly success. Each of these two mentalities allows, of course, certain exceptions.

TWO

On the Eminent Dignity of the Poor?

Do not lay up for yourselves treasures on earth, where moth and rust consume and where thieves break in and steal, but lay up for yourselves treasures in heaven, where neither moth nor rust consumes and where thieves do not break in and steal. For where your treasure is, there will your heart be also.

MATTHEW 6:19–21

WHEN in 1659 Bossuet titled one of his sermons "On the Eminent Dignity of the Poor," he was reasoning on the basis of an immobile society in which the disadvantaged had no chance of improving their lot. They nonetheless enjoyed a unique prerogative: they incarnated Jesus's suffering. They already constituted the city of God on earth.[1] Here the bishop of Meaux was using a rhetorical figure frequently found in Christianity: the inversion of values. Those who have nothing in this world will have everything in the next, and vice versa. "Therefore, O poor, you are rich, but O rich, you are poor."

The Glory of the Humble

Lucre, luxury, and lust: these are the flaws of the powerful according to Bossuet. The powerful are miserable, always hungry, prey to the furious throng of passions, ambition, avarice, pleasure, luxury, and indolence, while the calamities of the poor are privileges that make them "the first children of the Church" who have been promised the kingdom of God. The King of Glory, having "espoused the lowest of the low," having chosen what is most contemptible on earth, suggests that rulers should rely on the indigent to open the gates of paradise to them: "In that way grace, mercy, the remission of sins, the kingdom itself is in their hands; and the rich cannot enter there if the poor do not receive them."[2] Behind this majestic exhortation we do not find a call to subvert the social order. The redemption of the poor is promised only in the hereafter; they have to be saved from the bad example set by the better-off. In fact, the latter send society a powerful message: this life can be pleasant; there is no point in mortifying oneself. If part of humanity, because of its birth, enjoys the seductions of existence, it can tear everyone away from the catechism of resignation. What would happen if the citizens of a land wanted to have the same advantages as the well-off, if they demanded that this earth become a Garden of Eden instead of remaining a vale of tears? Then there would be a scramble of ambitions and appetites, a limitless thirst to enjoy, at the cost of forgetting God.

This danger has to be warded off by logical acrobatics: the ennobling of the poor man and the degradation of the nobleman, who is described as a "commoner of God." The humbling of the former is his claim to glory, and the glory of the latter is a sign of his fall. Saint Augustine already pointed out that it was the desire for wealth that was to be blamed as much as or even more than its use, exhorting the poor to endure cheerfully the loss of "the timid savings of greed."[3] Worldly opulence has to be exchanged for spiritual opulence. The rich man is bowed beneath the weight of a burden called abundance—in other words, having more than is necessary.

Death Presents Its Bill

As a good Christian, Bossuet viewed life from the point of view of death—that is, the leap into eternity. On the eve of death it is to God, who is both a justice of the peace and a prosecutor, that the rich man has to render account. To put it prosaically, the All Powerful presents His bill. This God of vengeance incarnates the twofold figure of the usurer who demands what he is owed and the torturer who punishes. Christianity condemned the usurer because that role was already occupied by God himself, who lends us life at interest. It is the poor who will play, at the Last Judgment, the roles of accusers and advocates, who will plead on behalf of the prosecution and the defense, indicting those who have neglected them, interceding on behalf of those who fed and clothed them. In Bossuet's view, poverty is a good in itself; it makes those who suffer from it "spiritual physicians."[4] On his deathbed, the bad rich man would like to attenuate the Lord's wrath by hastily distributing his goods, showing last-minute humanity. But it is too late. On the other hand, the good rich man, thanks to the alms he has given, has taken care of some flock of the afflicted, who will be able to plead his case before the Lord.

Death has the power to separate the wheat from the chaff, the immortal soul from the perishable body. It is the promise of a consolation in the hereafter: the just will have the first place, and the wicked will be relegated to the outer darkness. Here there is a double movement: condensing the whole of human destiny on the narrow crest of death, and inciting the rich to be generous only in order to spare them the torments of eternal hellfire. *Thus it is the fear of damnation that makes people good and not goodness that makes them generous.* The invocation of altruism is made in the name of the most selfish argument: the fear of hell. The Christian is supposed to scorn wealth and its empty promises and devote himself solely to the virtues of humility and charity. The rich, in their ridiculous pomp, would do better to serve the destitute, on pain of perishing in the flames—of being, after death, "powerful people powerfully tormented."[5]

This sophism makes us smile: sweetening the pill for the disinherited by explaining to them that they are the salt of the earth no longer works, especially among believers. As we have seen, with Protestantism, a new value has in the interim made its appearance in Europe: productive labor. Providing subsistence for himself and his family has become the duty of every self-respecting Christian. For moderns, the will to poverty, the taste for deprivation found in the mendicant orders, is nonsense. *Instead of the eminent dignity of the poor, people recognize the eminent dignity of work.* Instead of praise for destitution, they note the rehabilitation of wealth, so long as it is not shamelessly displayed and knows the wisdom of contentment (as Calvin urged). When Rome sees in the poor man the face of Christ and "heaven's gate-keeper," it is a question of bringing the poor out of their precarious situation by offering them work and at the same time condemning the idle, the beggars who take pleasure in their indolence. From this point of view, the Protestants were able to condone lending at interest so long as it were equitable, and the lender and the borrower shared the same risk.

Historians later agreed that there was an affinity between capitalism and Calvinism, the latter having developed the whole morality of success that is triumphant in today's United States.[6] Calvin reassured the powerful by putting them under divine protection: the Lord elected them among all others by rewarding them with his blessed manna. Earning money becomes an activity that is not only innocent, but recommended. Poverty retains its theological value, but as a trial addressed to faith. It has to be transcended and not celebrated as a virtue.[7] It must be circumscribed to keep it from spreading like a torrent and corrupting the very foundations of the city. With Calvin, it lost its sacred character and became something to be fought like a scourge that debases humans.

The Vampire and the Whore

This debate arose anew after the Industrial Revolution. Starting in the nineteenth century, new grievances were addressed to the Golden Calf: while for Christians it represented a competitor to God, for progressive thinkers it was the very blood of the poor, drained by their oppressors. It was, according to Zola, all the labor and sweat of France; among the fortunate, it thrives on what it has taken from the unfortunate. Being a kind of exploitation, pure and simple, it exhausts millions of individuals in a vampire-like act. Thus money has another defect, analyzed by Karl Marx: it inverts values, putting more in the place of less. "It transforms fidelity into infidelity, love into hate, hate into love, virtue into vice, vice into virtue, slave into master, master into slave, stupidity into intelligence, and intelligence into stupidity," Marx wrote. A strange criticism that might be taken for praise: money does not respect hierarchies. By facilitating the acquisition of virtues that do not properly belong to their incumbent, it becomes a delusion. It positions itself between people as a temptation, it makes it possible to buy dignity, honors, knowledge, the heart, the body. Marx explains: what I am, my qualities and the power of my being, are qualities of my money. "I am ugly, but I can buy the most beautiful woman for myself: thus I am not ugly, because the effect of ugliness, its repulsive force, is canceled by money. I am, as an individual, a cripple, but money provides me with twenty-four legs; thus I am not crippled . . . I lack wit but money being the real wit of all things, how can its possessor be a fool?"[8] Money confuses everything, transforming the slightest of my wishes into a reality; thus it is, Marx says, repeating Shakespeare, "the universal prostitute, the universal intermediary between men and between peoples."

A similar complaint was expressed by Emmanuel Mounier in 1933, from a point of view close to Christian personalism: money expels a person from himself. This impersonal machine snatches up governments, homelands, families. In the place of interiority it establishes self-interest and turns people away from their spiritual vocations. It denatures social life, which it subjects to simple economic calculations as much as it alters private life through the power of selfish calculation. Mounier offers a description of three human types engendered by capitalism: the rich man, the petit bourgeois, and the poor man. The first is subject to the regime of facility, nothing resists him: everything yields when faced by the irrepressible force of his desires. His material means allow him to buy illness, death, and even the appearance of love and friendship. The well-to-do man forgets the Other and impoverishes the world by thinking he possesses it. At his side, the petit bourgeois, fascinated by this model, is a stunted rich man who lacks the means to fulfill his ambition. The first seeks consideration, the second advancement. As for the poor man of olden days, he no longer exists; he has been replaced by the indigent person prepared to do anything for a few pennies, dislocated by unemployment, alcohol, need. "In the past, there was a people . . . it had no money . . . but it communed with a soul."[9] A retrospective idealization that has not the slightest historical basis but that is supposed to justify the a priori condemnation of money as the root of all evils.

A Dream of Abolition

On April 17, 1975, when the Khmer Rouge entered Phnom Penh, they were not satisfied to have evacuated in a few days the whole population of the city, even the patients in the hospitals, on the pretext of an imminent American bombardment. They decided, making a vertiginous temporal leap, to move without transition from capitalism to communism, and for that reason to abolish the very symbol of exploitation, money. They ordered goods confiscated, and abolished private property. It was decided to blow up the banks, and paper money, recently printed in China, was scattered in the streets, and no one thought to pick it up. In "real" life, people flock to seize bundles of money that fall from an armored car. In Cambodia, nothing of the sort: the riels (the Cambodian currency) rotted in the sun because they had not the slightest value. Anyone who picked them up would have been threatened with death. The old universe seemed to be dying in an iconoclastic act. It began with the destruction of money and ended with that of schools, hospitals, and temples; slavery was reintroduced, and people were treated as means of payment.

In his book *Utopia* (1516), the English philosopher and theologian Thomas More imagined a perfect society based on the common possession of goods and the suppression of money. He was invoked by the Bolsheviks in 1918, when the commissar for finances, Ivan Stepanov, set off a monstrous inflation and had money printed as fast as possible so that there would no longer be either rich or poor. According to

Keynes, Lenin had for a time entertained the theory of overthrowing contemporary society by corrupting its money. His comrade, Yevgeni Preobrazhensky, had in fact described the money-printing press as "that machine-gun of the Commissariat of Finance which poured fire into the rear of the bourgeois system."[10] The price to be paid for certain commodities was multiplied by two million. Poverty and hunger spread everywhere. Money was finally re-established, putting the country on the road to "socialist primitive accumulation" and a New Economic Policy. Leon Trotsky, reflecting on these events in 1936, wrote: "The deathblow to money fetishism will be struck only upon that stage when the steady growth of social wealth has made us bipeds forget our miserly attitude toward every excess minute of labor, and our humiliating fear about the size of our ration. Having lost its ability to bring happiness or trample men in the dust, money will turn into mere bookkeeping receipts for the convenience of statisticians and for planning purposes. In the still more distant future, probably these receipts will not be needed. But we can leave this question entirely to posterity, who will be more intelligent than we are."[11] The founder of the Red Army, then in exile and soon to be dead, saw in the watchwords about the abolition of the wage-earner and of money the symptoms of a mechanistic and not a dialectical mode of thought.

In Detroit in 1932, the Mexican painter Diego Rivera, painting a mural fresco for the Ford factories, wrote on these frescos: "Down with imperialistic wars," and this magnificent oxymoron: "Free money."[12] And in 1934 an ephemeral Worker's Republic emerged among Asturian miners, in Oviedo, in northwestern Spain: they put their goods in common and decreed the disappearance of money before disappearing in their turn under the blows of repression. Between 1958 and 1960 Maoist China also experimented with the Great Leap Forward and the forced collectivization of agriculture (which caused between twenty and forty million famine-related deaths), and a brief attempt to suppress monetary specie in numerous working class communes. Let us add, just for good measure, the condemnation pronounced by Friedrich Hayek and his disciples against money, judged to be too collectivist, and its replacement by private means of payment more in conformity with the individualist order.[13] A counter-example: ISIS, the Islamic guerrilla force, over-pays its fighters, issues money, draws significant revenues from the oil wells it controls, and its leader, al-Baghdadi, appears in rare videos with a large, ostentatious Rolex-style watch on his wrist. The Islamic State or the bling-bling caliphate of terror.

If money arouses so much anger, it is perhaps because it incarnates the very essence of modernity, the spirit of emancipation and mobility. It personifies flux versus permanence, the genius of circulation versus the demon of petrification, and it pushes people to want to improve their lot. In addition, it reduces the human condition to the sinister tonalities of calculation. If we believe the critics, a "quantitative ethics" is everywhere replacing the sense of quality, and life will henceforth bend under the gray mass of anonymous numbers. We weigh, we count, instead of savoring. Over time, money, a simple instrument of exchange that makes it possible to acquire goods, becomes the supreme good, "desired in itself and by itself" (John Stuart Mill). It bears man's desire for the infinite as a cloud bears a storm. The means becomes the end, the tool surpasses its use and arouses the desire to earn as much as possible.

Thus two great attitudes with regard to money emerge: that of its adulators, who venerate it, openly or secretly, and that of its denigrators, who hate it with a passion. The danger is that these two positions can be inverted, the ascetic becoming greedy and the greedy man becoming ascetic. It is no accident if the decomposition of communist societies after 1989 led, in the former Soviet empire, to wild corruption and the pillaging of public goods. The official hatred of capitalism had turned into its contrary, the will to seize wealth. All wisdom, if there is any, urges us to refuse to adore or to detest the base metal, and instead to calmly enjoy it.

THREE

France, or the Taboo on Money

Any attention paid to money matters was considered low and contemptible in the extreme in my family. It was, so to speak, an offence against modesty to talk about money; money was, as it were, a sad necessity of life, unfortunately indispensable, like water-closets, but which one must never mention.

STENDHAL, *La Vie de Henry Brulard*

What disgusts me is precisely what you all want, of which you are so proud, what you call by an ignoble name: ease. To be at ease, to put oneself at ease, to relieve oneself, that is precisely what I wanted to get at: one is at ease only on his pot.

GEORGES BERNANOS, *Les Enfants Humiliés*

EVERY Sunday, on the outskirts of Lyon, in the early 1960s when I was a child, the local notables came to mass in humble 2CVs, dressed in gray the better to melt into the mass of the parishioners. They left, discreet, contemplative, and then met, behind the high walls of their properties, their wealthy friends, their numerous servants, and their sports cars. In a fine symptom of its relation to money, the French bourgeoisie naturally avoids displaying its wealth.

In France, one has to seem humble to avoid arousing the envy of the disadvantaged. In the United States, on the contrary, wealth is flaunted. Patrician homes are displayed before everyone's eyes, without perimeter walls, whereas in France they remain hidden behind a curtain of trees or imposing gates. In America, the taboo on sex is predominant, in France it is the taboo on money. These two countries incarnate, in a chemically pure state, diametrically opposed archetypes.

Ordure and Mire

The American credo—*greed is good*—is opposed to the French cult of pleasures. The United States is obsessed by conjugal disloyalty, while France, horrified by the triumph of "materialism," shows a tolerance toward carnal deviations that has become an art of living. "France is elastic: people can rise again, even from a sofa," Lamartine said about his colleague in the Chamber of Peers, Victor Hugo, whom the constabulary found one morning in the arms of the wife of an official court painter. The Anglo-Americans counterbalance their prudery with an insatiable taste for profit that we pretend to disapprove of. In France, we live under the threefold heritage of feudalism, Christianity, and the Republic, each reinforcing the others. France, as a literary nation, combines aristocratic scorn for commerce with revolutionary egalitarianism. La Bruyère had, in his own way, anticipated this evolution: "There are dirty souls, molded in mud and ordure, infatuated with gain and self-interest, just as beautiful souls are infatuated with glory and virtue. . . . Such people are neither relatives, nor friends, nor citizens, nor Christians, nor perhaps men: they have money."[1] A terrible judgment: the order of possession expels you from the kingdom of being, and even from humanity. In this verdict, we must also see the nobility's fear of being dispossessed of its power by the new class of the bourgeois.

Our whole attitude toward money has its origin in the opposition between Rousseau and Voltaire. Rousseau assails luxury, which deprives the poor and corrupts taste and manners; he calls for virtuous and austere citizens. Voltaire, on the contrary, was a worldly man who traveled in a carriage, was a supporter of commerce and progress and a defender of tolerance; he wanted polite and brilliant men. We can say, like the young Jean-Jacques in his *Confessions:* "None of my dominant tastes consists in things that are bought. I need only pure pleasures, and money poisons them all."[2] But like Voltaire we can also consider the superfluous as "something very necessary": "What idiot, if he had a good bed, would have slept outside?"[3] For the author of *Candide,* comfort and courage are not incompatible; his whole life testifies to that. If in France appearances plead in favor of Voltaire, the subtitles are still inspired by Rousseau. Opulence is admitted only sotto voce, as a deplorable concession to the spirit of the world. These two minds illustrate this French discord.

In this regard, Rousseau has countless heirs: first of all, Jacques Roux, the red priest of the Revolution (1752–1794) and the author of the *Manifeste des enragés,* who saw in "the rich, that is to say, the wicked" a crowd worse than the classical nobility and demanded the guillotine for speculators, whom he saw as vampires starving the people.[4] In the nineteenth century, Balzac, who had witnessed the Revolution's despoliations and unauthorized transfers of patrimony, made Vautrin say in *Le père Goriot:* "The secret of great fortunes without apparent cause is a crime that has been forgotten because it was committed properly." Fraudulent bankruptcies, cooked books, inveigled inheritances, the deprivation of the poor—nothing excites the eloquence of the great novelist more than the description of the rapacity of his time. In 1854, the anarchist Proudhon denounced the stock market (along with the Jews), which "comes before school, the academy, the theater, political assemblies, congresses, before the army, before the judicial system, before the Church itself." Still in the nineteenth century,

Léon Bloy, a Catholic pamphleteer and an anti-Semite, contrasted the purity of Christlike blood with the nauseating pus of monetary flows.[5] For Bloy, who was more severe than Bossuet, it made no sense to speak of bad rich people because there are no good ones. They are all "devourers of the poor"—even those who appear to be the most devout—and fatten themselves on the suffering of the destitute. They are criminals de facto, if not de jure. "It would be less inhuman to put out their eyes and castrate them so that they would not in turn give birth to monsters."[6] Bloy even expressed hope that the 1908 earthquake in Messina, Sicily, said to cause as many as 200,000 deaths, would prove to have taken its greatest toll on the rich, causing them to meditate "in the vestibule of Hell on the delights and strength of riches."[7] For Charles Péguy, another fervent Christian, money, as the only reality that survived from the old order, is for the first time in history, facing God alone.[8] The instrument that must serve us to measure the world "has become the matter and the object of this world, a process as monstrous as if the clock began to be time." Its crime is the equivalence that favors "the immense prostitution of the modern world," which does not proceed from lust, but from "universal interchangeability."[9] Péguy went so far as to call for the abolition of the wage-earning class, which was to be replaced by a system of barter in which workers would give their labor to the city in order eventually to do away with monetary specie.[10] This amounts to an involuntary plea for the reestablishment of slavery—that is, of unpaid work. The only exception, and it is an important one, to this deluge of anathemas: Paul Claudel, in his book *Une voix sur Israël*, published in 1950, raises commerce and money to the rank of ontological categories and discerns in them the prefiguration of a spiritual existence.[11] And even if he denounces the false money that divides men and forgets "the sublime money

of charity," he also has one of his characters, Thomas Pollock
Nageoire, say: "Glorified be the Lord who has given the dollar
to man."[12]

Envious Hatred

The diatribes against money are part of our cultural treasure in
France and transcend the right/left division: "My only adversary, that of France, has in no way ceased to be money," General
de Gaulle said in 1969. François Mitterrand himself denounced
"King Money" at the Épinay Congress in 1971: "The true enemy
is monopoly, an extensive term for the powers of money, money
that corrupts, money that buys, money that kills, money that ruins
and money that rots even people's consciences." The pecuniary
instinct is always unworthy, even for the high bourgeoisie. Thus
it has to proceed under a mask: in this domain, as for religious
signs, the French choose discretion. Thus Françoise Bettencourt-
Meyers, at the trial concerning the possible spoliation of her
mother, a billionaire, by swindlers, made this incredible admission: "Among ourselves, we never spoke of money. Never."[13]

What the French reject is first of all the unequal distribution
of revenues. But they are also wary of success, which is always
suspect and results, according to them, from connivance.[14] Income taxes, and especially the wealth tax, become from this point
of view a fine that the privileged have to pay to excuse themselves
for having triumphed in a domain. Anyone who succeeds in
France has benefited from complicities in high places, or has
cheated. Everywhere *an envious hatred* accompanies the most spectacular careers. We are astonished when a person "coming from
diversity" (that is, not of European descent) piles up diplomas and
attains the highest positions. As if he had overcome a twofold

obstacle: the prejudices that are attached to the children of immigrants, and the difficulty in undertaking something without
falling prey to an asphyxiating bureaucracy. In the United States,
it is precisely success that makes you a hyperbolic American (as it
does in China or in India). The financial crisis of 2008 only exacer-
bated this anger. Didn't a supporter of "de-growth" and a Maximum Authorized Revenue propose to ostracize and deprive of
their nationality millionaires and billionaires who yielded to hubris and could no longer be compatriots like the rest?[15] Another
philosopher, who however rejected any moral approach to money,
regretted that a certain number of traders and rating agents
had not been hung from meat hooks after the subprime crisis in
2007–2008,[16] even though he doubted the effectiveness of the
measure. "Making due allowances (they are not murderers), mad
traders are as dangerous as Jihadists," a left-wing journalist explained with a keen sense of nuance.[17]

Jean-Luc Mélenchon, in his work *Qu'ils s'en aillent tous!* (2010)
suggests nothing less than kicking the rich out of France. The
back cover of the book is eloquent in this regard:

> Tomorrow, millions of people will take the powerful by the
> hair, exasperated to see them despoiling our country and
> condemning the population of the world's fifth economic
> power to the decline of all its social achievements. They will
> do so, revolted by the arrogant manners of the friends of
> money, not only this president and his government, but also
> the whole oligarchy: the outrageously expensive bosses, the
> wizards of money who transform everything human into
> merchandise, the financiers who are draining the lifeblood
> out of businesses, the media barons who have erased the
> people. Throw the bums out! Give us some air! I am calling
> for a "citizens" revolution in France to take power back from

the oligarchy, from the presidential monarch, from King Money.[18]

Even if Mélenchon suggests a maximum salary of a relatively comfortable 350,000 euros per year, beyond which a 100 percent tax would be levied, his extravagance shows the far left's inability to propose viable solutions for the malaise in France. The quarrel has even invaded show business; for example, when Gérard Depardieu announced in 2012 that he was moving to Belgium for tax reasons and opted for Russian citizenship, the left-wing actor Philippe Torreton replied in the daily newspaper *Libération:* "Shut your trap, take your dough and get out."[19] So let's go after the millionaires: on September 10, 2012, *Libération's* front-page headline was *"Casse-toi, riche con,"* this time addressing Bernard Arnault, who was suspected of having also applied for Belgian nationality, which he later denied. (This headline alluded to Nicholas Sarkozy's retort—"Casse-toi, pauvre con" [Buzz off, you poor jerk]— to a person at the 2008 Salon de l'Agriculture who had refused to shake his hand.) The simple spectacle of the rich and famous on television nauseates the left's good consciences. "Our fascination with the rich, Lagardère, Bouygues, Pinault, Bolloré, and others, the saga of power fills the columns of our newspapers. There is something obscene about the insistence with which their financial libido is offered up for the admiration of the *populo.*"[20] Besides, what does it matter that in France three-quarters of the taxes are paid by the 20 percent who have the highest incomes?[21] In other words, and contrary to the propaganda, it is in fact "the rich" who provide the fiscal backbone of the nation. How can one tolerate an element one scorns? By means of a psychological split, like everyone else. By condemning with the right hand what the left hand does.

Hide That Gold That I Can't Bear to See

A taboo does not forbid desires and pleasures; it reorganizes them. All these virtuous proclamations reflect first of all a certain pique in which one pretends to trample, out of envy, on what one cannot obtain.[22] A land of plenty populated by sixty-five million depressed people, France approves of the philippics of a guy like Pierre Rabhi, a militant supporter of poverty and a guru of happy sobriety, when he says that "gold has made humanity mad" and that "the ideology of omnipotent lucre" has subordinated "the beauty and nobility of the planet to the vulgarity of finance."[23] By a marvelous irony, Rabhi has become the darling of show business, from Marion Cotillard to Leonardo DiCaprio, and the bosses of the CAC 40 (the French equivalent of the Dow-Jones). Let us also recall that François Hollande made himself popular by declaring on June 8, 2006: "Yes, I don't like the rich. I don't like the rich, I admit that."[24] (He later regretted this remark.) And that he was elected in 2012 because he proclaimed in Le Bourget in January, during his first campaign meeting: "I am going to tell you who my adversary is, my true adversary. He has no name, no face, no party. He will never be a candidate, he will never be elected, and yet he governs. My adversary is the world of finance."

Hollande later forgot these principles and conducted an incoherent policy of fiscal bludgeoning followed by slamming on the brakes, an assiduous courting of the great financiers who give advantageous conditions to France, a declaration of love to businesses that had earlier been kept on the margins. The essential point is that these formulas won him the left's voters, who were expecting that the heads of the wealthiest would be put on pikes. Hollande may have lied, but in telling France what it wanted to hear, he showed a perfect knowledge of its soul. De Gaulle had already noted in his *Mémoires d'espoir* (1970) the extent to which social relationships had remained imbued with bitterness: "Everyone felt what he lacked rather than what he had," he explained in a very Tocquevillean phrase.[25] And Nicolas Sarkozy, declaring loud and strong his love of big money with a brazenness that shocked even Berlusconi, lost contact with the French.

The condemnations of money in France increase as the crisis grows. That is the very definition of ideology: turning the world upside down, taking the consequence for the cause, dreaming of a hypothetical exit from the market economy. Since a significant number of our compatriots no longer have enough to live decently, they will be told that prosperity is degrading, that true wealth is found in relationships and not in goods. In a period of crisis, the diatribes against the Golden Calf are a derivative. This explains the pamphlets against the rich that feed a whole industry of *lucrative indignation*. Take, for example, Michel and Monique Pinçon-Charlot who, for the past fifteen years, in book after book, have examined in detail the life of the big-business bourgeoisie. Their inquiry, instructive in itself, wins them high sales; they sound the powerful's way of life in order to damn it, in a striking alliance of hypocrisy and fascination. It is as if an archbishop spent evening after evening in the privacy of a brothel in order to be offended by its turpitudes. Here's an infallible rule: anyone who trumpets his scorn for the Golden Calf cherishes it in his heart. This pseudo-disdain is another name for a shameful passion. Genuine indifference to money does not need to proclaim its disgust.

Another journalist notes, in order to deplore it, that the governing left, from Lionel Jospin to François Hollande, has become

49

reconciled with money—that is, with the enemy—to the detriment of the promises and traditions of the socialist party.[26] And he compares this stunning turnabout to the French defeat at the hands of the Germans in 1940 as described in Marc Bloch's book *L'Étrange défaite*. The fact that the head of state took economic realities into consideration is supposed to be comparable to the French army's capitulation to the Wehrmacht's troops! The well-off exist to focus all this social rage on their persons. Let them leave or go to live elsewhere—in Europe, France has proven its mastery, along with Spain and Greece, in the art of exporting its riches (and its brains)—and people will point to the middle categories, describing their compensations as intolerable privileges. Thus in the autumn of 2013, the socialist government planned to decrease the salaries of professors teaching university preparatory classes, in order to create additional positions in secondary education. This proposal elicited such strong opposition that it was withdrawn. But the attempt itself was significant: incomes have to be leveled out if possible and reduced to the lowest common denominator. The hatred of the rich is descending; people begin by ranting against the billionaires, then the millionaires, and then the well-off classes; then they start loathing their next-door neighbors who earn a few hundred euros more than they do. Didn't Benoît Hamon, who was for a short time minister of national education, compare, in 2014, the success of children at school to "insider trading" because their families made use of connections, whether visible or concealed, to advance their kids in the system? Culture, work, and knowledge are said to be comparable to economic infractions and thus legally actionable. (Let us recall that teachers' children have a 92 percent chance of passing their baccalaureate exams. Should we therefore drag all teachers into court?) Hasn't President Hollande decreed that in France a person who makes at least four thousand euros a month could be considered rich? However, he himself declared assets of 1.17 million euros, just under the bar of 1.3 million euros for the ISF *(impôt sur la fortune)*. When he retires, the president's office noted in autumn 2014, he will receive a pension of fifteen thousand euros per month, a very comfortable sum for an enemy of the rich. Hasn't the minister of health, Marisol Touraine, an elegant upper-middle-class lady, distinguished "virtuous physicians," who accept low incomes, from "indecent physicians," who think that every effort deserves a good salary?

The Prohibition on Living Better

When Valérie Trierweiler, François Hollande's ex-partner, revealed in a best-seller on their breakup that he called the poor "the toothless" as a kind of joke, the press went wild: protest demonstrations by "the toothless" (as sans-culottes, one might say) were organized in various cities, all the left-wing groups as well as the right-wing Front National showed their indignation, and the president's popularity, already very low in 2014, sank still further.[27] The obsession with dental care became a joke throughout the country, a genuine social marker. People competed to show concern for the poor, opened their mouths wide to show the state of their teeth, and expressed their deference to those in precarious situations. We can wonder about this love of "the poor," which is so virulent in France, and ask whether it is not a way of abandoning them to their fate. They are enveloped in a nimbus of quasi-sacredness, the better to leave them in their current state. France is entering a market economy reluctantly, not without cursing it and swearing that it will never come to terms with it. It would be a mistake to ignore these anathemas, because they are not without influence on the way enterprises are run and the relations between capital and labor. The charm of Old Europe has to do with its immemorial anchorage in a pre-capitalist past composed of old-fashioned manners, strange forms of civility, and outmoded rituals. The charm of France is to have transferred the great aristocratic values to the domain of culture: among us, the desire for excellence, the worship of the great feat, is to be found in books, the theater, painting, cinema, and architecture. We are fascinated by the artistic trades exercised by men or women who combine creation and self-construction and rise to notoriety thanks to their talents. No matter how modest their incomes may be, these elites form a proud caste convinced that it is serving the country's renown. But this passion for liter-ature and language, this taste for the stage and the fine arts, goes hand in hand with an advertised disdain for mercantile concerns. On the one hand, France is very slowly liberalizing itself (even if public expenditures amount to 57.3 percent of the GDP, surpassed worldwide only by Finland), and on the other, it denounces the vulgarities of exchange: this linguistic camouflage is necessary to avoid antagonizing mentalities.

Consider the famous injunction attributed to Guizot, Louis-Philippe's foreign minister and then prime minister from 1840 to 1848: "Enrichissez-vous!" (Get rich!). It is still the object of outraged commentaries, a testimony to bourgeois greed, although others cast doubt on it, because Guizot, an austere Calvinist, is supposed to have left politics poorer than he was when he entered it. Lamartine had just uttered, under the July Monarchy, the fa-mous remark repeated by Pierre Viansson-Ponté in 1968: "France is bored." The country was languishing after the epic adventures of the Revolutionary and Napoleonic periods. Guizot responded by proposing a new watchword: "Enrich yourself by labor and by saving." According to historians, this formula can be understood in two ways. Either "Enrich France's material and intellectual condition," or "Enrich yourself by labor and saving and you will become electors," in a period subject to the system of *suffrage censitaire*, which limited the right to vote to those who met a certain standard of wealth.[28] The astonishing thing is that this imperative, which may in any case be apocryphal, could be held against Guizot as if it were an infamy. Taken in itself, the formula is not in any way reprehensible, much less than if it had said the contrary: "Impoverish yourself." (Deng Xiaoping himself said in 1978, as the Maoist torment was abating: "It is glorious to enrich oneself." But it is true that in China wealth is a source of happiness and in Shanghai, as Albert Londres said almost a century ago, it is "the first and the last material."[29]) But Guizot did not limit himself to recommending the appetite for gain; he made it the prelude to the nation's cultural and moral progress, once political and social rights had been achieved. Denouncing the rich is one thing, but why make the destitute feel guilty about aspiring to live better?

There is a constant ambiguity in the antifinance rhetoric: it seeks less to punish the upper crust—even if for a time they were threatened with a 75 percent income tax rate; the left has always confused the graduated income tax with a punitive tax—than to make the working and middle classes ashamed to express great ambitions.[30] It is easier to curse the nabobs than to lift the disinherited out of need. Instead, they are given a warning: "Don't try to live beyond your means; don't become a slave of social chimeras." The ideal society would be like the one in the former Soviet Union, where there were only the destitute (except for the *nomenklatura* for whom dachas and well-stocked stores were reserved). Then the desire to get rich, which is perfectly legitimate, is confused with corruption or wheeling and dealing.

But this soft Bolshevism—France is one of the last countries in the world where communism has long remained a seductive idea—is caught in an aporia. The French, so distrustful of the market, of free enterprise, would like to benefit from all the advantages of a developed economy—rapid transportation systems, free and effective medical treatment, safe housing, guaranteed incomes—and they want it without compromising with the "liberalism" they scorn. Lenin for the doctrine, Adam Smith for the results: hasn't it been said of France that it was a USSR that succeeded? (It combines the hypertrophy of the public sector with the atrophy of the private sector.) Capitalism, with its creation of wealth, but without capital. In France money always has an odor: it is the mathematical representation of the human cesspool. Wasn't it Zola who said in countless ways in his novel *L'argent* that money is both muck and an indispensable fertilizer?

Tartuffe in the Land of Robespierre

Every moralist is in danger of someday falling into the vice that he denounces, caught up by the object of his aversion. There is even a consubstantial link between the virtue that is trumpeted and the virtue that is trampled upon: authentic morality is modest and discreet. American commentary on politics and society is full of do-gooders, pastors, preachers, and politicians opposed to pornography, prostitution, adultery, and drugs. Sooner or later many of them are found in the arms of a call-girl or a minor, their nostrils full of cocaine. Then they have to spend their time repenting and swearing on the Holy Bible that they won't do it again. The Monica Lewinsky affair is emblematic of the sexual neurosis camouflaged behind a disapprobation of lying—even if North American puritanism is perhaps no more than a way of limiting erotic bankruptcy following the sexual revolution and of reviving a libido that is always haunted by exhaustion.[31] When everything is permitted, nothing is desirable anymore.

In the same way, the French allergy to money scarcely conceals a magnetic attraction to the financial idol that is revealed by the multiple affairs of corruption. No government of the Fifth Republic, including Hollande's, even though it claims to be exemplary, has been without its scandals (fraud, money-laundering, etc.), the most spectacular of which was that involving Jérome Cahuzac, the minister of the budget who swore before the National Assembly that he did not have any bank account outside France before retracting in 2013, and the most comical was that of Thomas Thévenoud, the ephemeral secretary of state for foreign trade, who in 2013 called upon tax cheaters to "do penance" whereas he himself paid neither his income taxes, nor his rent, nor his fines, allegedly suffering from "administrative phobia." Nothing serious, nobody died, but instead of accepting money and learning how to use it, the French demonize it in such a way that it reigns clandestinely and reappears furtively as a shameful appetite. It is true that in France, the caste of high officials, enjoying quasi-monarchical privileges, often feels that it is above the law. Let us recall that in 1766 Sweden instituted a principle of transparency regarding the incomes of ministers, representatives, and simple citizens, which prevented neither fraud nor scandals. We may also recall the famous Toblerone affair of 1995, when the number two woman in the Swedish socialist government was forced to resign for having paid for a chocolate bar with her official credit card. In this Scandinavian intransigence, we can also see an apotropaic act, a hardening before the possible abyss opened up by the nonrespect of the rules in the area.

A kind of phantom Catholicism continues to imbue the relation to money among the French: they venerate it like other nations, but in the mode of denial. "France is sick with money," Michel Rocard said in the *Journal du Dimanche* in 1988. A strange slip: for if France was sick, then it was, as it is today, sick with its hatred of money combined with an excessive indebtedness and galloping unemployment. These virtuous proclamations cannot take the place of politics in a modern nation that has become used to comfort and various services, and cannot consent to the latter's disappearance without serious damage. At the time when King Money is being denounced, it is instead a shortage of money that is predominant. Europe, especially southern Europe, is struggling with difficulties—unemployment, recession, deficits. Money is first of all what is lacked, by states, by public financial institutions, and by private individuals, and what really terrifies our compatriots is that they might slip into a lower social stratum. Thus in France there is a formal condemnation of wealth on the condition that we can enjoy its advantages all the same. Take for example the ex-soccer player Eric Cantona, who invited the French to empty their bank accounts on December 7, 2010, to overthrow the system and create a financial panic (and let us recall that at the time his wife, Rachida Brakni, was doing commercials for the Crédit Lyonnais bank).[32] We had heard about the red bosses who financed the Soviet Union; here we have a millionaire who denounces the rich, but without touching his nest egg. The verbal hatred of the system is all the stronger because people love to wallow in it. Posture and imposture coexist in the media. *The French are not a people of ascetics who reject luxury, they are a people of sybarites who pretend to love poverty.* The homeland of hedonism likes to clothe itself in the sackcloth of a rigorous Jansenism. Wasn't it the Maoist philosopher Alain Badiou who accused Voltaire of being a "wheeling-dealing scoundrel, a rich speculator, a skeptic and a sensualist"? From the fortune of the author of *Candide,* Badiou deduces his baseness.[33]

A Little Phenomenology of the Bank Note

Why, psychologists ask us, are we more reluctant to break a one-hundred-euro bill than to break five twenty-euro bills? Because when we break the larger bill, we have a stronger feeling of loss. We rank the figures, and a large bill seems to us to be worth more in itself than the total of the small ones that compose it. It shows the majesty of the large number the way a richly brocaded officer represents the whole of his army corps. Every bill comes to us in one of two forms: wrinkled like a rag or ironed like a clean shirt, shiny and smelling of fresh ink. This appearance can itself be subdivided into bills folded or in rolls. Some people carefully put their cash in their wallets, while others stuff it in their pockets. We have a tendency to spend the old bills more quickly than the new ones.[34] Dirty money, in this case, is old money; it looks worn out, it has passed through too many hands, while clean money has just come from the printing press, and you can imagine that you are the only one who has had it. It's another absurd feeling of property-ownership, the privilege of the first possessor, even though money can be possessed only by spending it. Unlike an object, money doesn't retain any aspect of its owner's soul. It is in principle an inert and neutral thing. But we try to keep it by attaching ourselves to large amounts. Many people like to feel the bills in their pockets, their silky crumple, more or less substantial depending on their value. They are given nicknames—in French, the old five-hundred-franc bills with a picture of Blaise Pascal were called "Scalpas," while in

Spain five-hundred-euro bills are called "Bin Ladens."[35] The matter that remains in money is what allows us to sympathize with it. Then it becomes flesh, it breathes under our fingers. It tells us: As long as I'm here, you have nothing to worry about.

Unlike a billfold overloaded with credit cards, the change purse immediately admits that it is the alms box. In the Byzantine world, the Christ child was compared to a coin in his mother's womb: the Virgin Mary's uterus was a moneybox full of gold.[36] In turn, the coins are the part of the available money that can be thrown away. The little god of piggy banks, when it jingles in its porcelain or metal container, produces a music sweet to the ear. What joy to find a substantial sum accumulated by adding up pennies. The coins' clatter is machine-gun fire that sounds and scatters on the floor when the piggy bank is overturned. If coins allow us to make exact change, they also embody the burden of something that is too heavy.

Inflation: the moment when bills are reduced to the status of garbage, colored paper. Commenting on "the debasement of money" in Austria and Germany in the 1920s, when an egg could cost as much as four billion marks, Stefan Zweig notes that a newspaper that cost fifty thousand marks in the morning cost one hundred thousand marks the same evening, and that currency exchanges made at ten o'clock in the morning could bring in ten to twenty times more at five o'clock in the evening. Softened, having passed through hundreds of hands, one day the bills join the class of rejects: having become mere tatters, they cease to enchant us. Finally, they become "pieces of paper of little intrinsic worth" (in J. K. Galbraith's phrase). Even if high-flying bandits, the geniuses of virtual finance, operate in abstraction, wealth will never be reduced to a series of figures on a screen; it will continue to take material form in rolls of bills, jewels, expensive watches, and diamonds. The petty criminals who with unerring instinct continue to rob banks, armored cars, and jewelry stores know that only too well. They are not going to steal a pure idea! As long as coins continue to wear holes in our pockets and bills to swell our wallets, money will remain a quasi-body as palpable as glasses, telephones, and prostheses. Bills and coins, miniaturized and easy to handle, are what remains of materiality in money. Money is a fiction that we need to touch in order to believe in it.

When a people claims to renounce money and the benefits it provides, that is because it also wants to renounce history. And that proves that it no longer has confidence in itself. Like many other nations, France lives between two systems of values: the gospel of Revolution and the iron laws of Capital, two opposed axiological systems. The one describes how we would like to see ourselves, the other the reality with which we have to come to terms. Between one and the other, there appears to be no compromise, even though this compromise is made in each of us all the time. The Republic claims to redouble its egalitarian ethos by praising spiritual greatness: it defends other cultural, literary, artistic riches as well as mercantile goods. We are in agreement on that. But in what way is a certain ease the enemy of the life of the mind?

FOUR

America, or Spiritual Money

*Faith is a certain confidence in what we hope for and an absence of
doubts regarding what we do not see.*
MARTIN LUTHER, HEBREWS 11:1

ON the other side of the Atlantic, everything seems to be reversed. In America, God loves the rich, not the poor. The imperial republic embraces money without embarrassment. Still more: it
seems to have established a quasi-sacred link between the nation
and the dollar, since the famous motto "In God we trust" is
written on every dollar. How can this be understood? We know
that the inscription of this formula was supposed to respond to
the trauma of the Civil War: put on two-cent coins in 1864, it
was abolished as a sacrilege by President Theodore Roosevelt in
1907. Although a few members of Congress were glad that God
would no longer be involved in secular transactions, others were
distressed by this abandonment. A congressman from Georgia
stated that the government should not coin "infidel money."[1]
President Eisenhower reestablished the motto by ordering it to
appear on all bills and coins—an extraordinary testimony to
America's belief that it enjoys divine grace, transforming the
marking of coins into a supreme act! For President Woodrow
Wilson, the destiny of the United States—the country of the
alliance between God and his people—was to redeem the world
by giving it liberty and justice, and to restart history on new
bases.

God in the Wallet: €/$

America's exceptional destiny is reflected even in its money: the greenback, bearing the staid image of a founding father and marked with the great seal, makes money a kind of impartial sanction, only the amount varying from one bill to another. This international reserve currency, *as good as gold,* is no doubt a burden for the rest of the world; as Treasury Secretary John Connally put it in 1971, "The dollar is our currency but it's your problem." It merely proves America's supremacy. As Milton Friedman asked in 1988: "Why worry [that America is living on credit]? The deficit is denominated in dollars and not in pounds or francs. In the last resort, we can always print more money."[2] Whence America's ability to tolerate a debt of almost 20 trillion dollars without being greatly inconvenienced, for the moment, because the debtor and the creditor are one and the same.

The identical dimensions of American bills is a puzzle: in all other currencies, the bills vary in size and color depending on their value. The dollar, remaining always the same, may perhaps thereby signify that the same dose of sacredness is inherent in the means of payment, no matter what amount is indicated: God is everywhere, even in the smallest bills. The monotony of the greenback, terribly symmetrical, with its imperial eagle holding war and peace in its talons, its Latin motto *E pluribus unum,* its truncated pyramid surmounted by a triangular eye like a Masonic symbol, is not a painting (though Andy Warhol made it one); it is an indefinitely repeated foundational act.[3] A majestic and austere currency, meaning that earning money is not just a vulgar diversion but a matter of the greatest importance, it does not need to be supplemented with a soul; the soul is in the bank note. The lollar is a paper Eucharist.

What a contrast with the euro, whose images, varying in size and color, no longer represent the great figures of the Old World, as did Cervantes on the old peseta, Leonardo da Vinci on the Italian lira, Goethe on the German Deutschmark, Pascal or Richelieu on the French franc, but instead bridges and arches, against the background of a map of Europe, a gigantic lobby where people from all over the world are invited to meet in a space without borders. This abstraction, whose colorfulness is more or less attenuated, testifies to the will to construct a political whole on the basis of the disincarnation of the peoples who compose it. The euro is a visual oxymoron that seeks to personify benevolent hospitality, even if it has retained a national symbol on the reverse of each coin. Europe has sought to construct itself on the subtraction of the nations that compose it and not on their synergy. That is why the euro, sixteen years after its introduction, still does not enjoy authority and arouses so much opposition. But currencies also tell us about the societies that issue them, their glories and their aspirations: Switzerland, for example, celebrates its musicians and its architects, Arthur Honegger and Le Corbusier; the British pound bears the images of Queen Elizabeth, Charles Darwin, Adam Smith, or Elizabeth Fry, a philanthropist who helped improve the condition of prisoners in the nineteenth century. Money honors the greatness of a culture, the high deeds of a history. Whereas the dollar combines verticality and inclusiveness—a money that is elected by God and covers the whole earth with greenbacks—the euro implies horizontality and confinement. A faceless currency flanked by bridges, vast marketplaces, it appeals to the unity of the human race but fails to establish itself on the worldwide level. In conceiving Europe as a "substantial vacuity," Ulrich Beck, a German sociologist, rightly saw airports and train stations as places of an empty conviviality, rechristened cosmopolitanism. A common currency adopted in the absence of supranational sovereignty, an economic act disconnected from any political act, is doomed to fail.[4] Although there are state banks, there is no prince to guarantee them. Europe dreams of being strong, of being capable of standing up to America. But by trying to exit History (even though at the moment it is being dragged back into it) it has desacralized its means of payment. It has been rightly remarked that the euro was introduced without any official ceremony, and this reflects a serious lack of symbolism.[5] The solemnity of collective membership was neglected in favor of a purely technical operation. And this creation, by leading to the disappearance of national currencies, aroused a feeling of dispossession everywhere.

Inversely, the dollar draws on a twofold source: from the past, with the effigies of the founding fathers, and on heaven, with the invocation of the Lord. Thus the smallest transaction is redeemed by God's blessing. In the United States, economics is a branch of theology. If in 1971 Richard Nixon was able to put an end to the Bretton Woods Accords and disconnect the greenback from gold, that is because the United States already had a gold standard: God himself. America: the alliance of prayer and prosperity, a materialism that remains constantly spiritual because it is blessed by the hand of the All Powerful. Over there, the bigot is also a businessman, and vice versa (pastors carry on business even during services; in the "megachurches," shamelessly, you can also buy "prayers as you go"). The supremacy of the dollar proves that only the nation-state, whether small or large, remains sovereign in the last instance, contrary to liberal or anarchist mythologies regarding the end of homelands. Money does not cancel politics, it derives from it. With the dollar, America has forged a *genuine spiritual money.*

To the immediate transcendence of the dollar corresponds the immanence of the euro, which is still desperately seeking its majesty. The dollar: the liturgical currency par excellence; the euro: the prosaic currency of an incomplete architecture. The nations that compose Europe have freely ceded part of their sovereignty to Brussels. But the Europe of twenty-eight countries has not reconstructed another federal sovereignty; it remains a market without a political project, a government, or an army. This construct, which is capable of setting the size of bananas or regulating the contents of chocolate in twenty-eight countries, cannot agree concerning sovereign decisions, which are left to the capitals of the main nations. The euro, in its fragility, is only a reflection of this hesitation. That is why France, and beyond it, the European continent, has had so much difficulty conceiving their future in the sense of a collective projection in time, as has not only the United States but also China, Russia, India, and Brazil, which are sure that they are called upon to make history. The United States exists in potential; Europe exists in nostalgia. The United States is a project; Europe is a regret.

The New Church of the Prosperous

In 1913, Freud associated money with sex, two subjects that involve duplicity and require a clear position on the part of the psychoanalyst: he has to ask patients to pay for being relieved of their reticence in erotic matters.[6] This argument is open to doubt: sincerity in one domain does not necessarily imply its equivalent in another. The proof of this is that the French, who like to be ribald, close up when financial questions are involved. Americans, on the other hand, are prolix regarding their incomes, but are coy when intimate questions come up, or else discuss them in detail with the cold precision of an entomologist. Over the past thirty years the criminalization of sex on university campuses in America has taken on frightening dimensions; any kind of intimate relationship seems at risk of being treated as harassment or rape, with neither mutual consent nor the age of the lovers being taken into account. Any penetration is a potential murder, and this opens the door to the worst kind of blackmail. The two sexes exist in a state of potential belligerence, aided by the judge and the lawyer, the indispensable third parties in all couples. Whereas in the Muslim world men are taught to beware of women, who are impure and perfidious, in the United States women are taught to beware of men, who are violent and brutal.

Americans have replaced their suspicion of eroticism with an immoderate appetite for profit,[7] which represents the goodwill shown them by the Creator. The great question of Calvinism is: Why bother to do good if we are already saved? Why try to limit evil if we are already damned? Faith cannot be proven, but it is attested by results which, if they do not provide an irrefutable answer, at least hint at it. In a deviation that neither Luther nor Calvin could foresee, in the United States the wealthy began to form an ostensible church that offered them a virtual certitude of redemption. Consider a remark made at the turn of the twentieth century by John D. Rockefeller (1839–1937), the founder of Standard Oil: "God gave me my money. . . . I believe the power to make money is a gift of God . . . to be developed and used to the best of our ability for the good of mankind. Having been endowed with the gift I possess, I believe it is my duty to make money and still more money and to use the money I make for the good of my fellow man according to the dictates of my conscience."[8] In the *Nouvel Observateur* for November 27, 1987, Françoise Giroud wrote: "In the United States, people display their fortunes the way monkeys show their sex organs. Who has the biggest one?" In this respect, she preferred French hypocrisy.[9] On the other hand, in the

United States it is clear that God does not approve of the indigent, and that is why Americans are reluctant to develop a providential state on the European model, even if they too have a system of assistance (the "welfare state," which concerns 12 percent of the population). It is one thing to say that the rich owe their prosperity to a divine commandment, and another to explain that the poor deserve their fate. Instead of looking for scapegoats, they should blame only themselves for their difficulties. "The best thing we can do for the poor is to leave them alone," Milton Friedman said. Let us also recall that America still sees poverty through the lens of the race question, as is emphasized in this famous statement by Larry Holmes, the former world boxing champion: "It's hard to be black. You haven't ever been black? I used to be when I was poor."

For Protestants, as we have seen, desiring privation is a sign of perversity. Thus Benjamin Franklin, the spiritual father of American capitalism, decried the ascetics of the monasteries, whom he considered absurd self-tormentors. The monk and the mendicant both insult God's glory and violate the duty of love for one's neighbor. In the United States, getting rich is a patriotic duty. "The chief business of the American people is business," President Coolidge was to say early in the twentieth century and went on to explain that "The man who builds a factory builds a temple. . . . The man who works there worships there."[10] Getting rich is the only way to pay homage to the Creator and to make his creation fruitful. This is an inversion of the Lutheran commandment: instead of money being the reward of virtue, virtue now consists in displaying one's money. This remains true even if the "robber barons" of the late nineteenth century, after a lifetime of rapine, ended up engaging in philanthropy, some out of braggadocio, like John D. Rockefeller, and others out of a guilty conscience, like Andrew Carnegie.[11]

The Lucky Sperm Club

The heir has merely taken the trouble to be born, and that is his tragedy. He belongs to the "lucky sperm club"—his existence is already masticated and predigested.[12] Unbearable "rich kids," who display their class haughtiness everywhere, think themselves far above average and trample on the laws, sure that Mom and Dad will come to save them if they get in trouble. That is why a certain proportion of them turn favor into malediction and sink into drugs and delinquency. For them also "one has to be pardoned for having more," as the Baroness de Rothschild said at the beginning of the twentieth century. The transmission of a great fortune, Andrew Carnegie remarked, is an unbearable burden for the beneficiaries, who rarely make wise use of it.[13] If you're a billionaire, what percentage of your wealth should you give your children? Even one or two percent represents a fabulous amount for ordinary mortals. There were 2,325 billionaires worldwide in 2014, and between now and 2019 there will be fifty-three million millionaires: the market of the descendants is enormous. From infancy on, they have to be trained to deal with this colossal manna that threatens to bury them. That is why the wealthiest (Sting, Bill Gates) are reluctant to leave their money to their children and prefer to invest it in charities. We know the cliché: the hideous group of brothers and sisters are waiting, perched like vultures, for the notary's decision and the reading of the will. Having expectations means wishing the death of one's parents.

What does Faust lack after having sold his soul to Me-
phistopheles in exchange for all pleasures? Precisely this:
the beauty of the path, the grandeur of the effort, the miracle
of the result. Only the money one has earned by one's own
labor is valuable. If all our wishes were granted and even
anticipated, we would be dead before we had begun to live.
Anyone who has not had to fight, who hasn't known hunger
and thirst, will never know the pleasure of victory. Unless
one belongs to a dynasty, being a son or a daughter of . . . is
to spend one's life taking one's patronymic back from one's
ancestors in order to appropriate it to oneself. The only
transmission from one generation to another that is worth
anything is that of the mind, of knowledge, of the love of
the humanities.

But an heir is not doomed to reproduce the past: he can
bifurcate, abandon the cozy affairs of his ancestors, go
elsewhere—like the philosopher Ludwig Wittgenstein, the
son of a German steel magnate who in 1913 gave his fortune
to his brothers and sisters. Succession is often secession.
Similarly, a rebel, thinking he is destroying oppression,
often prolongs it in spite of himself. Thinking he has made
a break with it, he limits himself to repeating or even ag-
gravating the old order. This has been the destiny of too
many revolutions that have merely substituted one dictatorship for another. We try to be rebels, and we end up being
conformists; we try to be loyal, and end up inaugurating, in
spite of ourselves, a new history. Even the most generous
legacy leaves a margin of uncertainty that is the margin of
liberty.

American Protestantism thus relapsed into the justification by works of which it accused Roman Catholicism. Wealth and, therefore, happiness in this world are the rewards of a particular way of life. This self-election on the part of the rich is not without arrogance, because it is essentially religious. A disturbing reversal that can be illustrated by a geographical example: at one end of Wall Street, a narrow, high-walled, and hypersecuritized artery in lower Manhattan, stands the Episcopalian Trinity Church. In it we can see a symbol of God watching over business, the Banker of souls protecting profane bankers. But it can also be seen as proof that the New York Stock Exchange has relegated the old God to a little house at the end of the street, the dollar having become the material holy sacrament. The outcome is undecidable: neither has the last word.

Beyond National Neuroses

Each nation is great only if it suspends its prejudices. If France were an ascetic country, it would be easier to understand its determination to relegate money to the lowest regions of experience. But Paris is not Sparta; in fact, it is the capital of luxury and fashion, and its determination to loudly proclaim values superior to materialism does not stand up to common experience: an appetite for goods and comfort, better accepted in the United States, is merely given a coat of moral varnish. Our public buildings are Old Regime palaces, and our ministers sit on Louis XVI chairs, under gilded ornaments and paneling. To devalue this vile metal, we would have to devalue merit, work, the taste for forms, for elegance, the love of good food—in short, we would have to unravel the whole national patrimony in favor of a utopia of asceticism very remote from our character. The commonplaces have to be recognized and reversed: if Americans venerate money, they also resent with increased anger its confiscation by a handful of people, as was shown by the ephemeral Occupy Wall Street movement, as well as by President Obama's warnings concerning the end of the American dream shattered by excessive inequalities. America is in danger of reliving, in the capitalist mode, Europe's experience of feudalism, the financial barons being the new aristocrats, without manners or blue blood. For a European, whether of the right or of the left, the American educational and health-care systems, which are expensive and easily accessible only to the wealthiest, and the incestuous proximity of Wall Street to Congress and the White House constitute a scandal and an enigma.

In America, what restrains the selfish appetite for well-being is the messianic patriotism and religiosity that brings the nation together in times of danger. If this bond were one day to be broken, there would be an explosion of violence aggravated by the enormous circulation of some 300 million firearms in the country. Remove this theological/political framework and the American Republic would collapse. In the United States, Tocqueville said, the poor and the rich share the same uneasy appetite for material delights and fear losing them.[14] He forgot to add that these desires are contained by the love of country that transcends each citizen and makes him a potential soldier in its service. Both France and America are complex enough to rise above their respective neuroses. Just as there is a French tradition of scorning finance, there is another that praises commerce and industry, from Montesquieu to Saint-Simon by way of Voltaire, Tocqueville, Frédéric Bastiat (1801–1850), and even the utopian pre-Marxist Charles Fourier, who praised wealth against the whole socialist

tradition: in his work, blessed money conveys passionate effervescence, and he celebrates, on page after page, the "thirst for
gold and hitting the jackpot."[15] Even Proudhon, the author of the
famous saying, "property is theft," paradoxically praised speculation and celebrated the stock market when it increases collective
wealth.

So why, then, is money condemned in France and subsequently admitted, though reluctantly, and why is money praised
in the United States, though subsequently subjected to contingent restrictions? To stress the dominant values of each society:
France sees itself as a universalist country, devoted to the arts of
the mind and to letters, while America sees itself as a land of opportunities where every citizen has the right to enrich himself as
he sees fit. In France, the constitution of national identity around
a venerated language, a passion of ideas, a will to address the
whole world, in the United States the cult of the frontier, the
desire for self-transcendence, and the certitude that by making
money each American is paying homage to the nation that has
witnessed his birth or been able to take him in.

Both the French and the Americans want contradictory things:
social protection for all, more in Europe than in the United
States, but also the right to live well, and thus social and occupa-
tional mobility and full employment. The Americans have created the myth of the self-made man, a Promethean individual
who leaves the past behind him and becomes the creature of his
works. Money is thus the sign of a freedom conquered, not of a
tradition undergone. America is one of the rare nations where a
collective sacredness binds citizens together and is in no way
governed by the laws of the market alone. What fascinates and
horrifies us on the other side of the Atlantic is a moral conserva-

tism coupled with hypermodernity: the continuing imposition of capital punishment in numerous states is accompanied by a scrupulous legalism, and the constitutive violence of the social contract does not prevent an omnipresent sentimentalism; puritanism cohabits with a great freedom of behavior, shocking inequalities with an eagerness to engage in enterprise, and familial traditionalism with a fascination with novelty. This archaism is what holds the republic together. Europe, on the other hand, is no more than a mercantile space without a political project. It has given itself over, bound hand and foot, to consumerist delights, without elevating them to a higher plane. France is more sensitive to the ambivalence of money. America reveres it, hedged in by strict patriotic and religious limits: the dollar works for the grandeur of the American nation and the glory of the Calvinist God, melancholic and hard-working.

Our French disapproval of money is twofold: we pronounce ourselves in favor of a fairer distribution of the pie, and at the same time denounce the very existence of the Golden Calf and dream of its demise. We never cease to oscillate from one to the other. When money flows freely, we denounce its base materiality. When it begins to be in short supply, when economic decline strikes, we censure the whole system.[16] A double postulate: If capitalism prospers, we hold our noses when faced with this profusion of ugliness and baseness; if it stumbles, we revolt against this second wave of iniquity. We want material wealth to be only what it is—the indispensable prelude to freedom—but we also want it not to extend to everyone. This oscillation is the mark of our ambivalence.

Most of the world is becoming Protestant (or at least adopting a puritanical variant of the Protestantism that has taken root in the United States), and it believes in the virtues of money and in

The Discreet Servant Complex

Is money a bad master or a good servant? This question—
which is attributed to Horace, was raised again by Alexander
Dumas fils, and has since been plagiarized countless times—
illustrates our malaise. As in the Hegelian master-slave dia-
lectic, money is supposed to be a recalcitrant servant who has
to be kept under control to prevent it from tyrannizing us.
First formulated by Aristotle, this process of inversion was
analyzed by Marx in a famous passage in *Capital,* where
he shows that in capitalism the classic commodity–money–
commodity cycle is replaced by a money–commodity–money
cycle, money having become an end in itself, independently
of what it allows us to purchase. It is supposed to be a *quasi:*
a quasi-end and a quasi-means, with an unclear status. Too
hot to be only a tool, too trivial to accede to the dignity of a
value. Assigned to fluidify human relationships, it is supposed to revolt against its status and aspire to the role of
intransigent lord. It is supposed constantly to lead us into
extravagance, offering our least reputable appetites a way of
giving themselves free rein.

It is too easy to attribute to money follies that are our own
fault. We alone decide to bow down before this demon. No
evil genius holds us in his power: in penal law, mad traders
are judged by their acts, not as irresponsible people possessed, victims of ultra-rapid algorithms. Money dictates
nothing to us that we ourselves haven't already conceived. It
is fortunate that humans invented it: it allows them not to
detest themselves too much. They can project onto it all the

passions that agitate them—greed, pettiness, lust, pride—and transform them into virtues, or else turn the advantages into defects and the defects into advantages. Money as folly and universal corruption. But it is a still greater folly to try to do without it.

A very fine, imperceptible line separates money as an end from money as a means. The task of consumerism and advertising consists entirely in constantly blurring that line. And our intelligence consists in reestablishing it when necessary. Thus it is up to us to keep money in a subordinate position. But to stay that way, there has to already be a lot of it. "The money one has is the instrument of freedom, the money one seeks is the instrument of servitude" (Rousseau). An erroneous argument, since one has to have sought and earned money; it doesn't rain down on us like manna. It may be a servant, but it is a servant that begins by dictating the conditions under which it will obey. The indifference to external goods advocated by moralists like Cicero, who was extremely rich, presupposes that one has enough not to think about them. "Money is of no importance; the important thing is to have some," as the character Marguerite says in the film of the same name.[17] It is still freedom when it is forgotten. It frees us from need but not from the need for money.

money as virtue. The latter does not do away with the political dimension; it is politics that founds the legitimacy of money, which is a simple projection of national power. If Europe had any kind of sovereignty, the euro would not be going through such a crisis. To Rousseau's question, "Do luxury and comforts extinguish the desire for freedom in man's heart?" the United States replies in the negative. This is proven by its worldwide interventionism, which is sometimes disastrous, sometimes indispensable, and its role as a "reluctant sheriff" (Richard Haass) in the world market. Tocqueville was mistaken when he described the citizens of this country as slaves to their well-being who were prepared to sacrifice their independence to it. Each time the situation has called for it, the Americans have subordinated their taste for business to the imperatives of engagement (even if they find an economic interest in it). They have saved the world's freedom at least three times, in 1917, in 1944 against National Socialism, and in 1948 against the USSR, and today they are in the vanguard, along with France and Britain, in the battle against jihadism. The expansion of a flourishing market in the United States has extinguished neither its concern for the oppressed nor its hatred of servitude, at the risk of sometimes allowing itself to go too far. From this we can perhaps derive an axiom: a nation that curses money is a nation that does not believe in itself and no longer believes in its future. We quibble about means when we have lost sight of the realm of ends. And the end, beyond private calculations, is always civilization.

PART II

Three Myths about the Golden Calf

❦ FIVE ❧

Money, the Ruler of the World?

In the end, civilization is merely the triumph of greed over war.
IAN MORRIS, *War: What Is It Good For?*

IN his novel *L'Argent*, which details the collapse of a Catholic bank in the grip of the demon of speculation in the last years of the Second Empire, Émile Zola presents a minor character, Mme. Conin, an "adorable blonde, all pink and plump," the wife of a stationer in the Rue Feydeau, who spends her afternoons, "during the hours when her good husband was doing his accounts, and when she was running around Paris, doing household errands," with lovers whom she never sees more than twice. The financier Saccard, the novel's protagonist, sees her coming out of a hotel with a young man, and propositions her in his turn. She politely refuses; he insists, offers her money, a very large sum; she declines, explaining that she loves her husband, that they will someday retire with a very nice nest egg, and that she gives herself to whomever she wishes, even "poor devils." Saccard is stunned: "What! So money could not buy everything! This woman others had enjoyed for nothing, and he could not have her, even at a crazy price! She said no, and she meant it. In all his triumph, he suffered cruelly over this, as if it had cast a doubt over his power, a secret disillusion about the power of money, which until then he had thought absolute and sovereign."[1]

79

The Last Romantic Illusion

Everyone has a price. It was, in France, after Balzac and, in England, after Jane Austen that the habit of assessing individuals in quantitative terms began to invade literature. People became calculating machines and something to be counted. This mania, which was contemporaneous with the improvement of technologies, began as early as the thirteenth century, along with numerology: the transition from Roman numerals to Indo-Arabic numerals, the use of zero, the reign of "pantometry," the universal measure that triumphed in astronomy, ballistics, clock-making, and especially the art of war, which put thousands of men in battle order.[2] In turn, the Enlightenment spread the idea of a calculus of pleasures and pains and began to evaluate human activities in terms of advantages and costs. This phenomenon of quantifying time and space culminated in the Industrial Revolution of the nineteenth century. Bodies and souls could be bought: "everywhere, civilization replaced honor with money."[3] For Balzac, the Revolution was nothing but the generalized plunder of the aristocracy's and the clergy's property and the ensuing confusion of the orders. He marveled at the "omnipotence, omniscience, and omnipropriety of Money," as if he had discovered the philosopher's stone of the new humanity.[4] If the two active principles of *La Comédie Humaine* are gold and pleasure, they conceal a great villainy: theft, expropriation, murder. The rich are respectable pirates. Balzac introduced the notarial dimension into literature. In his work, "destinies with little quantifiable amplitude" (in Bruno Tessarech's words) have no fictional quality.

The author of *La Cousine Bette* worked himself to death to pay his debts, and was the living proof of his system. So we might be tempted to say that without concern about money, there would be no great novels (a rule that has numerous exceptions, among them Henry James, Edith Wharton, André Gide, and Marcel Proust). However, Balzac's accounting was not always correct. The mathematizing of the world frequently goes off track, and the numbers are wrong: consider the black holes of several billions in national budgets or economic crashes, good examples of mathematics gone mad. There are few great novels about money pure and simple; it is novelistic only when it is mixed with other passions for which it is a mirror or an amplifier. Talk about money is always talk about something else: about loyalties and betrayals, meteoric ascents and spectacular collapses. Indifferent to the emergence of the working class, to the importance being taken on by productive labor, Balzac announces and foreshadows the financialization of the world. He issued his books like so many securities to flood the market and transform his ink into revenues.

Illusions perdues (*Lost Illusions*, the title of one of Balzac's novels)—French Romanticism posits, as a dogma, the opposition between the heroic dreams of youth and the vulgarities of the mercantile age. Life after the Revolution and the Napoleonic adventure is an ineluctable passage from hope to disenchantment. Under the gray skies of manufacturing and commerce, dreams are blasted, poetry is trampled. Glory has departed, sublime love gets bogged down in the conjugal stew. No prayer is answered, no aspiration recognized. However, there is one belief that Romanticism helped take root in our culture: that of the omnipotence of money. It is that cliché that I seek to challenge here and that haunts Marxists and leftists as well as Christians, conservatives, and liberals.

Saint Augustine, codifying the Catholic tradition, described three great sins committed by fallen man: the *libido dominandi*, the thirst for power, *conscupiscentia*, lust, and *avaritia*, the love of possession.[5] But, he added, each vice has the ability to check the others and to thwart their bad effects. Glory, power, and money are equally ignoble, but useful insofar as they can neutralize each other. As Moderns, we have forgotten this dietetics of the passions and have reduced it to a single dimension: self-interest. Our talent as clinicians, especially since Karl Marx, consists in detecting it beneath all the human machine's motivations. It is self-interest, an omnipresent medium, that is supposed to have triumphed and bent everything to its rule. Bankers, financiers, and brokers are said to be the "masters of the universe," to use Tom Wolfe's expression in *The Bonfire of the Vanities* (1987). We may find some consolation in the idea that, were there no master of the world, that would mean that history moves forward blindly, and that we are puppets in it. Morality, beliefs, knowledge, and authority are supposed to have been absorbed by the Golden Calf that imposes its law on us. Thus Michael Sandel, a professor at Harvard, pertinently argues that the domain of the activities that can be bought is expanding exponentially. For example, you can pay people to stand in line for you at the bakery and at the hospital (this practice already existed in communist Europe), or to stand in line to obtain passes to attend Congressional hearings; you can pay patients to take their medicine, and give children money for getting good grades at school or for reading books (in India, poor families who send their children to school are rightly compensated because in doing so they are depriving themselves of useful workers).[6] In China, you can pay a company to present your excuses, and in Germany if you don't dare tell your lover you want to break up, you can hire an agency to do it for you.[7] Everyone knows the classic and amusing example of the old man who sells his house *en viager* (the buyer to take possession when the seller dies) and who then suddenly recovers his health and buries his creditors one after the other.[8] Or that of insurance brokers who, having bet on the rapid death of their customers, are furious to discover that the latter have still not "arrived at maturity."[9] It is more shocking to buy the right to kill black rhinoceroses, an endangered species, or lions.

These examples, whether rapacious or comical, raise a real problem: to what extent does the commercialization of a good destroy its value? Does advertising in the schools undermine the mission of national education? For example, compensating children for sending thank-you notes defies good manners and virtually assures social difficulties later on.[10] In the same way, to pay them for going to school and promise them a reward for good grades, or to give them, as is done in Dallas, two dollars for each book read, is to risk discouraging children, who are sure that their parents do not think they are good enough.[11] Some kinds of compensation change the scale of values. We know the famous example of the director of a nursery school in Israel who, noting that parents arrived late to pick up their children, decided to impose a fine of ten dollars on them. Contrary to all expectations, even more parents arrived late: they were no longer constrained by any moral imperative, and were willing to pay a sum approximately equivalent to the cost of a baby-sitter.[12] The invasion of advertising on our television and film screens, billboards along the roads, and even on people's foreheads or arms, is rightly considered intolerable; but apart from the fact that this phenomenon is not new (men carrying sandwich-boards go back more than a century), it says nothing against money but everything against the poverty that leads a mother to have the name of a casino tattooed on her forehead, for example, in order to pay for her son's studies.[13] Thus it is not this vile metal in itself that is to blame, but its distribution.

Benjamin Franklin, or Virtue in Capital

The son of a Boston candle maker, the youngest in a family of seventeen children, Benjamin Franklin was a man of the Enlightenment: a great traveler, he was ambassador to France in 1776, where he visited Buffon, Hume, Voltaire, Mirabeau, and Robespierre. The inventor of the lightning rod, the Franklin stove, and bifocal glasses, an ardent abolitionist, and one of the authors of the Declaration of Independence, he is typical of a period that thought it could reconcile virtue, wealth, and learning. He was the first to propose a morality of money as the foundation of the new society. In his writings, he presents himself as an *exemplum*, in the sense the Romans gave that word, the edifying model of the "self-made man" who was concerned to devote himself to the community and to the American nation. He dispensed his economic advice to younger generations, dissuading them from falling into idleness, profligacy, lust, gluttony, or debt. He urged women to learn accounting, more useful than music or dancing, to protect themselves against the trickery of ill-intentioned people. He exhorted the young to enrich themselves because it was by work, sobriety, and honesty that one became a good citizen. He put all his talent in the service of others and asked himself each evening: What good have I done today? In what way have I been a useful citizen? He was born poor and was not ashamed to admit it, happy to have risen step by step to his present position.

He invented the genre of financial autobiography, offering prudential rules for the ordinary business of life. His *Poor Richard's Almanack* took the form of simple aphorisms: "Early to bed, early to rise, makes a man healthy, wealthy, and wise."[14] We can smile at these platitudes, at this long-forgotten Bible of the eighteenth-century good American. Franklin suspects the dangers to which getting rich exposes a person: a taste for luxury; intemperance; the vanity that leads us to conform to the judgments of others—"the eyes of other people are the eyes that ruin us."[15] But he hopes to contain these vices by simple discipline, moderation, and saving money. For him money is inseparable from ethics. After him, money and wisdom were to be forever dissociated. It's time to rethink the connection between them.

Money Is Always Secondary

The marvelous thing about money is that it performs miracles: it makes the impossible possible. But between this concrete power and the fantasy of omnipotence there is an abyss. In every financier, there is first a child who believes in fables, in the genies of legends, a deficient ego in the grip of the most puerile dreams. Consider this admission made by Jeffrey Skilling, the ex-CEO of Enron who was sentenced on June 21, 2013, to fourteen years in prison for fraud, conspiracy, and insider trading: "I've thought about it a lot. Only money matters. That's how you buy loyalty. Feelings no longer count. It's with money that performance is achieved." What is striking in this statement is not its cynicism, but its naïveté: if only money could buy loyalty and fidelity! The hope of using money to move beyond our condition is an illusion shared by its sycophants as well as its enemies. It is a mistake to minimize money's role, but it is also a mistake to overestimate it. Although money can do many things, it can't do everything. It always obeys our caprices; it is never their source. It isn't money that produces narcissism, the will to power, religious or political proselytizing, class inequalities, or self-interested motives. Financial poaching is supposed to infringe on the virgin territory of grand sentiments, honor, ingenuity? That's a good joke. At most, it's an accelerator, never a first cause. The market enters our lives with our complicity, it doesn't conquer our souls; they welcome it as a liberator. It begins by putting the world at our disposition: it offers us lifestyles and experiences centered on convenience and immediacy. A gigantic organization bends to my slightest desires and even anticipates them. The pleasure of money is twofold: it gives us time, spares us many boring tasks; but above all it offers each of us, democratically, in the form of personal trainers or janitors, the advantages that servants—coachmen, chauffeurs, major domos, and cooks— used to provide for their masters, but without moral or affective debts because they are not bound to anyone. What does service mean in the democratic age? A remunerated servitude in which those who help us are often treated inconsiderately. With this difference: the person in question can always leave. Service is a contract, not a property title. Everything that was subject to expectations or hierarchical relationships can be subcontracted to specialists: administrative and household tasks, baby-sitting, care for the elderly. In a democratic universe payment makes it possible to obtain what one wants before others do. The pleasure of the short-circuit: it adjusts supply to demand, and makes the instantaneous satisfaction of our wishes possible.

Our societies combine two factors: competition and convenience. One regulates competitive relationships and knows only the sanction of success or failure; the other outlines a simple and seductive contractual model that is valid for all kinds of connections. On the one hand, hard labor and the pain of rivalry; on the other, the ease of satisfying our slightest appetites without difficulty. The question is complicated by the fact that the market and the self as a small enterprise are congruent; in working on his personal development, in maximizing his talents, the individual is obeying the same principles of utility and rationality as the ones dictated by the economy. Each person becomes an asset that has to be made productive, and capitalism as a culture stimulates and accompanies individualism, which adopts its rhythms and benefits from its flexibility. To take an extreme example, the stars of showbiz, Jay Z, Beyoncé, Oprah Winfrey, Martha Stewart, Madonna, or David Bowie (who made his debut on the bond market in 1997), become their own brands and offer themselves as ways of life.[16] Money not only loosens our bonds to the group but also, by converting us into economic entities, forces us to sell ourselves, to convert ourselves into cash, since the self has become a value like any other, subject to the law of rise and fall.

However, this observation has to be qualified. Industrial dynamism or stagnation are determined by culture and the social bond understood in the broadest sense. That is why there are never economic crises in the strict sense of the term, only spiritual or moral crises. Schumpeter reformulated the paradox of the invisible hand this way: for the common lead of self-interest to be transformed into gold, it has to be supervised by institutions or by persons (judges, policemen, politicians, government officials) whose motives, put in the service of the public good, have nothing to do with those of *homo economicus*. To adopt the language of the Enlightenment: it is customs, a certain kind of people and manners, and the spirit of the nation that are primary, and the economic dimension is always derived. Capitalism functions only when it is channeled by the state, traditions, and customs that are governed by another logic. It is because society is not entirely a market that the economy can be one; a coincidence between the two would probably lead to reciprocal disintegration. A hospital, for instance, survives only because of the extraordinary devotion of its staff, which spares neither its time nor its generosity in caring for the patients. If money were the only thing guiding nurses (whose salaries are still scandalously low; from a Fourierist perspective, we should invert the salary scale and pay those doing the most thankless jobs the highest wages), we wouldn't think much of the patient's chances of surviving. There is no country in the world that is governed by the laws of profit alone. As we have seen, even the very capitalist United States balances its praise of free enterprise with a touchy patriotism, an omnipresent religiousness, and a keen sense of solidarities. Money is an atheistic machine that can turn everything into cash but is incapable of holding people together. The true bond is forged over the long term, in a community of citizens who share the same destiny and participate in a collective creation that transcends them.

There is a consubstantial relation between economic liberalism and political conservatism. On the right, the more technology and innovation seem to rule, the more people try to contain them by strict rules, the defense of the family, of morality, of religion. Instead of restraining the rules of the market, individual instincts are restrained. The left's calculation is the inverse: it wants to muzzle economic appetites to liberate people's desires, to redistribute prosperity among all so that everyone can cavort in his own Garden of Eden and deny himself no pleasure. Each camp is struggling with a fundamental contradiction.

A Moving Borderline

What has changed since the Old Regime is that nothing can be taken for granted anymore; in the name of liberty and equality, we have put our rituals, ways of life, and codes of politeness in jeopardy. Our values themselves are now the object of debate, whereas earlier they fell from the heavens, imposed by God or by tradition. The market now proposes itself as the miracle solution to individual or collective demands that are forbidden by law or limited by custom. If it is insinuating itself into delicate human activities (surrogate pregnancies, adoption, traffic in human organs, etc.), that is because it presents itself as the ally of our most infantile desires, whispering to us that we don't have to give up anything. It is always grafted onto fundamental aspirations that it promises to satisfy by getting around legislation, by brandishing the standard of freedom. It is these aspirations that have to be contested, not the medium. The market intervenes as a last resort when deliberation, consensus, or elections have failed to satisfy individuals' desires. Thus, in the face of the sterility of many couples, some economists tell women who want to have abortions for their personal convenience that they should keep their child and subsequently put it on the market. They also urge carefully selected female university students to donate eggs for $50,000.[17] If the baby business is expanding rapidly, with demand varying according to sex, race, eye color, and intelligence, it is also because the desire to have a child has become one of the most expensive pleasures in our societies. Payment makes it possible to accelerate procedures and broaden the range of options offered to parents on the waiting lists. But it in no way resolves the problem of the future relationships between parents and babies, any more than it foreshadows the future human's quality of life. Each time, it is not a trigger but a facilitator that serves our desires without questioning their legitimacy. It is invoked as if it were a miraculous solution, but it is a solution that is itself problematic.

Worldwide, over the past century democracies have been experiencing the contraction of the domain of prohibitions and the expansion of the sphere of freedoms. But this expansion cannot be unlimited without leading to anarchy or disintegration. Democracy is truly the universe of revocable truths, but only up to a certain point. In our regimes, apart from fundamental prohibitions such as murder, incest, violence, and slavery, we determine what is licit. That is precisely what is dizzying: at every point we have the power to decide what is permissible and what is not. There is no longer a supreme savior to enlighten us, but instead a more or less courteous confrontation of ideas. Faced by unreasonable demands coming from private individuals or groups, it is important to mark out the areas where money cannot impose its rule without damage: the schools, the judicial system, politics, procreation, and public service, but also the oceans, land, and outer space. The line between what is mercantile and what cannot be mercantile has to be negotiated and renegotiated collectively in each generation. Even if the borderline between what some people want and what society refuses is moving, it is the borderline that matters, and to do away with it would be suicidal. It alone makes it possible to decide which taboos to maintain, what kind of resistances to oppose to the often mad demands of individuals or lobbies, because it is better, as Descartes wrote, "to overcome one's desires than the order of the world." Such is the abyss of liberty.

It is obvious that not everything is for sale, that the market cannot replace political, educative, and amorous bonds and be applied to every domain of public life. Even if we wanted to extend the market in this way, we could not do so, and in this respect Hayek's utopia is as naïve as that of the communists. But we have to know how to rank the threats, and not put on the same level the practice of paying people to cut into line, renting advertising space in public toilets, and, more troublingly, buying votes in an election or corrupting a judge during a trial. Or again, the possibility of manipulating or influencing government, as in the United States since the Supreme Court granted, on January 21, 2010, business firms and labor unions a virtually unlimited right to bankroll electoral campaigns. Not to mention the immortality industry, a promise made to the wealthiest people, who reserve "parking" places for their cloned vital organs, cryogenically preserving their brains in the hope of surviving their contemporaries. These are incommensurable magnitudes, only the latter of which compromise the whole of the social contract. What is shocking about them? The fact that many things can be put up for sale in exchange for hard cash, or that whole nations remain in the grip of poverty, hunger, and violence? That whole groups of young people cannot get a good education because they lack the means to do so? That is the moralists' problem: they take offense at trivialities so as not to have to be indignant about true abominations. Their intransigence focuses on details to avoid seeing the worst.

On Anticapitalism as Unearned Income

Today, anticapitalism is the convergence of three theoretical forms of profit: clear-sightedness, anathema, and prophecy. It makes it possible to explain everything, criticize everything, and foresee everything. It confers on the person who professes it the advantage of a superior lucidity coupled with a strategic vision. It is a life program for several generations, especially since it has now co-opted new causes, including the environment. Connecting the climate change crisis with a criticism of the market kills two birds with one stone and enlarges the field for prospecting to the whole world. In the current demonology, capitalism plays the role that Satan played in medieval Europe. The list of its crimes gets longer every day. Everything that goes wrong can be imputed to it. Even in the camp of its enemies, the tribes are innumerable: we find those who are nostalgic about communism (Alain Badiou, Étienne Balibar, Jacques Rancière in France), critics of modernity (Slavoj Zizek in Slovenia, Toni Negri in Italy), messianic catastrophists (Immanuel Wallerstein in the United States), radical ecologists advocating economic de-growth (Naomi Klein, Nicolas Hulot, or Jean-Pierre Dupuy), religious believers (Pope Francis, the Salafist Tariq Ramadan), the red-brown movement (Marine Le Pen's Front National, Jean-Luc Mélenchon's Front de Gauche, Olivier Besancenot's Nouveau Parti Anticapitaliste). However, what is striking in these thinkers, economists, or religious people is the point to which their hatred of capitalism is still full of fervor for the system they want to destroy: they are against, completely against it. They want to maintain it to have the pleasure of denouncing it. People like them have been telling us for two centuries that it was going to die: "it is close to its end," Immanuel Wallerstein said again in July 2013 in the newspaper *L'Humanité*. But this end never ends. We await capitalism's fall the way other people await the Messiah, and if it is late in coming, it is just put off until the next year. Everything that contradicts this belief is seen as a means for reviving faith in the certainty of its disappearance. Let us beware of the closely intertwined couple of the capitalist and his opponent: rage leaves them welded to one another and the opponent strengthens the capitalist by criticizing him. Radicality always testifies to impotence: we embrace it when we have despaired of everything.

The Dictatorship of Money Was Worse in the Past

It has become a commonplace, peddled by the greatest thinkers: modern history is supposed to mark the defeat of the notion that anything is free of charge. As early as the eighteenth century, confronted by the influence of bankers and nouveaux riches in England, the concern arose that money would become "a bond more durable than honor, friendship, family, blood, or the union of hearts" (as Bolingbroke put it).[18] Against Montesquieu and his theory of peaceful commerce *(doux commerce)*, the theorists of liberalism led by Adam Smith denounced the decline of the martial spirit, narrow-mindedness, and scorn for learning.[19] In short, at that time the idea of weaving a society by means of commerce alone and establishing it as a third party in all relationships was already a pipe dream. However, we are obliged to point out a few banalities: today love cannot be bought, any more than in the past, nor can friendship (bodies and allegiances can be rented, hardly more), public office, honors, desire, or political esteem. The dictatorship of money was worse in earlier centuries: through slavery or forced marriage, a human being could be sold entirely without any possibility of emancipation. In Greece before Solon, a person could be seized, like a commodity, if he did not pay his debts. Some emperors bought their elections, as Charles V did. In the Middle Ages, the practice of ransoming prisoners was the nobility's principal resource, plunder and looting were the main attraction of battles, the armor and swords of knights who had been killed in battle were sold, and their families were imprisoned and released only in exchange for large sums. Finally, there were monastic orders that specialized in paying ransom to Barbary pirates who were holding Christians captive. In the fourteenth century, the kings of England Edward II and Edward III offered their friends as hostages to secure their debts. In 1340, the archbishop of Canterbury had to be sent to Brabant as security for Edward III's debt.[20] The French king John the Good, who was defeated and taken prisoner at the battle of Poitiers in 1356, was freed only in exchange for a ransom of several million crowns that bankrupted the kingdom and led the monarch to create the franc.

Dante himself excoriated the rapacity of the nobility, the clergy, and the bourgeoisie in fourteenth-century Italian cities.[21] The passion for gambling denounced by moralists was ferocious in seventeenth-century Amsterdam; in gambling dens and brothels as well as in palaces, people of all classes made wagers on the sex of a baby to be born, on the success of a hazardous expedition, on the probable death of a great person, on their own life expectancies, and on the ravages of the plague.[22] The tulip mania in Holland at the same period, a sort of erotic excitement mocked by La Bruyère when it spread to France, threw hordes of people into bankruptcy for a few bulbs of this flower from the Orient that everyone wanted to collect. It was an international fad.[23] Already, any object at all—even a bulb, but the bulb of a flower that had been raised to the rank of a work of art and that was more valuable than gold and diamonds—could drive people mad and generate a trade, a collective infatuation.

Today, it is in noncapitalist and nondemocratic countries that the most degrading forms of domination arise, involving even children. Let us recall that slavery (and its two substitutes, serfdom and indentured servitude) was abolished more than a century ago, at the very time that the modern market economy was being established.[24] Let us also recall that it was reintroduced in the twentieth century, first by the Bolshevik revolution of 1917, with its reeducation camps and gulags, where millions of people died (and which were later imitated by Mao and his followers in China and by Pol Pot in Cambodia), and again by the National Socialist regime in Germany in 1933, with its concentration and extermination camps, where prisoners had to work until they fell from exhaustion. In the same spirit, in the late 1970s Nicolae Ceausescu "sold" tens of thousands of Romanian citizens of German extraction to the German Federal Republic, giving rise to a lucrative business that brought in more than a billion German marks for the communist government. Every Romanian with even distant Germanic ancestry had to pay a tax to emigrate, on the pretext of paying the state back for the education it had given him or her. Since 2014, the Islamic State in Iraq has reestablished slavery in the territories it controls, setting the following rates: a Christian or Yazidi girl from one to eight years old is worth 138 euros, one from ten to twenty, 108 euros, one from twenty to thirty, 69 euros, and so on, decreasing in value until they are worthless after fifty. They are more expensive if they have blue eyes.[25]

A Civilizing Factor

The critique of the commercialization of the world is as old as capitalism. But money is also an incontestable civilizing factor: from Roman law's *pretium doloris* to reparations for war crimes or crimes against humanity, it is the payment of indemnities that avoids the cycle of vengeance or blood demanded as reprisals. Robert Musil has one of his characters, Arnheim, say in addressing God: "[Money] is spiritualized violence, a special form of violence that is flexible, highly-developed, and creative. Business is not based on deception and exploitation, on overreaching and exploitation; aren't those civilized, transferred entirely into man's interiority, and almost disguised as freedom? Capitalism, as an organization of selfishness in accord with the hierarchy of abilities in order to make money, is virtually the greatest and yet the most human order that we have been able to establish to Your glory."[26] By expressing debt in numerical form, money limits it and compensates in a different way those who have been injured: it is a pacifying factor. It has the virtue of turning the desire for vengeance into an appetite for retribution. It is precisely what prevents human sacrifice and distills it into sums. It is better to pay a fine, even a high one, than to shed blood. It is because of its status as an equivalent that it can be applied to beings and situations that are different in nature. "Humanity is born in man to the degree to which he is able to reduce mortal offenses to legal proceedings of a civil nature, to the degree to which punishment comes down to repairing what can be repaired and to reeducating the offender."[27] A wound, an incapacitation, or the mutilation of an organ cannot be undone, certainly not by mutilating the offender's corresponding organ ("an eye for an eye"). But a financial compensation, even if it does not replace the organ or the ability that has been destroyed, at least offers a substitute. "In the realm of ends," Kant said, "everything has either a *price* or a *dignity*. Whatever has a price can be replaced by something else as its equivalent; on the other hand, whatever is above all price, and therefore admits of no equivalent, has a dignity."[28] But people have a price only if they have dignity; one is the condition of the other, and not its exclusion. It is because we consider all human beings to have equal dignity that we can set a price on life (even if that seems immoral). Those who have no price are thus thrown into servitude or even destroyed. It was also calculating abolitionism that helped deprive the slave trade of legitimacy. Pierre-Samuel du Pont de Nemours (1739–1817), the physiocrat, compared the cost of slave labor with that of free labor and concluded that it cost more to enslave the blacks than it would to emancipate them—if not for the planters, at least for the colonial nations. A sordid cost-benefit analysis, but one that put self-interest in the service of virtue and supported the immense anti-slavery movement.[29]

There is a beauty in numbers: in Plato, mystic numerology made it possible to accede to the contemplation of pure ideas and to turn our minds toward the perfect abstractions that the circle, the square, and the triangle represented for him, and that he saw as existing independently of the material world.[30] Numbers not only make each object interchangeable, but also illuminate it; since the Renaissance, it has been the way the divine is represented because "mathematics is the alphabet in which God created the universe," according to Galileo. The defenders of the ineffable protest against the mathematizing of the world, forgetting that it provides immense services. Beyond a certain level, quantity is transformed into quality, as Hegel put it, since the quantitative refines our perception in the extreme and allows us to get down to the tiniest realities. In the fourteenth century, the invention of double-entry bookkeeping, with its active and passive columns, was like peddlers' and merchants' record books.[31] It was also a portable memory of their rigor or dissipation, almost a manual of good and bad conduct. The axiological neutrality of money and its convertibility allows it to embrace all the dissymmetry of human situations and descend to the infinitely small, to which it does justice.

The Impotence of the Market

Taken as a whole, the Western world is the one that put an end to the iniquity of the Old Regime, decided that human beings could not be bought, declared freedoms and fundamental rights, etc.[32] It has been misinterpreted: the period of full-fledged capitalism is also the one in which the protection of inalienable goods was extended, even if there is still an intense debate regarding the mercantile sphere's right to infringe on other domains. Thus it is not true that "markets rule our lives as never before" (Michael Sandel). One might even say that the reverse is true: the areas of involuntary bargaining have constantly shrunk over the past century. The slave trade was abolished in the nineteenth century, in the West marriage has ceased to be the subject of commercial negotiations and become an act of love (even if it has retained an economic dimension), and never have the great virtues—solidarity, charity, dignity—been so celebrated. Everywhere the demand for authenticity, sincerity, and respect is winning out over the play of masks and bonds of submission. Contrary to a thesis that is too widespread, modern societies have strengthened the circle of what is sacred, unlike Old Regime societies, which may have been religious (or rather, ritualized) but were founded on the depreciation of certain categories of humans—slaves, colonized peoples, women, children, serfs, peasants. The disapproval that continues to weigh on prostitution, the very lively debate regarding surrogacy, the shame attached to buying and selling babies, the indicting of traffickers in human organs who put the bodies of the poorest people at the service of the wealthiest, and the prosecution of smugglers who profit from the distress of migrants all prove that the mercantile view of the world is far from having triumphed. You can still try to sell your soul on the Internet: the risk is that no one might want it.

The fact that every human event has an economic dimension does not authorize us to place the economy above all the rest of our activities. As has been clearly shown by the American sociologist Viviana A. Zelizer, money is constantly reappropriated by human and social logics that bend it to their will.[33] All money is specific: bribes, tips, bonuses, salaries, theft, inheritance, each kind bearing the mark of its uses and its provenance, expressing social and family relations. That is why currencies vary in value depending on whether they manage private life or conflicts, mark rites of passage, or strengthen a collective identity.[34] Thus we speak of honoraria, wages, gifts, remunerations, defrayals, salaries, payments, and so on, different ways of referring to rewards. Far from "disenchanting" the world, in every society, in every group, money is the object of a remarkable adaptation. It does not exclude local cultures or particular uses, flexibly adapting to each individual's personality.[35] The much-feared uniformity gives way to a diversification of uses. Its plasticity adopts all the nuances of human feeling and in no way causes social life to dry up. Thinking that "finance" (this dubious word adds a conspiratorial dimension to the disapproval of money) governs the planet reflects a panicky need for clarity. There is no supreme power on earth, but instead a directorship of fragmented powers that negotiate with, influence, and restrain one another, including the megafirms (Google, Apple, Facebook, Amazon), which are too mutually dependent to be able to destroy one another. Money may be a "citizen of the world" (Paul Jorion), but to think that it might be its occult monarch is to confuse reflection with sorcery.

If only it could rule the world, things would be simple: the enemy would have a name and a face. It would suffice to neutralize it for the rule of harmony and love to be restored. But we have to recognize that although money is everywhere, in all regimes, in all periods, it is nonetheless only a small department of the human passions. If we examine the wars that are tormenting the planet today, we see a great deal of imperial ambition and religious fanaticism, but rarely the monetary motive isolated as such. Only a period—our own—obsessed by the economy could believe that money dominates humanity: *We begin by putting in things the faith that inhabits us and then are surprised to find it there*—even to understand phenomena as diverse as terrorism or fundamentalism.[36] For example, on November 27, 2015, Pope Francis explained the Paris terrorist attacks by attributing them to "an unjust international system for which not the person but money, the god money, is central." Clearly, the sovereign pontiff shows a very Jesuitical prudence with regard to radical Islamism; but on the part of the spiritual head of Christianity, this subterfuge is not commensurate with the stakes involved. Hatred lacks a reason or a cause. Justifying it by poverty, global warming, drought, or any other cause betrays an inability to think about it. The market is insidious insofar as it forces its adversaries to reply in its own language. Maintaining, as the far left does, that since capital and merchandise circulate freely, people should be free to cross national borders as they wish, is a way of reducing human beings to the status of merchandise. But humans are not beans that can be transferred from one container to another; they have a memory and a culture, they speak different languages and share different beliefs. That is why immigration cannot be subject to the sole criterion of altruism. As Bertolt Brecht put it, "being good is a terrible temptation." Angela Merkel's Germany, which confused lucid hospitality with compassionate narcissism, is in the process of learning that.

❦ ❦

Let us return for a moment to the hope of the Enlightenment: after emerging from the religious wars that brought Europe to its knees, Enlightenment thinkers assigned to *peaceful commerce* the twofold mandate of exorcising violence and dissipating instinctual drives through methodical activity. According to the eighteenth-century *philosophes*, self-interest, halfway between passion and reason, constituted the most social of the pleasures: it pacifies behaviors and replaces aggressive conduct with the prudence of accountability, a taste for acquisition, and the property instinct. For the man of faith and for the knight, who are inclined to be quarrelsome, it was necessary to substitute the man of needs, who was no doubt less glorious but also more peaceful. In this case, the ruse of history consists in the fact that self-interest has become in turn a passion capable of leading peoples to engage in lethal excesses.[37] Thence proceeds a twofold error: thinking that the desire for profit can extinguish the spirit of discord and that economic success transforms the most belligerent people into calculating lambs. From the oil-producing monarchies to the United States, everything proves conversely that prosperity has no direct effect on the culture of violence. A second mistake is to claim, like the Marxists, that war is borne within capitalism the way a storm is borne within a cloud, and that abolishing profit will do away with any source of conflict among people. That is once again to fail to understand human follies.

The twentieth century, to give just one example, was ravaged not by financial powers but by totalitarian ideologies: Nazism, fascism, and communism. The three genocides that occurred in it, against the Armenians, the Jews, and the Tutsis, were perpetrated by pure racial or religious aversion. Today the great torments of the planet are still fed primarily by the atrocities committed by Islamism, whether Shiite or Sunni, the irredentism of pariah states (North Korea), and the revival of empires. Barbarity is always ideological. ISIS does not recruit because it is rich; it is rich because it recruits thousands of fanatics attracted to its murderous message and its extreme cruelty. The billions it draws from its oil production, plundering, and slavery constitute only one of the attributes of its terror and its power.

What is to be feared in the twenty-first century is not the irrepressible extension of the market but rather its abandonment in favor of a battle unto death between hostile conceptions of the world. It is political, national, and religious passions that matter, and not the economy, which is now secondary. We will soon regret that money is not precisely "the master of the universe."[38]

Money Buys Only What Can Be Bought

There is only one domain where the Golden Calf seems to be predominant: the world of crime, which is moved by rapacious greed. On closer inspection, things are more complex. Even in the sphere of organized crime, money is a stepping-stone to power and the domination of families that want to reign supreme. The solidarity of the *mafiosi*, which is so striking, has to withstand prison, torture, even death; the respect for a promise made and loyalty to the clan or milieu are more valuable than the possible loot. There is nothing worse than a member of the gang who has allowed himself to be "bought" by an enemy gang or by the police; there is a merciless hierarchy, a blind obedience to the leader, and a respect for elders that reminds us of that surrounding great dictators. Even for criminals, there is a world of the promise and the contract that is superior to that of financial reward (whence the obsessions with betrayal, which is also characteristic of the world of espionage). Finally, the world of crime is a certain style, vulgar and flashy, a way of dressing, of driving around in big cars, of drawing attention to one's success—expensive watches, jewelry, extravagant parties, trophy wives. A desire to inspire fear as much as envy. Between blood brothers, relationships are not mercantile, they are based on honor, whereas people outside the clan are cheated without pity. It is a mistake to think that what defines the spirit of gangsters is the millions they've socked away: instead, the goal is to build an empire around a name (sometimes a family that comes from the same locality or neighborhood, like the Corleones and Toto Riina, the former head of the Sicilian Mafia). The underworld wants to dominate, and to that end it adopts quasi-military rules. The millions taken in are only the sign of its power. The extreme cruelty of the drug cartels in Latin America, the torture shows they put on, with heads cut off, bodies strung up and cut into pieces, their pleasure in large-scale massacres, and their incessant wars for supremacy can in no case be summed up in the simple desire for lucre. In the television series *Breaking Bad,* Walter White, a chemistry teacher who starts manufacturing methamphetamine in New Mexico to pay for his cancer treatment and ends up being so rich that he throws money away, explains the real reason he did it: "I liked it, I was good at it, and I . . . I was alive." For these criminals, who may be male or female and may even have lived to an honorable old age, life outside the law, rackets, hold-ups, being a mob boss, and the adrenaline of transgression are and remain their reason for living. It is life on the margins that motivates them, not mere metal. The recurrent theme of thrillers, the one last job (a burglary, kidnapping, etc.) that a retired criminal agrees to do to help his friends and that will bring him down, proves that being a wealthy retiree is not the bad guys' motivation. They want to burn with a white-hot flame in a state of permanent excitement.

That a certain affluence is preferable to destitution is proven by all the exoduses motivated by people's universal desire to live better lives and to escape poverty. If we only expected wealth to make life better we wouldn't be so alarmist. Indifference to worldly goods is admirable, but it cannot be imposed on younger generations on the fallacious pretext that "the industrial party is over" (Hans Jonas). By railing against the Golden Calf, week after week, as is too often done in France, by suspecting a spoliation or a theft in the slightest industrial or commercial success, we discourage the younger generations at the very time that they are dying to invent, to create. We push the most talented to go into exile, where their talents will be recognized and rewarded. The entrepreneurial spirit, the desire to take the initiative, and

On Art as Money

For Victor Hugo, "every great writer mints prose in his own image. . . . Poets are like writers. They have to coin money. Their image has to remain on the ideas that they put into circulation."[39] To which Paul Valéry sarcastically replied: "Hugo is a millionaire. He isn't a prince."[40] Curiously, Hugo was accused of the same offense by Paul Lafargue, Marx's son-in-law. Held in the Sainte-Pélagie prison in May and June 1885, he excoriated the poet's betrayals and especially the greed of "this reactionary, alleged good fellow [who] loved the poor and their big money so much" (letter to Engels).[41] To write a book, to paint a picture, to make a film, is to issue bills whose value the public alone will decide. The writer sells words for money, as did La Fontaine, whom Fouquet, Louis XIV's superintendent of finances, rewarded with a "poetic pension." In the end, art, like money, rests on this narrow base: the confidence, the certitude that one is not being deceived. That is what is meant by the phrase *prendre une histoire pour argent comptant* ("take fiction for reality," lit., "take a story for hard cash"): to listen to a story and believe it as simply as if one were calculating a sum. A stillborn work is a work that does not travel, which remains confined to a small group. A book, for example, can be a tombstone that no one moves aside, from which no Lazarus emerges, or it may acquire a greater wealth by passing through many hands. The same goes for a picture, a film, a piece of music. Their precious character proceeds from the approval they receive from the largest number: they have to be brought out into the bright light of the public, they have to be commented upon, heard, adulated. They are put upon the most unstable market of all, that of opinion, which is by nature fickle. Not only are we suffocating under an avalanche of novels, films, songs, and exhibits, but the same audience that adored you yesterday forgets you today with a disarming candor.

Mallarmé saw the poet as the alchemist of language, searching for linguistic gold far removed from the hackneyed words of the banker, whom he saw as a god without splendor. In his view, the work of art escaped the "salarial pact."[42] But doesn't this ideal poet who rebels against the system actually confirm it? The artistic world is the most Darwinian of all: it operates by elimination and selection. The artistic milieu, traditionally oriented toward the left, is also the one in which the laws of the market are applied mercilessly. Being a painter, musician, actor, director, or writer means owing your value only to other people's assessment of you. If it declines, you're described as a has-been. An artist's rating collapses as soon as people stop believing in him. There is a hiatus between the flaunted generosity of the great names in showbiz and the intelligentsia, on the one hand, and the ruthless cruelty that characterizes antagonisms among creators, on the other hand. In literary Bohemia and the avant-gardes, there is only the approval or the indifference of the public. Like the Roman emperor at a gladiatorial combat, it is the public who gives the thumb up or the thumb down. That is the price to be paid for having chosen freedom and imagination. The value of a work is established when it has authority, when it enlarges those who read it, look at it, or hear it, precisely in proportion to the multiple meanings that it thus receives. Then it escapes the alternation of infatuation and abandonment and shares in a kind of eternity.

the attraction of profit are not in themselves shameful. If there is dirty money, there is also and especially legitimate money when it is earned by work, intelligence, and daring. None of the problems raised by money is as important and serious as the problems raised by a lack of money. Let us ask the question: *given how long the world has been for sale, how is it that there are still things to buy?*

SIX

Does Opulence Make People Unhappy?

If money doesn't make you happy, give it back!

JULES RENARD

AIDED by a corrupt policeman and an indelicate treasurer, a gangster organizes, with his accomplices, a break-in at a race-track. The job, perfectly planned, brings in two million dollars, but when the men are splitting up the money they get into an argument and kill each other. Their leader escapes with his fi-ancée in an airplane, the loot stuffed into a poor-quality leather suitcase that he has to register at the counter in the airport. But on the tarmac, the cart carrying the baggage to the plane's hold suddenly brakes: by a cruel stroke of fate, a poodle has leapt from its mistress's arms and thrown itself under the vehicle's wheels. The suitcase full of money falls to the ground, the locks break, and thousands of bills fly away on the wind generated by the jet's engines.[1] A moving choreography: it's raining thousands of hundred-dollar bills. The suitcase, which incarnated the promise of a new life for its owner, now represents his loss.

A Freedom of Hard Cash

At the simplest level, *money frees us from money, in the rare moments when it is given to us in abundance.* Then it is a factor of carefree-ness and delivers us from the obligation to pay attention to it. It is the paper prison that we have agreed on to settle our transactions.

But this prison is also our summer palace, our vacation home. It is our despot and our liberator. For peoples doomed to exile, it constitutes a home that can be taken along in the form of jewels, bundles of cash, or gold. Finally, it is a promise of a future state that allows us to say "tomorrow" without fear, whereas being poor means not being able to project a future beyond the next week or month.

Nothing is more pleasant than having a certain amount of money in one's pocket. It's a reassuring, protective cushion, and safe-conduct to detachment. Liquid money is precisely what makes it possible to fluidify life, to spend the day without worries. It rounds off the corners, spares us complex calculations and nitpicking down to the last penny. "Money is minted freedom, and therefore, for a man completely deprived of freedom, it is ten times dearer," Dostoevsky wrote in 1862, in *The House of the Dead.* It is said that at certain points in his life, Sartre walked around carrying a million old francs, which he gave to people he happened to meet or who asked for money, taking a twofold pleasure in doing good and showing his scorn for wealth by squandering it. This is the generosity of an aristocrat on the one hand, and the grandeur of a libertarian soul on the other. Simone de Beauvoir describes Sartre at the end of his life, his funds exhausted by prodigality, worried about not having enough money or being able to take care of himself properly.[2] We spend our days handing out small sums like so many traces of our DNA. They are the equivalent of what we have to give up in order to exist; life exacts its tribute, no matter how small it may be, a minuscule hemorrhage that ends up being substantial.

Money produces joie de vivre when we forget it as such, and it is never so present as when it is absent. The person who responds to the question "How much does it cost?" by saying "It's no problem" proves only that for him this particular problem, which is essential for most people, has already been solved. And so much the better. The proper attitude toward money toes a fine line between serenity and concern. Like the silence of organs in the case of health, it's right only when it isn't heard. It requires a discreet vigilance, because it cannot be completely omitted, just as one can never be completely uninterested in one's body. That is why everyone calculates, including and especially the nabobs.

On Credit: Promises and Debts

The invention of credit in modern societies, starting in the 1920s in the United States and the 1950s in Europe, was first of all the invention of a new mode of desire. It began by inverting our relationship to time. Up to that point, to acquire something, households subjected themselves to the system of waiting, saving for years to purchase the house or the object of their dreams. Now we borrow from the future; we prefer immediate satisfaction to accepted frustration. Everything, right now: this byword of the rebels of 1968, which seems subversive, has become the byword of the market. It invites me to take what I want, when I want it. And for fear that I won't want enough, the market endlessly multiplies the temptations, launches into a commercial belly dance to prevent my appetites from drying up. By opening a window on the future, credit has made our generations terribly impatient: with it, all that is possible must become real. The least of my fantasies is enjoined to exist, at the risk of exceeding the limits of reasonable indebtedness.[3] And there is the rub.

There is more: we are born on credit, indebted to our precursors. To be born is to appear with others: we are always preceded, we owe life to others. Two types of society are opposed in this respect: traditional societies, for which debt is endless and has to be passed down from generation to generation; and modern societies, for which this duty of fidelity does not prevent individuals from getting off the ground, inaugurating something new. It is through education and work that people redeem their births, and they are no longer expected to reimburse their community forever for giving them the gift of life. Individualism was born at the same time as the merchant economy, in opposition to feudal society and its obligatory solidarities. It began by separating people, who then chose to reassemble, voluntarily, according to particular affinities: the Other no longer had to be endured but could be chosen as we wish, in amorous or friendly relationships. Having the audacity to invent another destiny, to speak in the first person (instead of being simply a part of a whole), is a certain way of freeing oneself from the bonds that hold us back. Classical, holistic societies are societies of redemption, while modern societies, which are individualistic, are societies of credit. In the first case we remain forever debtors, mortgaged to the clan, the tribe, or the family, constantly forced to give back what was bequeathed to us. In the second case we draw drafts on the future, freeing ourselves from tradition by granting ourselves advances.

Now we have to earn our living in order to have the right to lead it as we wish. Instead of remaining the property of others, each person has to pay with his own person to become his own master. Thanks to credit, which is a Faustian pact, we grant ourselves allocations of time, we live beyond our means by mortgaging our future, making it our debtor. Most American university students begin adult life with tens of thousands of dollars of debt incurred to pay for their educations. Some of them do not succeed in repaying this debt before they reach retirement age. Once they become parents, they have to start saving as well, to pay for their children's educations. The great promise of modernity was the abolition of original sin, the notion that *for every individual born on this earth, existence is now a gift, not a debt,* a marvelous privilege of which we can make use as we will. The classical man is a burden of obligations; contemporary man is a bundle of promises.

This promise is kept worldwide, with this drawback: as soon as I no longer have to worry about a heritage, about my ancestors, I become the pure contemporary of myself. I enter into the myth of self-engenderment. As the sole person responsible for my fate, I divide myself up the better to project myself, the creditor and the debtor now forming in me a single person. From childhood on, in the family, at school, we are urged to "assert ourselves," to avoid self-deprecation, and not to "go to great lengths" for someone who "is not worth the trouble." It's an ambiguous expression: we think of ourselves as a kind of money whose exchange rate varies, and we do not despair of being worth more in the future. A priori, this is progress: feeling that we deserve better is a strong incentive to transcend ourselves. This hoped-for destiny, thwarting the destiny imposed on us, constitutes what we call freedom. I would like a more wide-ranging, more beautiful life. But the mechanism of emancipation is twisted: apart from the fact we cannot construct ourselves without others, the self becomes its own debt. It must constantly avoid proving unworthy of itself, it has to make itself exist, seek its peers' esteem, and prove to them that it is "somebody, not nobody" (in Isaiah Berlin's phrase). Here it has entered into an endless mortgage in which it must accumulate proofs of its courage, its aptitudes, its intelligence, in order to convince itself and to convince the tribunal of public opinion. We can feel free of the past, but we are never free of the ideal of ourselves that we have set. Each individual begins life without a guarantee, seeking to make a name for himself against that of his parents and other people. If the weight of the collectivity is the traditional man's nightmare, the lack of certainty about his identity is that of the modern man. His independence is inseparable from the need for recognition and belonging. He expects others to confirm his progress or his talents for him, at the risk of never being able to repair his ontological insecurity.

Monetary borrowings appear to be the most difficult to pay back, even if in our societies many people are addicted to debt and start out only by burdening themselves with loans running to several figures and resorting to the craziest financial expedients. Petros Markaris, who writes crime novels, says that before the recent economic crisis the Greek banks sent their customers credit cards for all sorts of events, getting married, going on vacations, buying a car or a residence. Consumers no longer thought themselves obliged to pay back anything at all. The intoxication of spending was quickly sobered up by the repayment scandal. The United States is equally liberal in issuing credit cards of various kinds, each with its associated advantages and risks that invite the individual to use them by turns.[4] So long as a household has not reached its limit, it can be ruthlessly solicited; the shame then is not owing anything. Saving is rejected and even ridiculed. Some credit organizations grant you the freedom to take "payment vacations" in view of your past payment history. The billing fees for unpaid amounts are more advantageous for them than if you pay the total balance.[5]

In this regard, France is the country of the nest egg, and keeps its assets at hand; to an economy of squandering in the United States we oppose an economy of retention. Over there, credit is a way not only of acquiring property to compensate for the decline in salaries, but also of making money circulate, of digging up the

The Last Penny

After he was discharged from the army in 1924, Jean Mermoz, the famous aviator of Aéropostale, the pioneering French airmail service, passed through a period of extreme poverty. According to legend, he threw into the sea the last penny he had in order to start over from zero. As we have seen, Scrooge McDuck never parted with his fetish, his first wages, earned at the beginning of his career shining shoes. Dostoyevsky's gambler, having lost everything at the roulette table and having nothing but a single gulden left in his pocket, the price of a meal, leaves the casino and then goes back and bets it on the ball not going past 18. Twenty minutes later he leaves with 170 gulden: "What would have happened if I had let myself be beaten at that point, if I hadn't dared?" Three attitudes toward poverty: scorn, superstition, risk. Starting all over again, protecting oneself against chance, and making a leap of faith. In each case, a way of courting chance, by disdaining it or by defying it.

slightest dormant deposits. It's a question of making even the most modest households believe that they can have everything they want without worrying, at the risk of throwing a whole nation into a frenzy of acquisition without any relation to real profits, as was proven by the subprime crisis in 2008. And it is a practice that will begin all over again, no doubt, once the memory of it has faded—a feverish excitement in which money multiplied in a fictive way without any connection to labor, until an enchanting future gave way to an implacable regret. Debt that borrows against the future can also destroy the future, when it mortgages entire generations that have been sacrificed to our desires for instantaneous satisfaction.

The Confusion of Happiness and Well-Being

In a famous study published in 1974, Richard Easterlin, an American researcher, demonstrated the absence of correlation between countries' relative GNPs and their prevailing feelings of well-being.[6] Not only did elevated revenues fail to bring greater satisfaction, but they seemed to him to be prejudicial. The feeling of well-being could come "with significantly less economic wealth."[7] The fabulous advances registered in our societies provide no additional happiness. Rousseau was right in criticizing luxury: a good quality of life was not guaranteed in the past by the arts and sciences any more than it is today by computers, smart phones, and cars.[8] We are suffering from what David Myers calls a "spiritual hunger in an age of plenty."[9]

The proof? The great are supposed to be unhappy, according to a cliché that has crossed the centuries. In the past, they were said to be bored: forced to be inactive, they were exposed to the void and didn't know how to kill the time spent in the uneasy quest for new pleasures. Expiating a scandalous fortune by disgust, they were both desperate amid abundance and guilty of enjoying it while surrounded by a suffering population. These "kings without entertainments" were slowly dying of inanition amid gold and splendor. A convenient view, admittedly; it allowed the destitute to put up with their condition, since that of their masters was infinitely more painful. It was pointless to envy them or to overthrow them: they were already in hell.

This fable persists today: well-intentioned thinkers want to prove to us that wealthy people are mired in distress. The trick is a little crude, but it works, in a time of crisis, as a way of making people accept their fate. On the one hand, the rich are not unhappy, and still less repentant. Has anyone ever seen a millionaire on his knees asking to be pardoned on the eight o'clock news? On the other hand, boredom, recognizing no class barriers, has now largely spread to the world of work, and being active or unemployed provides no protection against yawn-producing, terrible monotony. It may be true that the rich are bored in their luxurious life, moving from their private planes to their yachts; but the poor are also languishing in their public housing projects. One shouldn't lose one's life in order to earn one's living, people said in 1968. Are we sure that it would have been better if we had earned nothing? Ultimately, the aristocratic disdain for work seems to have descended to the modest classes of today, at the very time when the well-off classes are sinking into overwork, putting in sixty to eighty hours a week as a sign of their superiority. Whereas the working classes aspire more and more to leisure, the upper classes embrace with delight the laborious slavery formerly reserved for the common people. If robots soon replace people and destroy jobs, if the digital revolution creates a mass of losers to the advantage of a techno-elite with fantastic salaries, we will be running a twofold risk: that of thereby undermining the social contract, and that of destroying the meaning of labor, understood as a patient maturation and transformation of the self. A majority of citizens, deprived of this advantage, would be reduced to the status of maintained serfs. One group would have the passion of shaping the world, the other would have the passion of consuming it—that is, of being no longer its builders but its subjects. That is the risk of the universal minimum income promised by both the Marxists and the economic liberals: monetary allocation seeks to be the salary for birth. My simple presence on earth deserves a reward. But are we still involved in free blossoming, or only in an almost noiseless survival, pacified by the bread and circuses provided for the crowd on public assistance?

A whole prolix literature thus gravely wonders whether money makes people happy. The question is idle: not a single author of these studies would be prepared to give up his salary on the promise that doing so would allow him to realize himself more fully.[10] But in this debate two distinct elements are conflated: well-being and happiness. The former is a statistical index that combines politics, the economy, housing, health, transportation, and the preservation of nature. The latter is a subjective feeling that pertains to each individual's temperament. To seek happiness amid material abundance is to continue this confusion and mix together two different orders. "How can we understand the paradox of a society that sets itself a goal that it always misses, happiness?" Daniel Cohen asks.[11] He concludes that happiness, after a long historical development, has never been so hard to attain, despite an expanding material abundance. The objection is strange, because it might easily be turned around: it is because our societies have set happiness as the horizon that they are exasperated by their failure ever to reach it.[12] A universe of obligatory beatitude can only sink into depression, so absurd is this goal.

Money Attenuates the Shocks of Adversity

It is not true that everyone seeks happiness, that Western illusion; everyone seeks to avoid unhappiness, which is quite a different matter. But above all, to set self-fulfillment as the sole end is to make moments of distress unbearable and the will to overcome them impossible. We are unhappy about not being happy all the time, a peculiarly modern folly. It is therefore a mistake to accuse the mercantile logic; the fault lies not in the economy, but in the spirit of the time. Consumerism and profusion are failing to satisfy us?[13] If we mean by that that they do not produce a feeling of absolute plenitude, we have to admit that apart from the joy of love, which is itself often brief, few things provide us with total satisfaction: we can be happy, Aristotle said, as much as a human can be—that is, intermittently.

For example, explaining that one is more fully realized at the age of seventy than at the age of forty, because one is freed of material things, seems a rather inadequate argument.[14] It postulates a correlation between retirement from one's job and peace of mind, forgetting at least two factors: demonstrations by retirees protesting against the cuts in their pensions, and the feeling of emptiness that follows retirement and constitutes the major problem of our aging societies. There is in truth nothing worse than the combination of the entry into old age and economic deprivation. Stranger still, some economists relapse into what they denounce by proposing to make happiness the new index of money.[15] According to them, we should mint "happiness coins" to testify to our "gross domestic happiness." This recalls the "gross national happiness" advocated by the king of Bhutan in 1972, before an economic crisis caused a precipitous decline in his fellow citizens' good humor.

Annoyed that they did not foresee the economic crisis of 2008, many economists seem ready to trample on their discipline and throw it in the trashcan. They tell us that we have been deceived. "*Homo economicus* is a walker who never reaches the horizon," writes Daniel Cohen; "Economists are complicit in an immense self-deception" that is supposed to satisfy our unlimited need for recognition, claims Jean-Pierre Dupuy.[16] Why not?

But this amounts to attributing to this discipline a dissatisfaction central to the human condition. What is life if not a magnificent illusion, a mad adventure? According to these disillusioned thinkers, we have to return to more authentic values: friendship, cooperation, solidarity. But how does that make economic science obsolete? These writers seek to draw up a different mental map, to lead us toward the high ground of idealist speculation, where people are supposed to live on fresh water and beautiful thoughts—an old ascetic song that fools no one. When *homo economicus* weakens, the whole society falls ill. Elias Canetti put this very well when he explained that inflation in Germany in the 1920s made people superfluous: "[It is] a witches' sabbath of devaluation where men and the units of their money have the strongest effects on each other. The one stands for the other, men feeling themselves as 'bad' as their money; and this becomes worse and worse. Together they are all at its mercy and all feel equally worthless."[17]

We have to free ourselves from happiness as an imperative, from the mad quest that forces us to fluctuate between bitter frustration and fatuous hope. Greek mythology reminds us of this. We waver between Tantalus and Midas. The former, known for his wealth, commits the offense of taking revenge by cutting up his own son and serving him at a banquet of the gods; Zeus condemns him to spend eternity in Tartarus, on the banks of a river that dries up as soon as he tries to drink from it, and under a tree whose branches are blown out of his reach by the wind as soon as he tries to pluck its fruit. Above him a delicately balanced rock threatens to fall and crush him at any moment. Midas is the king of Phrygia. A drunken, obese old man named Silenus, whom he has taken under his wing, offers to grant his dearest wish. Midas asks that everything he touches turn to gold.

The Specter of the Repentant Trader

The epidemic of frauds, one after the other, that have punctuated the life of finance for the past thirty years, with banks working against their depositors (notably Goldman Sachs) and selling them junk bonds, coincided with the appearance of a new figure: the repentant broker.[18] He cheated and extorted his clients like a pirate, with the implicit consent of his superiors, and was the dominant figure in "pillage capitalism." Now he is returning, clad in the sackcloth of the penitent. There is an atmosphere of sacredness in the great halls of finance. Isn't the London Stock Exchange located on Paternoster Square? The life of a trader is close to that of a monk, and implies first of all the rupture of familial and amorous ties: crazy work hours, scheduled down to the last second, and confinement in trading rooms, with all the amenities at hand—gyms, fitness centers, doctors, dieticians.

This asceticism sometimes flips over into its opposite, and the brilliant toiler sinks into debauchery: a villain with a human face, a charmer who makes countless promises. He urges you to join him in making juicy profits. Caught with their hands in the till, some of these rip-off artists have the decency to commit suicide by jumping out windows on Wall Street.[19] Every crook has his rhetoric, his way of charming his marks, using obscure acronyms. Every kind of scam is acceptable, including running a "boiler room" where stock values are artificially inflated to encourage investors, and then abruptly resold. That was the specialty of Jordan

Belfort, who inspired Martin Scorsese's film *The Wolf of Wall Street* (2013), and who bilked more than fifteen hundred clients. Or "spoofing," which makes it possible, using an algorithm, to place enormous buy or sell orders and then cancel them at the last moment, which pushes the market up or down depending on the positions taken. The differences are pocketed.

The atmosphere on the trading floors is hysterical, with the swaggering of the "golden boys," the "big swinging dicks,"[20] explosive machismo, the use of cocaine, amphetamines, private jets, call girls. These young people are caught up in a monotone over-excitement, always on alert, feverish 24/7. Recruiting is combined with a total loyalty to the firm. Some people have to work twenty hours a day for three days in a row without faltering, which accelerates wear and tear and throws them in the trashcan at the age of thirty-five, like athletes and models.[21] It is a highly addictive game. These fops in suspenders think they are the kings of the universe. Making use of "high frequency trading," a tool that issues thousands of buy and sell orders in the blink of an eye and can detect the slightest movements of the market, they enjoy an unlimited power to do harm. Having been conditioned and crushed themselves, they use their operations to crush the weak and cause collapses without flinching. A stock market crash is the purgation of a system saturated with too much activity.

It is a supreme paradox: when superpowerful computers issue buy or sell orders in a few nanoseconds, money simply has no value anymore. We enter into mathematical panic.

Millions, billions are swept away in an instant, in "flash crashes," stock market Waterloos, transformed, as Mallarmé put it, into "grandiloquent figures." These are disasters that take place in the bright light of a rampant technology that no one controls, but that everyone wants to accelerate. Traders will soon be replaced by robots that will sell and buy in a millisecond. Will these supercalculators then be accused of fraud, of insider trading? Profit turns into a rout: pushed all the way, extreme greed flips over into squandering.

But all this excess voltage is compensated by detox clinics, seminars on ethics, yoga, Zen Buddhism, meditation, even prayer. At a meeting of the IMF held in October 2014 the Archbishop of Canterbury, Justin Welby, asked the world's young bankers to take a year off in a community of prayer and ethics and devote themselves to the poor. Spontaneously, the money man speaks of morality and solidarity. In his case, the remorse is as ambiguous as the sin. It was with Jérome Kerviel that the trader was transformed into a martyr.[22] The accused becomes the lamb that bears the sins of finance. We have to recognize that Kerviel is a brilliant stage director and has an acute intuition into symbolic mechanisms. He knows that in a Catholic country, a sinner who repents is forgiven more than a good man who has never sinned. *Felix culpa.* His pilgrimage to Rome, his audience with the pope, the triple consecration by the far left, the Front National, and the Church in the person of Msgr. Di Falco, who headed his support committee, are worthy of a great artist. We would be wrong to laugh at this; just as the police and the judicial system dismantle gangs by making use of members who agree to testify against them, we need these turncoats to foil the octopus's evil spells. For instance, the computer expert Henri Falciani, an ex-croupier, black-mailer, manipulator, and mythomaniac who in 2008 stole from the HSBC bank's home office in Geneva computerized listings that revealed the bank's fraudulent practices. Or again, the criminal former bankers who have become policemen and know the mysteries of the profession better than anyone. In every group of criminals, even among the jihadists, there are always traitors. Sometimes they are paid, as in the United States since the Dodd-Frank Act (2011), which allows informers who reveal criminal acts in financial matters to receive between 10 and 30 percent of the fine imposed by the authorities. Money stops money, at the price of transforming the bonus hunter into a remunerated informer. France is considering identical measures. The traitors are asked to shut down corruption from the inside. They have committed offenses but are ready to redeem themselves, in exchange for absolution and revenues. They are ethical thieves. Former hoodlums make the best policemen.

Immediately the water he tries to drink and the food he tries to eat are transformed into nuggets of gold. The world around him is petrified, and to rid himself of the curse, Midas has to purify himself in the waters of the river Pactolus, which begins to carry away the precious metal. Not being able to satisfy one's needs is a scourge. But satisfying them is also a scourge. Lack is as great a trap as satiety.

Money does not "make" people happy, in the strict sense of the term (nothing, no recipe or technique, makes people happy), but it attenuates the virulence of unhappiness and allows us to keep it at a distance. It is a shield against the blows struck by fate. Being able to receive care, to get a good education, to be decently housed—these are what it authorizes, among other things. It wards off the inevitable side of adversity by giving us the means to fight it. In this respect, it is irreplaceable.

Envy, the Sickness of Equality

Envy is the suffering felt when observing the happiness of others. What will give them pleasure will cause us pain. This ugly sin was limited, in the Old Regime, by social status. The "would-be gentleman" could ape the nobility, but he was banned from it because of his low social status. The aristocratic universe maintained an unbridgeable distance between human beings. By declaring the equality of all men, the French Revolution generalized the competition of all against all. In such a society, the success of a minority and the stagnation of the rest are intolerable. By promising everyone wealth, happiness, and plenitude, modernity legitimates the covert war waged against each other by people who are resentful and happy by turns, depending on their fortune. This, combined with the poison of comparison and with the bitterness elicited by the spectacular success of some and the stagnation of others, draws everyone into a cycle of desires and deceptions. What exacerbates this all-too-human malady is the proximity of those whose physique, salary, love life, or elegance one covets. Constantly living among people who are more well-off and dynamic, and who emphasize your limits, can only rub salt in the wounds. "Being poor in Paris," Zola said, "is being poor twice over." Our poverty would be more bearable if we were not constantly witnessing the happiness of the wealthy strutting about. Everything feeds envy: other people's bliss, their fortune, their social position, and even their misfortunes and their illnesses, which make them more interesting than we are.

There are two kinds of societies: those in which disparities are stimulating and those in which they are discouraging. When people from different milieus live side by side, astonishment and also rage can arise from their confrontations. "A house," Karl Marx said, "can be large or small; so long as the neighboring houses are of the same size, it meets all society's expectations for a residence. But if a palace is built next door to the little house, it is reduced to the rank of a hovel." Envy is a passion of proximity and not distance. That is why in France success is often attributed to connivance, to a complicity among elites, whereas in the United States entrepreneurs go to malls to talk about their careers and encourage their listeners to follow their example.

Consider this typical situation: a marina where crowds of people come during their summer vacations to wear shorts and flip-flops and admire the wealthy living the good life on their yachts. The sudden telescoping can elicit several reactions: I will do anything to become one of them someday. Or else: I'm going to fight to ensure that nobody has the right to display his wealth in such an obscene way. Or again, a wiser position: I'm happy for these lucky people, but I don't gauge the grandeur of a life by the display of material goods. The rich themselves are caught up in the mechanism of covetousness toward those who are wealthier than they; alongside the ordinary well-to-do, there are the great tycoons, the munificent people whose pomp offends others and who raise the bar to an inaccessible height. As soon as the American and French Revolutions opened the Pandora's box of equality and the right to the pursuit of happiness, they set loose the monster of comparison, and thus of competition.

Through the mechanism of ostracism, the ancients sacrificed valuable human beings in order to heal envy and halt discord. Thomas Wolsey in the sixteenth century and the intendant Nicolas Fouquet in the seventeenth century were themselves exiled, by Henry VIII and Louis XIV, respectively, for having tried to (among other things) rival their sovereigns in splendor. The same society that elicits envy nonetheless creates the mechanisms capable of restraining it. The perverse pleasure taken in the poverty of others, for example, on the evening news, helps us tolerate our own, which seems more bearable. If the media display before our eyes handsome, wealthy, tanned people, they also register, with a certain sadism, celebrities' slow decline, the bags under their eyes, their wrinkles, the problems in their love lives, their career setbacks. They exalt people's splendor as much as their volatility: these living gods reign unchallenged for a few years before one day tumbling into the dust. Other people's joy wounds me when it is too ostentatious, too demonstrative. The bursts of laughter coming from a happy group sounding in my ears remind me of my solitude, of my bilious temperament. Recall the aphorism written by Jules Renard in his *Journal:* "It's not enough to be happy: it's also necessary that others aren't." Happiness is a good whose value consists in its belonging only to me. The envious person is always watching out, with perfidious greed, for the fall of his models and competitors. He takes in this a morose pleasure that is close to resentment, as he waits to find new persons whom he will court and detest at the same time.

The only way out of the hell of envy is through admiration. Other people are not only rivals whose brilliance wounds you, but also prompters, in the sense that this word has acquired in the theater. They inspire us; they suggest countless ways of living our lives differently, of blazing new paths. The venomous breath of jealousy can then be converted into emulation, into curiosity, and others can become conductors of desire rather than intolerable obstacles. They take us out of ourselves and broaden us.

The Specter of Satiety

If it is impossible to despise money and impossible to venerate it, that is because it is also an abstraction. It puts us in the position of God after the creation of the world, puts at our disposal all imaginable goods. It almost offers us the gift of ubiquity, enlarging space and prolonging time. That is why the joy of earning is often superior to that of having. It is the excitement of the short-circuit: amassing, while very young, a large fortune at top speed, without setting any limits. Earning one's living is a burden; getting rich quick is a game close to erotic madness. Becoming a millionaire at the age of thirty is an exploit that can leave us unsatisfied if it is not prolonged by other objectives. There is, of course, no special despair among the rich. But there is a potential problem: the specter of satiety. Money becomes so desirable that it makes everything else insignificant. Nothing can rival the potential lack of limits that it incarnates. Then what do work, worldly beauties, affective and carnal relationships matter? We no longer know what we want when we can have everything. Money does not desire for us, it enjoys itself. We can enjoy possessing it without possessing anything else. Insofar as it is dematerialized, it seems to lose its brutality; but that is probably when it is most dangerous, because it has acquired the force of a pure idea.

Anyone could write an autobiography of happiness in which he would relate the amount of his revenues to the feeling of self-fulfillment experienced in each period. It is not clear that the two coincide, or that they diverge, because so many other parameters must be taken into account: health, age, recognition, love life, family life. A certain shortage of money in one's youth does not have the same significance as financial difficulties in one's fifties. This is how fortune is seen: everything we have, less what we owe, plus what we hope for. At twenty, one can live like a prince in a hovel; at seventy, one can live like a poor wretch in a palace, crippled and lonely. We are familiar with the pathetic figure of the well-off person who no longer has time to spend what he has accumulated. Money flows over such unfortunates like a calamity; even when they think they are losing money, they are amassing it.[23] They are sated by the world before they have tasted it, and amid abundance they experience a shortage of pleasures. They would almost welcome some setback in order to start over again from zero, to recommence the exciting odyssey of social ascension. Their fortune was exhilarating only on the condition that it never took concrete form. "I die of thirst beside the fountain," as the medieval French poet François Villon splendidly put it. Schopenhauer took up the metaphor again, comparing wealth to seawater, which makes you thirsty when you drink it.

We end up lacking lack, the vivifying source of desire, which is always curious about everything. Since there are too many choices, too many possibilities, there is no longer any place for attraction. Our true fear is that we will see the fervor that binds us to the world weaken. We might say about the abulic rich person what Chrysippus said about the fool, that he needs nothing but lacks everything—and above all lacks the most important thing: the ability to desire again, to fix his choice on the goods of this earth.[24] He suffers from a terrible ambivalence: money is simultaneously the way to pleasures and the wall that cancels them. A burning frigidity, it deprives us of the capacity to transfigure the everyday, which is the real poetry of existence.

Money illustrates marvelously well the following paradox: Every procedure used to achieve happiness can also make it disappear. Or rather it retreats as soon as we imagine that we can touch it. We think it is going to come land on us like a bird, once a certain amount has been amassed; it is a false totality that is constantly disintegrating as it is being elaborated. To enjoy happiness, you have to accept the fact that it comes to us and leaves us, visits us like a kind of grace and evaporates almost as soon as it has been recognized, as staggering as it is ephemeral. There are people who have more talent for money than for happiness, who prefer multiplying figures to grasping the shimmering sweetness of each instant. Haven't they chosen to make money precisely because they don't know how to do anything else?

Extinguish Desires?

Detachment with regard to material goods: that has been the moralists' leitmotif since time immemorial. They consider our passions to be follies, and when confronted with a procession of gold and silver they exclaim, like Socrates, "How many things I can do without!"[25] In arguing that we should despise ambition, the vanity of riches, and the madness of the torments of love, philosophers fulfill their role as spoilsports. However, their wisdom is another name for renunciation. If everyone followed their advice, society would sink into neurasthenia. Doesn't true human poverty consist in the extinction of desire rather than in an explosion of appetites?

Money is in fact a malfunctioning seismograph of the contemporary psyche. It bears within it the contradiction of democratic societies: the will to accede immediately to all kinds of pleasures, followed by fear of doing so too quickly. Money is first of all what I always lack, whether I am rich or poor. How can you recognize a millionaire? By the fact that he complains about never making enough and would feel more comfortable if he had at least twice as much. If he has five million in assets, he would like to have ten, and if he had ten, he would want twenty. Nothing can calm his concern, or produce the subjective sense of well-being he seeks.[26] As he tells it, the cost of living is too high, restaurant prices are prohibitive, real estate is out of sight, and the initial deposits required for certain bank accounts are so high that they discourage applicants. We all look above ourselves to assess not what we already have but what we do not yet have. Money is a truth serum that brings out everyone's defects and fears. Connected with needs and with the fear of dying, it compensates in an imaginary way for all the evils of existence. It adds to the human condition a tenacious illusion: the certainty that we are rising above the herd and the disconsolate awareness that this is not true, that a rich man suffers and dies like everyone else.

The worst thing that can happen to each of us is the plethora that stifles our appetites. In matters of food, for example, the United States is typical of a country persecuted by its own wealth, where the abundance of food draws its citizens into overconsumption and obesity. Instead of learning moderation, Americans push their digestive systems to the limits of their capacities, consuming excessive portions at every meal. Whence two strategies that are deployed to cope with the excess of goods: restriction and overbidding. To get rich, Epicurus said, what we have to do is not add to our money but cut back on our desires, construct a peaceful home for ourselves, without fear or sorrow.[27]

Anti-Semitism, from Left to Right

Describing, for the newspaper *L'Humanité* on June 17, 1967, the parade of Israeli troops after their victory over the Arab armies, the labor union leader and French communist Benoît Frachon wrote: "The presence of certain figures in high finance would confer on this ceremony a meaning different from that of religious fervor. . . . Even the Golden Calf was there, still upright and, as in Gounod's opera, contemplating in the blood and mire at its feet the results of its diabolical machinations. In fact we were informed that these saturnalia had been attended by two representatives of a cosmopolitan tribe of bankers well-known throughout the world: Alain and Edmond de Rothschild. At their feet, the still bleeding dead."

What is money, according to the current cliché? It is the Jewish vice par excellence. In January 2006, the "gang of barbarians" in Bagneux kidnapped Ilan Halimi "because a Jew is rich," demanded ransom, and tortured him for three weeks until he died. Or again on September 10, 2015, on the France Inter radio station, the French film director Philippe Lioret attributed the crisis of the migrants from Syria in part to Israel and to the Six Days' War, and more generally to all those "who have money." In 1892, Léon Bloy said of Jews: "It is through them that this algebra of turpitudes that has been called Credit has definitively replaced the old Honor on which chivalric souls relied to accomplish everything."[28] And in the 1930s, Georges Bernanos denounced the "Jewish conquest," referring to "the masters of gold" who "imposed themselves by their very vices, which caused their downfall so many times in the past, the frenzy of display, the impudence, the cruelty of the satrap. As early as the middle of the nineteenth century, in the leading positions in the Administration, the Bank, the Magistracy, the railways or the mines, in short, every place where the heir of the great bourgeois, the bespectacled graduate of the École Polytechnique, became accustomed to find these strange fellows who talk with their hands like monkeys, nonchalantly looking over columns of figures and stock quotes with the eyes of a doe in love. . . . With their black hair, their features chiseled by age-old anguish, the savage itch of a marrow worn out ever since the reign of Solomon dispensed in all the beds of shameless Asia."[29] Excluded from all the trades in Europe, the Jews, as we know, became bankers, money-lenders, and were hated all the more because they were indispensable. When at the end of the fifteenth century the Inquisition was tracking down the *conversos* and suspected them of secretly carrying out Jewish rites, King Ferdinand of Spain tempered the investigators' ardor by alluding to the Jews "who are our coffers and are part of our patrimony."[30] As for Marx, mentioning the "chimerical nationality" of the Jewish people who had found a home in the abstraction of the market, he promised the Jews emancipation only once capitalism had been destroyed. We could fill whole libraries by inventorying monetary anti-Semitism, which is only a department of general anti-Semitism. Jewish malfeasance is inscribed in the demonic power of gold. The Jew is the incarnation of our sins and the vector of their redemption. That is why Léon Bloy, a paradoxical anti-Semite, also wrote *Le salut par les Juifs* (*Salvation through the Jews;* 1892), in which he sees Israel as the cross to which Jesus is eternally nailed, the dike that raises the level of the global human river. The Jews must therefore be evacuated for our own redemption.

A protean, immemorial passion, in full expansion today in both the Arabo-Muslim world and in the European far left, especially since the creation of the state of Israel, anti-Semitism includes numerous dimensions in its spectrum. But the detestation of finance, which is so present in the socialist movement, always runs the risk of spilling over into the detestation of the fantastical Jew, the bearer of our sins, both scapegoat and pariah of the nations.

This is, in truth, a sly strategy. Is it a question of pure abstinence or, more subtly, a way of reviving desires by temporarily drying them up? There is a second path: multiply the temptations. One hates to mention the obvious fact that civilization is not the diminution of appetites but their multiplication, their extreme sophistication. The goal of our desire has value only if it remains out of reach, just as the feeling of love does not exhaust the plenitude of the beloved. To the passion for money, which is desiccating, we have to oppose the money of the passions, as a fluid that allows them to flourish and multiply. The passions are not a malady that has to be overcome but an opportunity to embellish our earthly home and escape the burden of boredom. The genius of a great culture is primarily and above all the development of beauty, the feeling of an endless exuberance from which we cannot escape without suffering grave damage. That is the secret of a good life: Never run out of things to wonder at. Quench thirst only the better to reawaken it.

SEVEN

Has Sordid Calculation Killed Sublime Love?

"Pray, my dear aunt, what is the difference in matrimonial affairs, between the mercenary and the prudent motive? Where does discretion end, and avarice begin?"

JANE AUSTEN, *Pride and Prejudice*

When poverty knocks at the door, love goes out through the window.

AFRICAN PROVERB

DURING the summer of 2014, an American woman wrote to an investment consulting firm:

I am a beautiful young woman of 25, well brought up, and I have class. I wish to marry a man who earns at least half a million dollars a year. Do you have in your files the addresses of a few unmarried men (widowers or divorced) who earn $500,000 or more? Perhaps also the wives of rich men could give me some advice? I have already been engaged to men who make $200,000 to $250,000, no more . . . but $250,000 is not enough for me to live in the best parts of New York. I know a woman in my yoga course who is married to a banker. She lives in Tribeca and yet she is not as beautiful as I am or as intelligent. But then what has she done that I have not done? How can I attain her level of life?

An advisor, a banker by trade, replied to her:

I have read your letter with great attention, and after studying your request at great length I embarked upon a very careful financial analysis of the situation. First of all, you're not wasting your time with me, since I myself make more than $500,000. Allow me simply to sum up the facts: you are offering your physical beauty, and I am offering money. Unfortunately for you, this is a very bad bargain. It is certain that your beauty is going to fade and disappear someday, whereas at the same time my income and my fortune will very probably continue to grow. Thus "in economic terms," you are a passive who is undergoing a depreciation, while I am an active who is producing dividends. Hence you are undergoing a depreciation, but since the latter is progressive, your value is diminishing faster and faster! To be more precise: today you are twenty-five years old, you are beautiful, and you will probably stay beautiful for another five or ten years. But each year you are a little less beautiful, and when you later compare yourself with a photo taken today, you will see how much you have aged. This means that you are currently in the "growth phase," and thus it is the right time for you to be sold but not bought. In economic terms, the person who possesses you today has an interest in having you in trading position and not buy and hold position. However, the latter is what you are offering.

Consequently, to continue in economic terms, marriage (which is a buy and hold position) with you is not a good bargain in the middle or long term. On the other hand, renting might be, in commercial language, a reasonable arrangement that we could discuss. I think that if you provide the guarantee "well brought-up with class and marvelously beautiful," I might very probably be the renter of this "product." However, I wish to try it out first, a practice very common in business.[1]

In other words, human beauty can be assimilated to a "shrinking currency" (*Schwunggeld*, a term invented in 1916 by a German economist, Silvio Gesell) that depreciates over time. Gesell, a disciple of Proudhon, was the finance commissioner of the ephemeral Bavarian Council Republic in 1919; he was hostile to both the nationalist right and the Bolsheviks. Very impressed by the denunciation of unearned income, he stressed that a currency that diminished in value would circulate faster, and would prove more productive than a hoarding currency: "Thus we must make money a worse merchandise if we want to make it a better means of exchange." Gesell proposed that bank bills be stamped by the post office, which would regularly register their decline in value according to the length of time they were held (local exchange trading systems, or LETS, in accord with this principle, apply negative interest and issue time-limited bills).[2] This inverts the old adage. It is now money that is time, and it disappears at the same rate. It has to be spent for fear that it will evaporate. Along the same line of thought, in 1923 the Austrian anthroposophist Rudolf Steiner imagined "aging moneys with limited validity" so that loans would gradually be transformed into gifts and would not drive debtors into bankruptcy. All debts were thus supposed to be canceled at a given date in order to restart a virtuous circle.

How could a woman sell her charms in Paris "while still dressing like a good bourgeois wife?" Balzac asked in *La cousine Bette*. It takes a great deal of talent and luck, a great city full of idle, blasé rich men, fine manners, and wit, and an unshakeable appearance of fidelity certified by a husband who is in on the game. These "Machiavellis in skirts" constitute the worst kind of courtesans: the ones "with an ingenuous face and a heart like a strongbox."[3] Expert at forgery, they pass off the counterfeit money of their inclination as authentic affection. One declares one's love to such women by murmuring to them: "I love you like a million."[4] Similarly, the professional seducer has to have an advantageous physique, the gift of gab, endurance, and an ability to take aim at heiresses, like Maupassant's Bel-Ami, before he loots their bank accounts. A man's or a woman's aesthetic capital is accompanied by an erotic capital that allows them to move at lightning speed. In the same register, Zola explains that the wife of a bigwig in the Second Empire gave herself to lovers for one hundred thousand or two hundred thousand francs, thereby acquiring a "rarity value" that forestalled the accusation of prostitution.[5]

In the 1970s, Pierre Klossowski, claiming to be a follower of Sade and Fourier, also wanted to establish a "living currency" based on people's erotic potential, and especially that of women, who were supposed to be exchanged freely like so many priceless fantasies.[6] The value of each "industrial slave"—that is, each employee—would be determined by the emotions she aroused in others. For Charles Fourier, desire is at once the engine and the currency of his "new world of love," and pleasure is the salary, always recompensed a hundred times over, that is paid for it. "Where we go wrong," he said, "is not by desiring too much but by desiring too little." Following Fourier, Klossowski denounces ignorance of the mercantile character of the passions.[7] Carnal arousal has never been disinterested; it presupposes evaluation, bids, and therefore a price to be paid. Desire is in fact the raw material of the whole society, and nothing is more fatal to enjoyment than being free of charge. However, such proposals evade the problem of aging: what should be done with women (and men) who, after a time, find themselves outside the enchanted sphere of desires? Must they be considered unfit to be on the social scene? As often happens, the most subversive proposals come from an aristocracy of youth and beauty that sets aside the immense majority of the population. This panmonetary utopia merges desire and money, without considering the more prosaic question of ordinary needs and affections.

The Three Axes of Contemporary Marriage

For a long time, Romanticism contrasted two systems: on the one hand, the noble passions, impetuous ardor, fervor, poetry; on the other, the ignoble passions, calculation, prudence, nit-picking accounting. Grand feelings on the one hand, pettiness on the other. For Robert Musil, conversely, from the beginning of the twentieth century on, all human relationships already borrowed the language of political economy. One of the main characters in *The Man without Qualities,* the very rich Arnheim, explains that "Today, all intellectual relationships, from love to pure logic, could be expressed in the language of supply and demand, of discounts and reserves, at least as well as in psychological and religious terms."[8]

Political economy has not killed the purity of our feelings; it has allowed us to understand certain mechanisms of love and of religion. Money is a general translator: everything can be expressed in its language even if not everything can be reduced to it. The naïveté of the nineteenth century was to subordinate the heart to revenues, and even to see in them the *ultima ratio.* Today's naïveté is to subordinate the married couple to desire and forget the old financial balm. The double trap of crude materialism and triumphant idealism. In Europe, until the middle of the twentieth century people got married for financial or dynastic reasons, and the value of a wife was calculated with reference to her dowry. Now the decision to marry is made on the sole basis of free choice and passion—a passion that since the Second World War has been accompanied by a sexual dimension seen as indispensable to the couple's fulfillment. Our mistake, in the 1960s, was to think that the monetary question had been eliminated from conjugal relations. However, even when dazzled by love, spouses never cease evaluating, weighing the pros and cons, wavering between attraction and reticence. Cooing is also calculating.

To put it another way, contemporary marriage reconciles three dimensions: self-interest, love, and desire. None of the three wants to surrender. Financial considerations, initially relegated to the background, often reappear during a separation, when the couple is on the skids. Failure in love can then turn into wild speculation. Judicial records are full of magnates or oligarchs who grant their wives several million dollars when their marriage breaks up, the wives having used detectives and law firms to build a solid case against them. What is true of the well-off is also true of the ordinary citizen. If divorces have become the site of such bitter financial battles, that is because they constitute a full-fledged business whose goal is to convert sorrow into cash. As in past centuries, marriage proves to be a good bargain, and separation to be a restructuring plan that ensures a comfortable retirement. Love is a fog that indemnities dissipate. It was vague, uncertain of its intensity; now it becomes transparent to itself.

Lovers sometimes behave like usurers who lend their hearts and mercilessly capitalize on wrongs or worries. Their attachment was a gift that requires restitution, in one way or another. The compensation demanded is a way of making the other partner pay, in the strict sense of the term: he has to heal the wounded narcissism of the person who feels duped and is asking for the payment of arrears. Then a couple's life together, even it if lasts twenty years, resembles a career pursued in common, in which retirement credits have been accumulated that will be recapitulated by judges and lawyers when the case ends up in divorce court. In its aridness, money symbolizes the fear of being stolen from oneself: the other person has broken into me, turned my life upside down, and I have to get myself back in the form of offerings, salaries. A prenup has at least the virtue of making things clear: by setting before the wedding the amount the wealthier party will pay to his or her spouse in the event of a separation, it avoids confusions. But negotiating favors is nonetheless not excluded, hence the denial of sex used by women since time immemorial (in Aristophanes's play *Lysistrata,* to stop the war between Sparta and Athens). This form of militant abstinence is a way of putting pressure on males in order to obtain various advantages. Some feminists have advocated that the "conjugal duty" be paid for in cash, seeing it as an act of exploitation on the part of the husband/boss, and some very wealthy mothers on New York's Upper East Side receive bonuses paid by their husbands to reward their domestic work.[9] Here we see the prostitutive mentality silently triumphing among those who want to free women and are merely extending commercialization to the most intimate relationships. Old attitudes persist: for a majority of women, it is still men who have to pay the bill, even after "liberation," whereas many men consider it degrading when a woman pays and humiliating when she makes more money than they do. Money is the remedy and the poison, it has an emancipating power that can turn into a lethal disease. When lovers act like shareholders disappointed in their own couple and fall into the dance of moneybags, they are capable of the worst, even bankrupting the other in order to teach him or her a lesson. The love that doesn't calculate makes up for it when it ceases to be love and casts on the marriage the pitiless light of the bills to be paid.

For a long time—and in France, until the 1960s, when women were finally allowed to have bank accounts and checkbooks, major transactions remained the husband's prerogative.[10] Nevertheless, the family economy had devolved upon the wife, especially in working-class households (for example, in the coal-mining areas of northern France); the husband handed over all or part of his wages to his wife to pay current expenses, and to take care of the household and the children. It was also a matter of avoiding squandering the money in a café or bar. The battle for control of the purse strings was a major subject of public debate in both Europe and the United States, and the household's money became a "controversial currency in the late nineteenth century." The wife, the guardian of affects, also had to become a manager and learn to spend without waste. If she earned a supplemental income, it was considered pocket money to pay for "her trinkets."[11] When consumerism began to offer young wives all the temptations of the great department stores, their pecuniary requests started to shoot up; this was already the theme of Zola's novel *Au bonheur des dames*, which was contemporary with the opening of the Bon Marché department store in Paris, and it has since been the subject of countless comedies of manners. For a long time, the only thing that mattered was the income of the husband, the breadwinner, who was simultaneously a protector and a provider who held others' fate in his hands.[12]

Everything changes when the two spouses work together and begin to share resources. The comparison of the spouses' respective incomes can lead to happy cooperation or to muted rivalry. Either they contribute to the common fund and draw from it when they need to, or they manage their revenues separately, have separate accounts, and arrive at temporary arrangements depending on the purchases to be made.[13] Then life in a couple becomes a constant calculation in which the slightest expense is prorated in accord with each partner's means.[14] Doing the accounts: an exercise in which almost every couple, no matter how much in love they might be, has to engage. It is not, however, in any way degrading; on the contrary, it is a vital necessity. In a happy marriage, passions and interests converge. Money suspends neither solidarities, nor charity, nor love; greed and desire can get along well, as we see in certain couples that are small businesses all by themselves, even if eroticism is often the commodity that reaches its expiration date the fastest. Self-interest, by its foreseeable nature, can strengthen the solidity of a marriage, whereas moods are changeable. Modern conjugal life resembles a diplomat's shuttling back and forth: it looks like constant improvisation, everything is negotiated all the time, from sleep to the divvying-up of errands, domestic tasks, childcare, and erotic interludes. Nuptial harmony also implies a certain passionate prosiness, an ability to go into the least glorious details. It's a matter of defining the respective territories, of making constant adjustments to avoid frictions. Otherwise grievances accumulate like so many dirty dishes next to the sink.

To those who accuse the "disastrous and invisible hand of the great Moloch Baal Mammon" of breaking up our marriages to make money and increase growth, we must object that for many couples divorce is synonymous with a collapse of their standard of living, especially for women.[15] If self-interest alone were involved in separations, and not only the authenticity of feelings, no one would want to compromise the family assets by leaving his or her spouse. Money, far from being the corrupter that devours affections, is the ally of time: it allows the couple to survive over the long term. The proof *a contrario:* couples who are too poor to separate and who remain under the same roof, eaten up by rancor. Economic life is the humus from which our lives derive their magnitude, their regularity. *Eros does not get along well*

Simulate Poverty?

Marcus Aurelius, the philosopher-emperor (121–180 CE), who was introduced to Stoicism when he was still a child, had the habit of sleeping on a mat on the floor to harden himself. The Stoics did in fact practice a special spiritual exercise, *praemeditatio,* which simulated poverty, hunger, and physical suffering. The point was to "resist the seduction of the sweet aspects of life" (Cicero), to look upon pleasure from the point of view of pain, and on abundance from the point of view of penury: to force oneself to eat gray, hard bread while lying on a pallet, and to wear coarse garments so as not to suffer from their loss. "We shall be rich with all the more comfort, if we once learn how far poverty is from being a burden."[16] Let us recall that Seneca was colossally rich, since his assets were considered to be equivalent to one-sixth of the Empire's budget.

The intention here is twofold: to prove that good food and beautiful clothes are luxuries that one can do without, but above all to defy adversity. The artificial character of these practices is obvious: depriving oneself of food, dieting once a week, and purging oneself of foods that are too rich is a parenthesis that allows one to continue to live in affluence. Wasn't it the environmentalist Nicolas Hulot, surrounded by spiritual leaders of all denominations, who in June 2014 recommending fasting once a month for the climate and to unlearn how to consume? Shams that are about as useful as dancing to make it rain.

Schopenhauer claims that those who are born with money withstand the buffeting of fate less well than those who are born poor and have known a little wealth.[17] The latter have acquired a twofold confidence in their luck and in their ability to bounce back. For them, poverty is not a bottomless abyss but a natural point of departure. There are people who have retained the habits of hard times even when they have become well-off, like homeless people who continue to sleep on the ground when they are offered a bed, or like the author Jean Genet, who had become famous but persisted in living in shoddy hotels, keeping his belongings in a small suitcase. Resilience is a form of capital that is eroded with luxury. Tocqueville maintained, not without pretentiousness, that a noble cares so little about the material that he could live just as well in destitution. "All the revolutions that have troubled or destroyed aristocracies have shown how easily people accustomed to the superfluous could get along without the necessary, whereas people who worked hard to achieve wealth can hardly live once they have lost it."[18] Really? One doesn't move from the status of a grand duke to that of a chauffeur or a worker—consider the White Russians in France after 1917—without a sense of having fallen. There is a certain presumption in believing that one has been immunized against all ills simply by force of habit.

Pride is the Stoic sin par excellence. According to Cicero, if one is a real sage, escorted by moderation, courage, magnanimity, and patience, one can do without everything, appearing indifferent to the birth or death of one's children or happy even though blind and deaf, but also appearing indifferent under fire and torture.[19] Such a man is not a sage, he's a monster! The problem with such statements is that they are made by people who have never lacked for anything (even if Cicero and Seneca died heroically, in a way worthy of their philosophy, the former offering his neck to the executioner and looking him in the face, the latter slitting his wrists on Nero's orders).[20]

The remorse of the sybarite, *praemeditatio* betrays the desire to control all the stages of one's life, even reverses of fortune. We have to imagine the worst in order to confront it without flinching when it comes. Believing that one can defy death, illness, and privation by preparing oneself for them day and night is enormously naïve. It is always inadvertently that we are struck by misfortune, ruin, or illness, even if we think we can defuse them by anticipating them. We are always surprised by what we have foreseen.

with poverty. Our love lives are naturally compromised without being cynical, a heritage of composite tendencies, and trying to isolate one element while deploring its disappearance or preeminence is not to see the interweaving of drives that inhabit us. We are not "disappointed Romantics" (Pierre Manent) but prudent Romantics, too aware of the vulnerability of feelings to debase them in a thoughtless fusion. The contemporary duo is a very singular alliance of ardor and stew: lyrical flights, carnal follies, feverish conversations, and household triviality.

Marriage as a Prison and an Escape

In the nineteenth century, marriage was incontestably a transaction, to which the woman brought her dowry in exchange for the protection her husband owed her. We see it in English-language and French novels: the woman is caught between four estates—the saved wife, the lost old maid, the suspect widow, and the accursed prostitute. She is subject to the authority of her father or her brothers, and it is the nuptial bond, a guarantee of well-being, that ensures her self-fulfillment; and since women do not work, except in exceptional cases, she has to make a success of her marriage, which is the great business of her life. Whence the importance of finding a husband, if possible one provided with a comfortable income.

"Single women have a dreadful propensity for being poor, which is one very strong argument in favour of matrimony."[21] In this novelist, weddings are a redoubtable test whose laws and motivations must be known in order to take the best advantage of them. She herself thought she was doomed because at the age of twenty-three, she was still not married, not having any capital. She began writing, despite the social disapproval she incurred, in order to help defray the household's costs and not to be a burden to her family.[22] In 1817, shortly before her death, she added up, with a housekeeper's attention to detail, the revenues she had received from her novels: 684 pounds and 13 shillings, a modest sum in view of her later fame.[23] (F. Scott Fitzgerald made a literary genre out of the account book, since many of his short stories are simple coded registers in which the debits exceed the credits.)

Three characters resist the proper functioning of this business: the philanderer, who wants to seduce without marrying, the dowry-hunter seeking to win an heiress of the gentry, and the idealist young woman dreaming of a partner more exciting than the official suitor.[24] It is security and not the quest for happiness that is supposed to preside over these kinds of arrangements, even if the couple, once married, may experience an honest felicity. All the rituals—courting, flirting, the official proposal—are carried out before the eyes of others and in the transparency of the mutual patrimonies. The value of people on the matrimonial market is connected first of all with their wealth. Young women sometimes seem like livestock put up for auction by their parents. The best-suited couples are those that have accepted an amicable companionship based on mutual respect and common interests. Only women who are wealthy or intriguers can occasionally escape this kind of negotiation. An honorable man should not undertake to approach a young woman unless he intends to marry her. In Jane Austen each family, especially if it is composed of girls, forms a community of matchmakers: each girl participates, at her own level, in the others' weddings, comments on them, anticipates them, makes wagers. It may even happen that only one of them, like Emma, "beautiful, intelligent, rich, and endowed with a good character and provided with a very comfortable home," finds that she has matchmaking talents and gets involved in the neighborhood's romantic affairs, rather than searching for a husband for herself.[25] The delight of love, in Jane Austen, is the art of weaving between minds and bodies: pairing couples, studying the compatibilities of characters, establishing delicate relationships among friends. Love consists mainly in the preliminaries to love, insofar as a good marriage will benefit the family in turn and assure the security of the household. Let us add that these enterprises took place in Europe in the "golden age of security" that lasted up to the First World War. During this period currencies were stable, inflation was virtually nonexistent, duration was assured, and confidence unshakeable.[26]

Jane Austen catches her heroines in the nets of a gigantic matrimonial agency, with happy or disastrous outcomes, depending on the initial advantages and the opportunities encountered. One could suffocate in these carceral novels that trap young people, shape their hopes, and transform the map of the Land of Love into a notarial cadastre; but in them we breathe the air of freedom and intelligence, a freedom that is subject to conditions and makes its way through the labyrinth of conventions. In her own way, Austen foreshadows in a way Gary Becker, an American who won the Nobel Prize for economics, who defined marriage as an investment in human capital, the result of competition in an imperfect matrimonial market where the costs of the encounter and the education of children are compensated by a satisfying return on the investment.[27] And if Austen, who never married, condemns marriages of convenience, purely mercenary unions, she is also wary of the flights of passion. If possible, one has to reconcile reason, the heart, and money.

Like Austen, the American novelist Edith Wharton explained that for a pretty girl in the United States of the end of the nineteenth century who had neither money nor a vocation, "only marriage could prevent [her] from starving to death, unless she met an old lady who needed someone to walk her dogs and read her the parish bulletin."[28] It was the way to salvation.

❀ ❀

On the other side of the English Channel, Balzac had a no less realistic view. Just consider the advice that Rastignac gives a girl: "Get married . . . my child. For a girl, to marry is to impose herself on a man who makes a commitment to maintain her in a more or less happy position, but one in which the financial question is resolved. I know society: girls, mothers, and grandmothers are all hypocrites in peddling feelings when they're really talking about marriage. None of them is thinking about anything other than a fine position. When a girl has married well, her mother says she has made an excellent bargain."[29] The difference is that the French novelist deplores this state of affairs; his cynicism is a disappointed idealism, whereas Jane Austen accepts it as inevitable. In Balzac the passions disrupt the social order and destroy proprieties. In Austen, proprieties restrain the passions and civilize them. Balzac offers a dismayed view of these transactions; Jane Austen a calmed one. Reading these two novelists, we can gauge the immense progress represented by the generalization of work for women and the emancipation of manners. Women emerged from dependency through paid work that liberated them, even if most of them still earn less than their husbands.

What both Balzac and Austen emphasize is the *patrimonial endogamy* that presided over marriage in Europe and has not ceased to do so in the interim, despite the so-called "sexual revolution" (in which men remain the winners, since they still have, among other things, the possibility of remaking their lives with a younger woman, while the inverse is less frequent). Most people marry in their own milieus, and the heart, despite its capriciousness, remains the servant of the established order. Working women have broken the bond of servitude that formerly connected the wife to her husband. It makes it possible to purify feeling and distinguish economic need from authentic affection. It also accelerates the divorce rate in the event of discord, since the wife can fend for herself. Financial independence is a guarantee of liberty.

F. Scott Fitzgerald, or the Distress of the Lowborn

There is a misunderstanding about Fitzgerald. He has been made the herald of the Jazz Age, of surprise parties, insolence, the Côte d'Azur, burdened by alcoholism and a feeling of decline. But there is little eroticism in his work, transgressions remain conventional, and the fall is foreseeable from the first books on. Fitzgerald is a Calvinist writer in a democratic country. "The rose-tinted spectacles of drunkenness" hardly conceal his belief in predestination, the certainty that the rich form a brilliant caste to which the fine things of the world belong by inalienable right. They are not humans but a tribe of demigods that we have the right to admire, not to approach. And among them, young women with voices "full of money" constitute the paradigm of a domain that does not tolerate any misalliance, where all the Gatsbys of the world are sent away after having amused the audience. Desiring them is already a sacrilege. Even though she is bipolar, the beautiful heiress ends up leaving the doctor who saved her and whom she throws away like an empty shell, preferring a man of her own caste (*Tender is the Night*). Happiness is a treasure guarded by a heavy door that everyone wants to open. Those who get a foot in the door are the ones most violently struck. They glimpse paradise and are driven out of it as intruders. "The poor fellows mustn't dream of marrying rich girls . . . when you take people out of their milieu, it turns their heads, no matter how brave a face they put on it." Only the very wealthy have an exclusive property right to pleasure; everyone else is doomed to the mediocrity of work, to the whirlwind of chimeras.

All of Fitzgerald's books convey the malaise of the man who is not at home in his class, too ambitious to accept women of modest background, too modest himself to have access to the women he dreams of, and forced to play the eccentric, since he cannot violate the conventions. His best novels recount a cheerful disaster in which the collapse happens under the auspices of luxury and parties, where alcohol and illness cut down people in the spotlight. He spent his life trying to find work for newspapers and studios to glean a little money and pay some of his debts. According to Fitzgerald, neither youth, nor grace, nor humor could compete with these dynasties of tycoons who were moved by nothing. Even hastily won fortunes don't make you a member of this very special race, especially if they were destroyed by the crash of 1929. In the work of the author of "The Diamond as Big as the Ritz," social barriers are so many sacred barriers that no audacious person should ever dare to cross. He has been seen (by Cioran, by Deleuze) as an existential and literary bankrupt, a "night of the soul." But his "flaw" resides first of all in his puerile belief in money as a sign of election.

In that respect, he is in no way romantic. This movement was a protest against the rule of manufacturing and calculation. Fitzgerald suffered from sharing the values of those who rejected him and relegated him to nothingness. His whole work is an allegory of the American Way of Life and its frenetic cult of the greenback. His modern epigones (Jay McInerney, Bret Easton Ellis, Robert Goolrick, et al.), all of whom are as fascinated by the cynicism of the rich as he was, redouble this fascination by ferociously criticizing them. That's because in the meantime the 1960s happened. It seems that all it would have taken was a step sideways, precisely the emancipation of manners, to allow Fitzgerald to escape the glacial theology of the dollar, that divine seal that separates the elect from the outcast, and to recover a freedom of action. But without this poor man's dream, this poor dream that bears within it its own defeat, there would be no tragedy and thus no artwork, no masterpiece.

Our Love Is Always Impure

It is said that the rich are never loved for themselves, that their wealth interferes with the friendships they arouse. That may be true, but it is also true of most human relationships. Feelings exist only in situation, in relation to shared projects, common tastes. Every attachment to a person comes in the form of character traits or physical traits that we prefer. Would you love me if I fell ill, if my face were suddenly disfigured by a terrible leprosy, if I suffered a reversal of fortune? Here we encounter the eternal materialist contradiction: giving self-interest the last word in affairs of the heart. By clarifying ambiguous feelings, money claims the privilege of lucidity: where we thought there were effusions of feeling, the pitiless law of the dollar or the euro reigns supreme. This clear-sightedness is a delusion, however. This is well shown by Adrian Lyne's film, *Indecent Proposal* (1992), in which a wealthy man offers a beautiful young woman—married and in love with her husband but debt-ridden—a million dollars to spend a night with him. With her husband's agreement, she reluctantly consents. Their marriage soon falls apart, not because she has lost her "soul" in the exchange, but because she has developed feelings for the man who has rented her. But after divorcing her husband, she realizes that she has made a mistake, and ends up going back to him. It isn't money that has killed love, it's love that has distorted the transaction and made it unduly long.

Feeling raises the question of value. If the other person loves me, I am saved from my contingency, I am cleansed of the sin of existing. If the other abandons me, I am overwhelmed by the gratuitousness of my being. I am *worthy* only if I am justified by the other's desire. We could, moreover, continue the metaphor for every stage of a relationship. The evaluation of a person who pleases us, the weighing of defects and qualities, sometimes resembles a job interview in which one tries to maximize opportunities or at least minimize losses. As for the formula "I love you," a marvelous confession, it is also a pact through which we try to tame the other person to make him or her our equal. Saying "I love you" is a way of synchronizing our feelings, of putting the other in the same time zone we inhabit. But this revelation is not an oblation pure and simple: the love that I profess demands reciprocity in accord with the old formula of Roman law: *do ut des.* I give so that you give. If the other does not respond in kind, the declaration of love is in danger of turning into a declaration of war or a deception.

The sexual encounter itself implies a sharing of pleasures. The Kantian formula, which is so brutal in its realism—"Marriage is the appropriation of the other's genitals"—has as its counterpart the fact that each partner benefits from this possibility. If the man behaves in a selfish way, he will be incapable of satisfying his companion. In the sexual encounter, the woman teaches slowness, she needs to be gradually aroused and begs her lover not to exhaust himself too fast. Male eroticism is brief and parsimonious, female eroticism is complex and generous. Love stumbles when it ceases to give without keeping score and starts storing up the slightest blunders as evidence for a legal proceeding.

Remembering offenses subjects the most harmonious marriage to a list of one's spouse's shortcomings. Confidence gives way to reproaches, credits become debits. And this calculation is the direct result of egalitarianism, the monetary principle par excellence, which requires an emotional, educational, and erotic symmetry. It triumphs in the highly symbolic domain of household tasks. Cooking, housekeeping, and errands are just so many exhausting activities that erode the flaming wall of passion on a daily basis. Its invisibility makes the economic model all the more significant in our couples. The sweet shadow of tenderness is supposed to solve all problems. In everyday life, love is a continual exchange of favors, from housecleaning to shared emotions and sex. In love, one is never out of debt. In fact, a good marriage is precisely that: the temple of reciprocity is constantly renewed, like a sacred flame. Little attentions, kisses, and gifts stand out against the background of this ongoing trade without which no conjugal relationship is successful. The feeling of not being paid back (a marvelous expression) in life with one's partner, the fear of being cheated, sabotages a couple more than financial problems as such.

In short, a time comes when money as a metaphor is everywhere except in money as a reality. I've given you everything, sacrificed everything, the disappointed lover says, and this reproach proves that he gave nothing for free, but was hoping for a return on his investment. This gift was a loan from which he expected dividends. The logic of calculation is redoubtable in that it makes our affective life undecidable. It is in fact impossible to say what in our couples is devotion, habit, vanity, or arithmetic. Our love is always impure; that is our destiny.

Venal Love, Immoral Love

Walking in the Bois de Boulogne amid horse riders, financial barons, and duchesses displaying themselves in their carriages, Georges Duroy, alias Bel-Ami, greets a "parvenue of love" who is passing by in an elegant carriage "with two grooms seated behind her." He admires this "bold luxury earned between the sheets," and feels himself close to this courtesan whose audacity contrasts with the hypocrisy of the other visitors to the park. The solidarity between the gigolo and the courtesan who are proud of their success.[30] Why do our societies disapprove of venal love? Because, received opinion says, it transforms those who practice it into slaves. But what if it is freely chosen or practiced discreetly and episodically? When it is disguised as marriage, for example, for those who admit that they are seeking financial security?[31] A young woman, a "sugar baby," marries a man in his fifties or a wealthy man in his sixties, a "sugar daddy" who is prepared to pay for her studies and provide her with an apartment and a car—what should we call that? Pure tenderness, a mad passion for an aged body, or a judicious investment? And the European, Canadian, and American women who go to West Africa, the Caribbean, or southern Europe to find vigorous lovers whom they pay for their services—what does that look like? Are we going to attack female sex tourism because women are now customers as well? There are countless ways to pay for love, and Stendhal's definition of marriage as "legal prostitution" is far from being outdated. "How much love costs old men" was set forth by Balzac in his novel *Splendeurs et misères des courtisanes*. He compared the women who terrified and plundered old lovers to the bleeding that was supposed to relieve bodies of excess blood: a way of irrigating commerce with hundreds of thousands of francs, of "repairing the misfortunes of

Avarice and Cupidity."[32] An unauthorized redistribution carried out on couches and sofas.

As early as the nineteenth century, socialists and feminists began to expect that the disappearance of the bourgeois family would result in the erosion of prostitution. Freedom of choice in sex and love were supposed to guarantee the end of erotic servitude. Women are incontestably more independent today, at least in democratic countries, and yet venality continues to thrive. There are at least two reasons for this persistence: economic necessity and some individuals' unequal access to pleasures (because of their physical unattractiveness, their illnesses, their age). For such individuals, paying for sex is a way of overcoming this injustice—unless sexual help for the handicapped is deemed a crime, and they are forced to observe an obligatory abstinence. It isn't money that kills love, it's a lack of money that throws it into transactions and compels some girls in Kinshasa, in the Congo (to mention just one example), to take multiple lovers in order to provide for their needs. They are prepared to have sexual relations in exchange for ten dollars and a good meal. This is what the Congolese novelist Marie-Louise Bibish Mumbu calls "the culture of chic, check, shock," a combination of financial wealth, elegant clothes, and sexual savoir-faire.[33] Is this prostitution in the strict sense of the word, or an intermediary state that excludes neither feelings nor sincerity?

When "escort girls" (or "boys") offer their services for an evening, when students sell their charms to get through the end of the month or to pay for make-up or costume jewelry, are they professionals that have to be penalized or fearless young women who are coping with the difficulties of paying for their educations? Take for example the expression "Don't forget my little present." Through a pretense that fools no one, venality seeks to retain the appearance of a gift.[34] In this way the dignity of the buyer and the seller is respected. Money disinfects the sexual exchange of any affective adherence. Once it's over, everyone is quits. Prostitution is diffused throughout society and increases our perplexity regarding erotic exchange: with it, we enter into the universe of uncertainty where everything is done in a complex mixture of disinterestedness, oblation, and indirect payment. Money espouses the anarchy of desire and increases it. What difference is there between a kept woman and a call girl? *The permanence of the customer*, the former's obligation to put up with having her benefactor around 24/7 and to show him her gratitude.

It is pointless to try to embellish it. As a destiny, prostitution remains a thankless, sordid trade. It exposes those who practice it to the bullying of their customers, the arbitrariness of the police, the violence of their pimps, the insufferable compassion of kind souls, and the blame of others. The tragedy of this profession is the easily earned money that makes a return to "civilian life" harder and saving difficult. How can you put up with a small salary when you can make as much as $10,000 a day by prostituting yourself? Formerly disqualified in the name of vice, prostitutes are now qualified as victims who have strayed and who have to be saved from themselves. They used to be criminalized; now they are infantilized. We don't want to hear their demands on the ground that they are allegedly being manipulated. The fact that call girls, rent boys, and transvestites are fighting, in "sex workers'" labor unions, to improve their condition, not to abolish it—that is what appalls the moralists.

So what should we do if we know there is no good solution? Choose the one that does the least damage: Grant a status to people working in this trade; allow them to enjoy the fruits of their labor and to get out of the business when they want to. Choose regulation that monitors and protects rather than abolition, which would force entertainment women into hiding and leave them at the mercy of gangs (as has happened in Sweden, a supposedly "virtuous" country that has driven prostitutes off the streets and into the arms of the mafias and the Hell's Angels).[35] Even if the goal is to punish the johns, it is the better to make prostitution invisible, to spare decent people the sight of them. It will never be completely anodyne to rent one's body—or rather a part of one's body, since prostitutes, whether male or female, do not kiss and limit very precisely the zones their customers are allowed to caress. But there is no obligation to make prostitution a crime, to imprint "fateful distinctions" (Balzac) on those who practice it, and relegate them to "peripheral humanity." This activity ought to be relieved of its debasing mythology. Venality terrifies a society that thought it had emancipated Eros and now sees that nothing has been resolved. A twofold opprobrium is cast on prostitutes: the genital continues to serve as a synecdoche for the female body, the part being taken for the whole. Man *has* a sex organ, woman *is* her sex organ. For a woman, to give it without limits is to be lost: that is why being a gigolo is less shameful than being a whore, even though they practice the same trade.

Just as the nineteenth century feared the confusion of a woman of the world with a courtesan, the former setting the tone for fashion and luxury, we fear the "mixture of kinds," we want to distinguish pure love from base commerce. But prostitution is in the gray zone where feelings converge with money, where desire oscillates between the free gift and a monetary transfer.[36] It is a catalyst that reveals what is really going on. Even in an ideal society without major inequalities, men and women would choose to offer themselves, in exchange for a salary, for the pleasure of potentially belonging to everyone and anyone (that is the argument of Kessel's *Belle de jour,* and it is the foundation of Fourier's utopia). "Some women have more success selling themselves than giving themselves" Stendhal remarked brilliantly.[37] Even an ugly person

Gambling, a Secularized Version of Grace

No gentleman gambles for the sake of the money, Dosto-evsky said, or to satisfy the "plebeian desire to win," "even if he might have lost his last penny."[38] What is it that motivates a gentleman facing the thalers and louis d'or on the card table, "burning like hot embers"? The desire to thumb his nose at destiny, "to stick out his tongue" at it: to find the win-ning formula that will defeat the unknown on its own ter-rain. Hadn't Pascal and Fermat, the inventors of probability theory and the ancestors of insurance, set forth the discovery of a certain order in the irregularities of history and stressed the risk of seeing a disaster recur at fixed intervals? It is not the hope of finding a mathematical recurrence in games of roulette or dice that matters; it is the impossibility of the project itself that attracts Dostoevsky's gambler, and leads him, contrary to all reason, to go to the casino, where he bankrupts himself, swears that he'll never do it again, and then starts all over. With a snap of his fingers, he wagers his life, double or nothing.

At first, the lottery resembles the definition of a second marriage coined by Samuel Johnson (1709–1784): the tri-umph of hope over experience. What motivates it is the ambition to improve one's life by betting against fantasti-cally high odds: one chance out of tens of millions. Perhaps it is because the jackpot is out of reach that people become addicted to the lottery. The bettor could say, like the faithful, "I believe because it is absurd." With this differ-ence: no one has ever seen God, whereas winners exist and keep the legend going. The system provides, in addition to the jackpot, a whole series of consolation prizes that prevent discouragement and increase impatience. What number should players choose? Their birthdates, or those of their family members? Since the result is uncertain, they become obsessed with figures, to which they lend a personality. Believing the impossible to be possible simply because we want it to be—the lottery is a good example of a process familiar to psychoanalysts: negation. I know that it is unlikely that I will win, but I try all the same. The game makes it possible to relax the pressure of reality, delivers us over entirely to the caprice of fortune, with its twofold sense of chance and wealth. If there is deception, in this case we are its accomplices; we don't expect the lottery to change the social situation or to correct inequalities. And of course it is better for a state to levy a little on millions of modest incomes than a great deal on a small number of high ones.

We still have to distinguish two kinds of gambling games: those that depend on us and presuppose skill—cards, baccarat, horse races—and those in which the players allow their fates to be decided by the anonymity of balls rolling in a machine or the whims of aggregates of numbers. The former can bankrupt us, the latter are less harmful because of the periodicity of bets and the relative modesty of the sums involved. If we lose, we lose only our bet, not our shirts. This gives the ritual visit to the tobacconist, where people scratch their cards or fill in the squares, a simultaneously feverish and calm aspect: improbable winnings, minimal losses. The thrill is democratized, but without the dizziness of the fall:

addiction lite. What really keeps people playing is the crazy idea that they are going to challenge fate on its own territory, that it might have chosen us, and us alone, among millions. The lottery is a secularized version of Grace.

Often there is something worse than losing: winning. Wealth that falls from heaven is the most dangerous. The beneficiary has to be immediately taken in hand, advised. Having become the target of swindlers, he is in danger of seeing good luck turn into bad and ruin him. The marvelous thing about gambling is that it is one of the "emergency exits" (Theodor Fontane) that relieve us, free us from the choice between success and failure. Neither moral nor immoral, it is a way to entrap fate, to create uncertainty in order to avert it. The gambler is a warrior of the imponderable. In the ordinary world, the dice roll only once: why not allow oneself to begin over and over? In that regard, betting on the existence of God is the only game in which one can neither lose nor win, because the answer presupposes the death of the gamblers.

who offers himself or herself elicits a certain emotional turmoil by suggesting a scandalous possibility in the coded universe of social relationships. Amorous hospitality implies a dissolution of individual barriers that makes each person's body potentially the property of everyone. And what is money, if not the whore with a heart of gold par excellence, who belongs to no one but gives herself to everyone?

PART III

Richesse Oblige

EIGHT

Should Bourgeois Values Be Rehabilitated?

Two new Russians meet. The first says: "Look! I've got a new tie, it
cost me five hundred dollars." The second replies: "You imbecile, I
know a place where you can buy the same kind for eight hundred."

MARIE FREYSSAC, *Ma Vie Chez les Milliardaires Russes*

THE historian Norbert Elias tells us that one day the duke of
Richelieu gave his son a well-stocked purse so that he could learn
to spend money like a great lord. Shortly afterward, the young
man brought the purse back to him, full. Furious, his father threw
the purse out the window.[1] For the nobility, saving money was a
reflex of commoners, base merchants. It was better to ruin oneself
giving splendid parties than to limit luxury or resort to degrading
work. "One is all the more a man of the world the less one is a
man of money," Taine wrote. But this disdain arose from pillaging, war, and the labor extorted from peasants and serfs. The
aristocracy had to dissipate the gold that it otherwise scorned:
saving it up was the height of vulgarity. And when funds came to
be lacking, the aristocrats had to resort to money-lenders, even if
it meant never paying them back or throwing them in prison.

Inversely, there is one person who works, accumulates, and
seeks to enrich himself through constant labor. Read all the literature of the nineteenth and twentieth centuries: it is one long
indictment drawn up by the revolutionaries, monarchists, and
Romantics against a new human type: the bourgeois. Paunchy,
hideously ugly, calculating, he was and has remained for the past

three centuries public enemy number one. Who is he? An unprepossessing fellow. Not content with parodying the aristocracy, exploiting the peasant and the proletarian—whose name in Latin refers to a person who can count only on his children in order to survive—he imposes a way of life whose monotony is rivaled only by its pettiness.[2] In contrast to the old sumptuary feudalism, he marks the triumph of meanness. He can be summed up in a word: he is *base*. "Big and fat, naïvely ingenuous," as Balzac says of his père Goriot at the beginning of the novel of the same name, before unveiling the sublime soul within. The bourgeois is entirely obedient to an economy of confinement. He restrains his passions, his élans, only to give them free rein in the only activity that matters to him: making money, the only kind of blood that runs in his veins. Didn't Benjamin Franklin say that to lose a pin every day was to lose five pennies a year and all the profit that could be drawn from them?[3]

Having become the dominant class, the bourgeoisie never ceased to ape the nobility while destroying its values. Insisting too much on man's pettiness, the seventeenth-century moralists paved the way for the demolition of aristocratic honor and facilitated the Revolution of 1789. With their devastating lucidity, Pascal, La Rochefoucauld, and the Jansenists foreshadowed, without knowing it, the advent of the accountant with limited horizons, propitious for the blooming of capitalism. There was no longer anything grand or noble in humanity's firmament, only the selfish impulses that Freudianism reduced to the fundamental drives of sexuality and anality. But the bourgeois is flexible: to the straight-laced type of the nineteenth and twentieth centuries, as hypocritical as he was moralistic, succeeded, starting in the 1960s, the new-look bourgeois, " 'straight' by day, 'swinger' by night," who slaps onto the economy the ideal of enjoyment inherited from the revolution in morals.[4] The goal is no longer just to work, it is to consume with a view to well-being. The notion of prudence is replaced by that of expenditure. The market is put in the service of our self-fulfillment: that is the post-war period's innovation. The capitalist order, guilty of having expelled the poetry of the world, was an order of disenchantment (Max Weber). Today it has given way to the order of entertainment, the convergence of the work ethic and hedonism. The appearance on both the right and left of bourgeois bohemians who reject the divorce between their cultural ambitions and their professional reality: The left-wing bourgeois bohemian aspires to live an artistic life while at the same time retaining his prerogatives, sheltered by his protected quarters; the right-wing bourgeois bohemian seeks the thrill of license without losing any of his respectability. Both of them want justice for everyone and the maintenance of privileges only for themselves.[5]

The Big Pie

At the beginning of the twentieth century, the banker John Pierpont Morgan explained that he would not trust a firm whose boss earned twenty times more than his employees. These days CEOs set their own remunerations or decide to increase them through boards of directors that support them, and receive five hundred, a thousand, or two thousand times more than their employees. Far from being connected with merit, their remunerations are due primarily to connivance or competition with other members of the financial elite, especially their Anglo-American or Chinese counterparts, with whom it is felt necessary to keep up. A recurrent figure in modern capitalism is the big boss who wants to freeze the salaries of his workers while he pockets a bundle, or, better yet, to carry out massive layoffs accompanied by an increase in salaries. With this kind of booty, we are no longer in a logic of competence but in *a logic of gluttony:* today, the elite expresses itself in stratospheric figures that are described using all sorts of astonishing names worthy of a mad grammarian. These "remuneration packages" include annual bonuses, exceptional bonuses, pluriannual bonuses, stock options, free stocks, phantom stocks, signing bonuses, welcoming packages or "golden hellos," presence bonuses, indemnities on departure (golden handshakes), transactional indemnities, noncompete clauses, in-kind payments, and complementary retirement pensions. You think you're dreaming when faced by this newspeak consisting entirely of euphemisms. The same might be said of the bankers' jargon, the preciosity of the great priests of money, with their acronyms that are incomprehensible even for those who created them, a linguistic barrier intended to intimidate the novice and strengthen class spirit. Why should we be astonished by the shareholders' rebellion? It would take a Molière to set to music these new manners typical of capitalism gone wrong. Add to that the transfers of CEOs or, in another order of ideas, athletes, soccer players and others, from one club to another, sold as "human assets."

Let there be no doubt, there are countless good reasons for a big boss to grant himself such emoluments while at the same time demanding that others tighten their belts: notably, the ferocious competition between major managers on the world scene who are sought like spoils of war. But to run a firm is to be concerned about cohesion; it's to set an example, and not to establish an unbridgeable distance from one's troops. The Sadian axiom according to which to be rich is first of all to take delight in what others don't have is truer than ever. When are salaries too high? When it is felt that there is an intolerable interval between those who earn the most and those who earn the least. Like a society, an enterprise has to respect a proportion. When this proportion is lost, there is no longer any common world. In addition, the disproportion has to be publicized to be validated: those receiving the top salaries have to proclaim it loud and clear, even though negative reactions are to be feared. It is not the classic lure of profit that motivates such amounts, but more simply the desire to dominate, to rule in Olympus. In an enterprise, how can one join in a common effort when differences are so vast? For the salaried employees and the managers: the constraints of success, of ruthless competition, the ordinary universe of capitalism; for the bosses: "socialism for the rich," co-optation among the happy few and connivance between shareholders and managers.[6] To justify compensations running to seven figures, the privileged invoke the laws of the market. Their "liberalism" is another name for conservatism: it is supposed to legitimate inequalities by reference to an invisible hand that combines immanent justice with redistributive justice. Today, almost all sides have espoused the egalitarian ethos that remains the symbolic horizon of our societies; all actual inequality is supposed to be justified by arguing on the basis of a hidden but equitable order.

The appalling imbalance of compensations is transformed into a simple reflection of competencies. Contemporary neofeudalism presents itself in the guise of merit: "Because I'm worth it," as the L'Oréal ad says. The market is a plebiscite that sanctions the best of all possible worlds. Money that has been earned becomes the judge of personal qualities: the elect will never say that they are rich, but only "comfortable," tormented by the fear of ridicule when confronted by so many crowned heads that are better off than they are. But in order for society to work, the gap between the highest and the lowest cannot seem insurmountable. An overwhelming disequilibrium destroys all hope of social ascent.

According to the IMF's economists, in 2015 the immense wealth of a few people was supposed to be inimical to growth for all. On the global scale, the concentration of wealth is spectacular; almost half of the world's resources, or about 110,000 billion dollars, is controlled by 1 percent of the population. In other words, the "good society" or the "good enterprise" is not one that reduces all talents to the same level but increases everyone's chances, allowing them to develop with a view to the future.

Even if most contemporary rich people did not inherit their wealth,[7] they demonstrate the simple power of wealth in all its brutality. Their bank accounts are the only things that sets them apart from common mortals. Their delights and their leisure activities are the same as ours. They no longer aspire to high culture, but are content with ordinary distractions. The distance that they cultivate is purely spatial, not mental. Nietzsche had sensed this development, presenting the poor and the rich of his own time as the rabble below and the rabble above, one and the same vulgar crowd with the same tastes.[8] Subversion by "venomous envy" among the former, relentless labor among the latter, who are tormented by "insatiate avidity." Such is the contemporary world: rubbing shoulders with competing plebeians who are engaged in a ferocious battle for recognition.

The Artist and the Rogue

The old model, the one of the frugal, puritanical bourgeois, the last hero of the original capitalism (which may be a reconstruction owed to Max Weber's talent), has become a foil. The rich man should live modestly, said the millionaire Andrew Carnegie at the beginning of the twentieth century; he should avoid luxury and extravagance and become "the mere agent and trustee for his

The Greedy Person, the Hero of Simplicity

What we call greed may be nothing other than an easy solution. Money provides the material conditions for a good life without, however, dictating it. It lends an immediate meaning to life: it is easier to pile up millions than to make a success of one's destiny. Material wealth should precede spiritual wealth, but many people do not move beyond it, because they are not capable of doing so. The greedy man is one who has a single passion, but it is insatiable: he desires, figures, calculates the decimals with a joy close to intoxication. Stock market operations, purchases, mergers, takeovers; he lives in a state of effervescence punctuated by adrenaline highs. Money is a belly of inexhaustible fertility that does not know the term "enough." For every risk run, the greedy man feels the pleasure of decline or glory. When a large group of people is moved by a single concern, a single motive, it no longer has either the time or the leisure to devote itself to other subjects that are insoluble or painful. If there are no "more innocent ways of spending one's time than employing it to earn money," as Samuel Johnson said, that is because while doing so one thinks of nothing else.[9] The greedy person lacks imagination and has isolated, in the complexity of human affairs, one element and only one, to which he devotes himself.

The acquisition of a fortune follows an ascending path that reminds us of the Platonic ascent of souls, even if parodies the latter. For example, being on the list of the richest people is a way of reassuring oneself regarding the quality of one's life. Hence two possible uses that can be made of it:

living a better life thanks to one's money, or making as much money as possible without being able to take advantage of it. Enjoying things in their diversity, eating and loving with delight, cultivating oneself, spreading the arts and letters, dressing elegantly, traveling the world—or, on the contrary, multiplying one's fortune. "Our age doesn't know what to do with its money, with its labor, if it is no longer money, no longer labor" (Nietzsche). In life, we have to choose between cash flow and capital: one passes, the other inflates. The former offers the enjoyment of its passage, the latter the enjoyment of its increase.

poorer brethren, bringing to their service his superior wisdom, experience, and ability to administer, doing for them better than they would or could do for themselves."[10] In April 2013, a French newspaper expressed its surprise that until recently, old-school bankers in Geneva still dined "on a thin soup and a stuffed tomato: eating a third dish would have been considered gluttony."[11] But the dominant classes have changed their imitation, as a direct consequence of the hedonist revolution of the 1960s, and reconciled themselves with their perennial enemies, the rogue and the artist: one violates the laws, the other the forms and codes. Consider, for example, the advent of capitalist hippies (of whom Richard Branson might be considered the emblem), cool billionaires in jeans and flip-flops, all or almost all of whom are tax exiles ardently involved in the battle against global warming, poverty, and AIDS. Their teachers are now wealthy painters, prominent athletes, sometimes organized crime figures or even dictators (consider the fascination that Fidel Castro or Putin exercise on our elites). Art, which is in theory the most disinterested activity, has become the most profitable. These days, capital is an artwork and the value of the value, a square of painted canvas. It has become an element of social status as much as an authentic appetite for beauty. Priceless canvases painted by masters are hung on vast surfaces, intended to attract the attention of visitors. The name of the collector is almost as important as that of the artist, provided that the earlier owners were prestigious. For example, Liu Yiquian, a Chinese taxi driver who became a billionaire and bought at Christie's, for 170.4 million dollars, Modigliani's *Nu couché*. By purchasing a Picasso or a Degas, buyers also acquire a notoriety increased by the revelation of the amount of the bids. It is war booty that honors them. Similarly, people pay fortunes to buy the works of a young painter who has made a dazzling debut on the market. The movement goes in the opposite direction: the artist seeks the panache of insurrection as well as comfortable revenues. He seeks to win on the level both of symbolic subversion and of the well-stocked bank account (Jeff Koons, Anish Kapoor, Damien Hirst). Didn't Salvador Dalí have himself photographed with a ten-thousand dollar bill on each cheek after signing a book contract with Simon and Schuster in the 1950s? The *nec plus ultra* is to invite creators to dinner, to get a showbiz star to attend one's birthday party or to have one's portrait made by the greatest artists, as princes used to do, in order to become oneself a work of art: Kate Moss sculpted by Marc Quinn as a siren in solid gold weighing over a hundred pounds, in a complex yoga pose, or Pierre and Gilles immortalizing the bearded transvestite singer Conchita Wurst, haloed with light like a saint.[12]

Life was too tranquil in the bourgeois cosmos; now it has to be exciting. Sensitive to the artists' criticism of capitalism, some members of the elite joined in the demand for authenticity and liberation implicit in this milieu.[13] Now we see the bourgeois being disgusted with himself, loathing his pettiness and his morals, and wanting to be seen as a bohemian. He is overtaken by "a ravenous hunger for unlimited experience."[14] He keeps a covetous eye on the great innovators whose sense of invention and boldness of execution he admires, as Luc Ferry has clearly seen.[15] The bohemian wants to act like a bourgeois, and the bourgeois wants to go slumming. The latter swoons before the art market, dreams of being freed from all ties, and wishes that he too could experience the intoxication of borderline situations. Formerly criticized for his mediocrity, he is now accused of a lack of moderation, his strange folly. He has broken with "the goddess Temperance," and left forever the golden mean, the management style of the good paterfamilias.

Another temptation: organized crime, which increasingly contaminates the ordinary economy and has in some countries led to an alliance between industry and the underworld.[16] Didn't Pablo Escobar propose in 1989, after a campaign of terror intended to influence the presidential elections in Colombia, to reimburse his country's foreign debt?[17] Wasn't Chávez's Venezuela already a mafia-state whose leaders behaved like gang bosses? The fall of the Berlin Wall has allowed new mafias to develop in Eastern Europe, and especially in Russia, and they are experts at theft and plundering, picking up where the former communist *nomenklaturas* left off. The journalist Roberto Saviano has shown that the Neapolitan Camorra has penetrated the great industrial firms of northern Italy and the tourist sector in Spain. As for the Scandinavian thriller, its main theme is the murderous excesses of the ruling classes. A "criminal system energizing both the lower and the upper strata of society" is being set up, playing on the weaknesses of the parliamentary system.[18] The manager, the CEO, the notable, and the banker make "villainous pacts" with organized crime and embrace the gang boss's transgressive ideal of life, whereas the gangster dreams of transforming himself into a "bankster." It is the same movement that drives stock-market swindlers, constructing Ponzi schemes on the naïveté of the uninitiated, whom they fleece in every way. It is typical that the gang boss, who combines predatory behavior with intelligence, can become a model for some nabobs who are trying to increase their power with total indifference to human laws.

The criminal, a Nietzschean figure par excellence, is the exceptional being who does not allow himself to be intimidated by herd morality. He was encouraged by the loosening of morals in the 1960s, and he contradicts its anthropological optimism. Our desires, people said back then, are good by nature, and nothing should limit them; the only terrible thing is the prohibition that represses them. We have to admit our mistake: the ruse of reason, according to Hegel, consisted in achieving sublime goals through brutal passions. The ruse of modernity consists in creating brutal situations through reputedly sublime drives. Contemporary hedonism intersects the new delinquency, which offers it an opportunity to develop and move into new areas of transgression. In the future, everything will be played out there, in the opposition between the criminal bourgeoisie and the virtuous bourgeoisie. By nature, the hedonist is more permeable to moral perversion than the conservative, since his only criterion is his own pleasure. Let us recall Hannah Arendt's formula, written in an entirely different context, that of the rise of Nazism: "High society is falling in love with its own dregs."

The End of Money, the End of Economics?

"The day is not far off," Keynes wrote in 1946, "when the economic problem will take the back seat where it belongs, and the arena of the heart and the head will be occupied or reoccupied, by our real problems—the problems of life and of human relations, of creation and behaviour and religion."[19] Thus society would have to take an interest in ultimate goals, such as happiness, and ignore means, such as technology and growth, those detestable poisons. A strange tendency in an economist, decreeing that his trade is on the way to extinction, once prosperity is automatically produced by the industrial machine. This reminds us of Karl Marx's wish in *The German Ideology* (1845), where he explains that in a communist society, abundance would be such, and so well regulated by production, that people would be able to hunt in the morning, go fishing in the afternoon, and indulge in criticism in the evening without ever being either hunters, fishermen, or critics. Astonishing prophecies on the part of individuals who devoted their whole lives to economic problems and who suddenly declare them to be superfluous. The specialist in curves and statistics dreams of poetry and love. A counterexample: all the people in the literary and artistic world who claim to despise money but who incessantly talk about it, obsessively, like a symptom.

Others argue for the end of money, at least in its material form, and the expansion of its electronic form, the "megabyte currency" reduced to a chip inserted behind the ear or under the skin. This would eliminate counterfeit money, the theft of cash, attacks on armored cars, and the Mafia's money laundering. Cell phones would become portable banks, making it possible to offer financial services to the most destitute in villages and ghettos.[20] These arguments are correct, though very widespread electronic fraud still exists. However, the terms remain imprecise: it is not the end of money that we are witnessing, but rather its metamorphosis. Since we cannot extinguish human passions, we try to abolish the accursed sign that conveys them, hoping that this change will erase our turpitudes. Moreover, the preference for cash shows how much the dematerialization of money remains a utopia. Can you imagine handing a homeless person a credit card to give him a euro or a dollar? Whether we aspire to abolish money or transform it into an electronic currency, the goal is the same: to disembody human existence. But to achieve this sublime state, we still have to enter into long economic, monetary, and financial explanations, and thus resuscitate the very thing against which we are rebelling. Keynes again, adopting a prophetic tone: "When the accumulation of wealth is no longer of high social importance, there will be great changes in the code of morals. . . . The love of money as a possession—as distinguished from the love of money as a means to the enjoyments and realities of life—will be recognized for what it is, a somewhat disgusting morbidity, one of those semi-criminal, semi-pathological propensities which one hands over with a shudder to the specialists in mental disease."[21] Perhaps! But the invocation of the future as a place where consolation is to be had is always a subterfuge. It is a way of seeing humanity not as it is but as one would like it to be. We have to stop using the term "end" this way: it is never the end of the world, of religion, of the nation, of history. It's the end of *a* world, of *a* view of history, of *a* form of belief. Physical money is not about to disappear, any more than human morbidity is.

Puerile Felicities

In a lecture given in Vienna in March 1937, Robert Musil explained that the artist and the writer have the right, contrary to ordinary people, to be foolish in all innocence.[22] They are permitted to be immodest because of their position. They can allow themselves what others cannot: the free development of their narcissism in the form of sublime inanities that are received as revelations. This is also the advantage of wealth: it makes its elect children who are permitted to do anything, or almost. They can, for example, elevate their little problems to the level of tragedies. "The poor man is forced to skimp on his pain. The rich man displays his pain in full" (Charles Baudelaire). The well-off are surrounded by a nimbus of fervor: near them, one breathes the invigorating air of success (whereas the unfortunate spontaneously disgust us). We all know people who are paralyzed by the grandeur of the establishment, whose friendship is determined by the prestige of their acquaintances, and who are prepared to do anything to be admitted to their circle. This is a dangerous game: to rub shoulders with the rich, out of mimicry, is to take the risk of opening a wound that will never heal. It is the royal road to bitterness, is shown, for example, by Lily Bart in Edith Wharton's novel *The House of Mirth*. A beautiful but impoverished orphan living in New York at the beginning of the twentieth century, Lily is attracted like a moth to the flame by the select world of her friends, who end up rejecting her because she has not mastered their codes.[23] The privileged seem to be saved during their lifetimes. They are blessed by the versatile goddess Fortune, in her double role as the source of abundance and chance. Dispensing delights, she is the sister of Need and Sumptuousness. They emanate a power that reaches far beyond their means. By frequenting them, we might benefit by ricochet from their aura.

The superrich are monarchs whose whims divert us or outrage us.[24] Ignoring the usual constraints, they believe they belong to a different race. When they fall, following a corruption scandal, they may comically exclaim, as did Robert Diamond Jr. the former general director of Barclay's who was dismissed after the scandal concerning the manipulation of the Libor (the interbank interest rate) in England: "I never did anything for money. I never set money as a goal. It was a result."[25] His successor, Rich Ricci (a fateful name) explained that it is impossible to live in London or New York with less than one hundred million dollars. In 1951, the magnate William Randolph Hearst asked to be buried in a coffin in the shape of a safe to prolong his passion for money into the hereafter. In 1899, the American sociologist Thorstein Veblen laid it down as a law that financial power had to be associated with conspicuous consumption. "Beauty is commonly a gratification of our sense of costliness masquerading under the name of beauty." At that time, the Vanderbilts were having huge private homes built in New York (the one on 57th Street had no less than 137 bedrooms). In 1882, Cornelius Vanderbilt gave Marble House, the "marble palace" in Rhode Island, valued at eleven million dollars, to his wife Alva for her birthday. Meanwhile, an unskilled worker was paid about two cents an hour.[26] J. P. Morgan had bought his first Vermeer painting, not because he liked it, but because it was expensive and could impress his peers.[27] It seems that in the 1970s Aristotle Onassis, who was involved in an expensive battle against his rival Stavros Niarchos, had the bar stools in his yacht covered with sperm whale foreskins, and installed solid gold water faucets and a swimming pool that could be transformed into a dance floor paved with mosaics.[28] These are "big boys' toys," as the luxury magazines call them.

Now as then, plutocrats sink into a phallic rivalry in matters of cars, boats, and houses: their yachts become ocean liners with landing pads for helicopters, inside and outside swimming pools, and a miniature submarine; their houses are gigantic, not to mention the private jets that crowd airports and lead to aerial traffic jams.[29] Every extravagant desire has to be satisfied: arranging for one's daughter to marry in France, as the Indian Lakshmi Mittal did in 2004, inviting a thousand people to the wedding, privatizing the Tuileries Palace in Paris and the royal château at Versailles for the sum of seventy million euros. (In 2013, a wealthy Indian industrialist similarly staged his daughter's wedding in Cannes, but failed to obtain authorization to parade down *La Croisette* on elephants). Peer pressure is pitiless and leads to an escalation of excess. Tycoons are divided between the 1 percent of people with extravagant incomes and the 0.10 percent of people with very extravagant incomes: there are no words to describe these hierarchies; superlatives no longer suffice. The crowd of well-to-do aspirants who are mired down in "mass luxury" have to be left behind, and to do that one has to spend more, slap down dollars by the hundreds of thousands, by millions, in order to keep one's place and one's rank. Money makes its possessors advocates for their status. And what does it matter that this rivalry leads the middle classes, the "almost rich," to compete with the upper classes in sumptuary expenditures, at the risk of falling into debt?[30] Opulence materializes our most infantile desires, our wish to stupefy our contemporaries by engaging in mind-boggling waste. Ever since Adam Smith we have known that to seek wealth is to seek other people's recognition and good will, it is to want to be loved and envied. Whims make sense only in relation to other people with whom we have to keep up.

But money liberates as much as it enslaves, it leads tax "dissidents" to move abroad, and those who hold all the aces to live with their own kind, like the South American or Russian upper bourgeoisies, barricaded behind gates and guard towers, sealed up in their deluxe fortresses. Their curse is to be doomed to live among their peers in a rarefied space. They close the door to the unexpected, derive no benefit from the urban mixture, from that marvelous porosity of the great cities that makes sitting in cafés, meeting people by accident, and strolling around so exciting. Proust, referring to the dining room of the Grand Hotel in Balbec, describes it as an immense aquarium in front of which the workers, fishermen, and petty bourgeois crowd to admire "the feast of the marvelous beasts," the dukes, countesses, and bankers dining there. It is not certain that this "feast of marvelous beasts" would still make us salivate, or that felicity and surprise have taken up residence exclusively in the upper crust of our societies, which are doomed to be closed up. Money, a malicious divinity, circulates only the better to petrify those who possess it, to congeal them into statues made of salt.

The Miser and the Spendthrift

"Angela Merkel," Sigmar Gabriel, the president of the German Social Democratic Party, remarked one day, "is like a miserly old aunt who keeps her bag on her knees so no one will take her money, but Germans like that." There is a difference between the spirit of thrift, tinted with moral philosophy, and avarice, which is a retentive disorder. To prudently let go of one's cash is, after all, to put it back into circulation. The miser is peculiar in that he transforms his gold into substitute organs. Letting it go would be tantamount to agreeing to dismember himself. Money is his skin, his nerves, his muscles, neither more nor less; he fabricates a body made of an inert, atemporal material that will survive him. He is his fortune more than he possesses it; it constitutes him. He accumulates it only to forbid himself to benefit from it: no pleasure could equal that of possessing it.

Consider Molière's Harpagon: at once odious and naïve, he betrays himself by burying his money box containing ten thousand crowns in his garden. Cunning, he lends money at exorbitant rates; cynical, he wants to marry his daughter to a fifty-year-old man who accepts her without a dowry. He is, moreover, pretentious; he wants to marry a girl of twenty who is, however, in love with his son. Possessed, he seeks in the proliferation of his money a fountain of youth, just as he wants to regenerate himself by marrying a tender young thing. Molière's miser scorns other people. Classically, *avaritia*, from which the word "avid" is derived, was associated in the Middle Ages with greed, the mother of usury. Then it signified a rapacious passion for life and people, and not the petty meanness that we have denounced since Molière. Even in hell, in the iconography of the Last Judgment, the miser keeps his purse around his neck amongst the tormented. He worships his moneybag even in eternity.[31]

Rich people's stinginess is an astonishing phenomenon; it is as if they wanted to combine all conditions, the prodigality of the wealthy and the parsimony of the indigent: it seems that J. Paul Getty, the California oil millionaire, had a pay phone for guests installed in his London house and was never the first to leave a meeting so that he would not have to pay for the taxi. Perhaps he wanted to avoid the weariness of being rich by acting as if he were starting over again and had to count every penny. Avarice is a mathematics of subtraction, an ice floe of the heart. The miser realizes with terror that his money never really belongs to him, that it is a fugitive, unstable entity, which he has to constrain by his meanness. It may be there that the Freudian metaphor of anal retentiveness is pertinent, through the liking for retention. But it is outrageous to claim, as Ferenczi did, that money "is nothing other than odourless dehydrated filth that has been made to shine," or that the love of money is related to the death instinct present in fecal matter. [32] Dry excrement and rub it—you won't get a louis d'or, a sou, or a euro!

The spendthrift is opposed to Harpagon the way drunk money is opposed to sober money. By spending money wildly and visibly, the prodigal never ceases to emphasize how little he cares about it. No party, no banquet or expensive purchase stops him. As he throws money away he is hoping to see others ecstatically watching him, consecrating him as a great lord. The big spender likes to squander money and criticize the stinginess of his fellows. Serge Gainsbourg, protesting taxes by burning a five-hundred-franc bill on television, on March 11, 1984, was defying the law and showing his contempt for the Golden Calf. The spendthrift's insistence on spending heavily proves that he is not completely detached from the object of his scorn. His generous gifts are deceptive; he is engaged in an endless settling of accounts with fortune.

The miser and the spendthrift are two sides of the same coin. Aristotle saw this, opposing to both of them the liberal man who gives as much as he should, when he should, and with pleasure, under the double auspices of virtue and enjoyment.[33] And still more the "magnificent" man, who excels in the great and noble by his considerable giving, which no one can surpass. We all oscillate between miserliness and generosity: we sometimes quibble over a ridiculous sum, spend heavily on a whim, and are niggardly about trifles. The right relationship to money is to have several: that is the sum of our uncertainties about it, so much does it seem inhabited by significant powers.

Are Taxes for the Poor Alone?

It is by rejecting social rules and first of all that of paying taxes that the new oligarchies show their inclination to move beyond the common world. Expert at evading taxation and at competitive relocations, they employ armies of tax specialists and lawyers to escape obligations to which ordinary citizens are subject. Some prefer to no longer invest in their own countries, thus nine thousand American expatriates chose to renounce their citizenship after the Foreign Account Tax Compliance Act (FATCA) was passed in 2011. This law obligates foreign banks to communicate to the IRS all information about accounts held by United States citizens. Money laundering in tax havens and optimization in large corporations have become the rule, even in countries where the tax burden is lighter than elsewhere. (On average, in Europe Amazon and Google pay far less tax than in small corporations, 19 percent as compared to 35 percent).[34] To the point that Warren Buffet and other billionaires published an appeal to President Obama in the *New York Times*, "Stop pampering the filthy rich!," demanding that the government increase taxes on everyone who makes more than a million dollars a year. In general, this appeal made by these "generous" billionaires met with an indignant response on the part of the superrich who consider taxation an archaic practice only for the common people. In 1989, Leona Helmsley, the queen of the New York hotel industry, was prosecuted for tax evasion and sentenced to a year in prison without parole. During the trial, her housekeeper testified that she had heard Helmsley say, with delicious naïveté, "We don't pay taxes. Only the little people pay taxes."[35] A marvelous formula that sums up the whole spirit of an age. Part of the wealthy classes would like to maintain the fiction that they are an isolated group of superior minds living above common humanity. An excessive tax burden can be questioned, but there is something shocking about privileged people who refuse to repay society a fraction of what it has granted them in the form of education and care. What is a personal enrichment that does not contribute to the enrichment of all and does not take the form of foundations, schools, hospitals, and actions useful to the collectivity? What is at stake here, in a dramatic way, is no more nor less than the survival of the middle classes, which are caught between the hammer of proletarianization and the anvil of opulence, and are, for their part, compelled to pay their taxes, cash on the barrelhead.

There comes a time when money has to be defended against the rich themselves, who protect themselves and co-opt each other, exercising a veritable monopoly in defiance of any competition (Joseph Stiglitz). If the market is characterized by creative destruction, to adopt Joseph Schumpeter's famous expression, it is also characterized by a destructive destruction. Some sectors of finance, with their "vulture funds," their raids, their rating agencies caught in the act of lying, and their dismemberment of the finest firms, seek to liquidate the system for the benefit of a few people.[36] This makes their culpability overwhelming in the current crisis, because they are weakening the economy and prohibiting access to the market for all. In this epidemic of devastation, it is the classic bourgeois, who may be petty but is still responsible, who is disappearing; the bourgeois of whom Milton said in the seventeenth century that he alone could still observe virtue.[37] Capitalism is not a desire to demolish but the fusion of calculation with audacity, the desire to reinvest profits in innovation (Max Weber). Isn't it time to reinstate self-interest's titles of nobility? Etymologically, "interest," derived from *inter-esse*, means to be among people, to form a society with them, to combine reasonable self-love with concern for others. Adam Smith said it well: wealth and grandeur go hand in hand, they imply fame, morality, an aptitude for governing, setting an example for others. What good is wealth without virtue, without a civic sense, without the will to help the community? Money, Balzac said, is a power only when it exists in disproportionate quantities. It civilizes but only up to a certain point. Beyond that point it becomes an ally of barbarity, when it puts considerable means at its service in an epiphany of violence, as is shown by the epic of the violence of gangs and terrorists.

The old bourgeoisie was constantly destroying the dominant class in order to feed on it, according to Fernand Braudel. The nobles sold "their rusty titles to financiers' daughters."[38] It may have lacked flair and did not always avoid ridicule. But at least it remained more or less fascinated by high culture and felt the need to invoke and propagate it; it knew how "to excel in the useful and the pleasant" (Voltaire). The bourgeois, described as an antihero (Huizinga), petty (Bataille), and moved by fear, knew how to improve himself. He proved capable of thinking against himself, of participating in the demolition of his own stereotype. So that these days the true bourgeois is a person who despises his own class, plays the rebel, and takes pride in constantly belittling himself. Thus the bourgeoisie constitutes, as Thomas Mann said in *Buddenbrooks,* "the nobility of merit," concerned about progress and well-being. Nobility is no longer something that falls to us by birth, but something that we grant ourselves on the basis of our constancy, labor, and talents.

The puerile exuberance of our elites should not make us forget that in every age the rich have incarnated and borne an exemplary art of living. Today they should be reproached not for wanting to rule the world, but for lacking ambition, for having exchanged a vast mission for short-lived pleasures. "A highly evolved civilization is inseparable from luxury and wealth," Oswald Spengler said. It is the role of the great patrons—the Medicis and the Rothschilds, the Camondos, the Péreires, the Onassises and the Niarchoses in Greece, or today, Bernard Arnault and François Pinault in France, Jeff Bezos and Elon Musk (for the

A Tulip Named Bankruptcy

In the eighteenth century, the sultans of Constantinople, who were passionate about flowers and gardens, developed a variety of tulip with marbled colors that they named "Sahipkiran," which means "bankruptcy."[39] There is no better proof of how much speculation sometimes desires its own ruin. The attraction of a crash is like the urge some people feel to jump off a cliff. It has become a genre of its own; it even has its symbolic geography. Wall Street is inseparable from New York, the city of exuberance par excellence, whereas Silicon Valley, the cradle of the new technology, is located in an area of great seismic activity in California. The stock market has been described as a circus, a casino of reckless passions. But what is particularly striking is its monotony with predictable variations, which makes it possible to regulate current business, to invest, to borrow. Everything would be simple if finance were not as indispensable for the health of a country as it is for a household, the scarcity of money strangling an economy as much as a war does.

Nouriel Roubini, one of the few experts who predicted the 2008 collapse, called economic crises "creatures of routine." How do people, who think they are pursuing their interests, provoke such a debacle? At a time when planet Finance has grown larger than planet Earth (Niall Ferguson), money always ends up taking us back to the truth of figures. That financial practices must be regulated, put under political control, and everyone's access to credit assured— that much is obvious. A large mass of money in the hands of a small number of adventurers is quickly transformed into an appetite for disaster. Excess capital has to be purged. Having embraced money, humanity has embraced progress, but it has also pointed a weapon of mass destruction at its own head.

conquest of space) in the United States, Adrian Cheng and Liu Yiqian in China, the Tatas or Azim Premji in India—to put their immense fortunes in the service of human beings, to transform the base metal into beauty and generosity. Only thus will the elite be able to avoid the aridness of the money men who have sacrificed everything to a mathematical idol.

NINE

Getting Rich Is Not a Crime
(and Falling into Poverty Is Not a Virtue)

If you see a Swiss banker jump out a window, jump after him; you can be sure there's money to be gained.

VOLTAIRE

A bank is an institution that lends you money if you can prove that you don't need it.

BOB HOPE

EUROPE and North America live in fear of the return of the impoverishment that marked their history and the first stages of capitalism; we are the spoiled children of a growth that cost our ancestors terrible suffering. The vagabonds, the proletarians, whose uprooting Karl Marx described, and whom Jack London, Émile Zola, Charles Dickens, and Victor Hugo made the heroes of their novels, the dispossessed people torn away from the old rural solidarities, from the regulated life of the countryside and the ancient cantons of old Europe, continue to haunt us. We descend from so little, that is our fear.

Four Stages of the Poor

Four memories of the poor cohabit in us. In the Middle Ages, invested with sacredness, they were the pilgrims of God, who make use of the world as if he were not making use of it. Starting in the Renaissance, when the mendicant orders of the Church became suspect, the poor were slow to join the Reformation without the cruelest punishments being inflicted on them. They were transformed into lazy idlers who had to be brutally reeducated.[1] They were no longer God's emissaries but "the dregs, the cast-offs of the Republic." With the advent of modern times and the Revolution, there was another transformation: the poor became the insurgent people, an actor in its own destiny, the founder of the nation, or the proletarian rebels sung by literature. But the communist movement tried never to assimilate the working class to the poor, the latter constituting the disorderly mass of the *Lumpenproletariat*, which was always ready to sell itself to the highest bidder. The revolutionary project must not suffer from the bad reputation attached to the destitute. The poor man then became, in the rhetoric of the defenders of the "third world," the *guerrillero*, the exploited peasant, the colonial, to whom a coefficient of sympathy is always attached because of his distress. The Christ of nations, he is sacrificed on the altar of History as its redeemer.

Today, indigence signals a failure of modernity. Formerly a condition common to most people as contrasted with a handful of nobles ("for one very rich man, there must be at least five hundred poor ones," Adam Smith said), it became synonymous with failure as soon as a middle class established itself halfway between utter destitution and extreme opulence. There is something dreadful about the way the disinherited are reproduced, even though in the West, where the welfare state takes responsibility for them, their condition has nothing in common with that of their nineteenth-century counterparts. If until recently the poor man was promised redemption thanks to progressive forms of messianism, he is now reduced to a surviving relic that has resisted waves of prosperity. Such stubbornness suggests a bad attitude. The poor man is a dunce who persists in poverty, which social welfare plans, humanitarian organizations, and great institutions examine year after year, swearing to eliminate it. Even if absolute poverty has diminished throughout the world, thanks to the expansion of the market, the objective of transforming the condition of nobodies remains for the moment out of reach. We will never see the total eradication of poverty, for a mathematical reason: even if the needy doubled their standard of living, the gap between them and the wealthiest people would remain very large, since the latter's incomes continue to rise. In the nineteenth century, the possessors and the dispossessed were called "the fat and the thin." Protruding bellies and chubby cheeks were signs of prosperity. These days, it is the poor, devoted to junk food, who suffer from obesity, and the rich who take care to remain slender. Finally, increasing population and medical progress automatically increase the number of mouths to be fed and make resolving the problem more difficult.

Countless solutions have been proposed to do away with this scourge: no-cost or low-cost loans, easier access to property ownership and to reliable financial institutions rather than to unscrupulous usurers; encouraging women to engage in entrepreneurship (Hernando de Soto Polar), extending education to both boys and girls; granting study scholarships to the children of the most impoverished; setting up institutions responsible for schooling, vaccination, and transportation, as governments in developed countries do.[2] However, it would be wrong to reduce poverty to economic parameters: that would exclude, in the primary sense of the term, the person for whom work, no matter how onerous, is simply a means of subsistence. But it would also exclude the person who is "poor in world," to borrow a term from Heidegger, the person who lacks relationships, knows no one and is known by no one, finds himself relegated to his place without being able to modify it, and is forced to constantly scale back his ambitions. (In this sense, many so-called underdeveloped countries have constructed, despite their poverty, a rich social society and mutual aid networks that leave no one out.) Poverty is first of all symbolic; it is a privation of abilities, to adopt Aristotle's rhetoric (reformulated by Amartya Sen). That is why communism, by establishing an equality in need, arouses nostalgia in many people. It clipped the wings of a virulent passion among Moderns: envy. If we are all poor, it is pointless to desire what others have, since just like me, they have nothing.

All the same, it is reductive to oppose poverty and wealth term for term. The nuances and gradations are infinite, and statistical science fails to render them. Their confrontation is blunted precisely by the creation of the middle classes as a *sociological shield halfway between poverty and abundance*. The middle classes alone, endowed with doors and antennas, and capable of openness and tolerance, form democracies' center of gravity. Already celebrated by Aristotle and Milton as emblems of the intermediary, they prevent societies from being divided into two hostile, antagonistic castes. If they disappeared, it would be all over for our regimes, all over for this very particular mixture of law and prosperity that characterizes Europe (in the United States, the middle classes, which are being impoverished, have already lost their role as a demographic and economic pillar). It is always the triangular structure that saves us from Manicheanism: just as the invention of purgatory made it possible to escape the opposition between hell and paradise, the middle classes save us from hostility between the well-to-do and the disadvantaged. For many of us, it is uncertainty that is predominant; we don't necessarily feel poor because we earn little or fulfilled because we have a good salary. As Aristophanes said a long time ago, a certain state of difficulty is indispensable. If everything were given to us from the outset, no one would make use of his ingenuity. It is not bad that things cost us something: as soon as money becomes the metaphor for human perfectibility, it encourages us to transcend ourselves.

A Perverse Idealization

It remains that these days, in Europe as in the United States, a militant neopauperism is declaring itself to be a "value of well-being." Not being able to eradicate poverty, we begin to find good sides to it. It is a very French temptation to erect our failure—unemployment and apathetic growth—into a model and to propose it to other peoples. Nothing is more perverse than the praise of misery offered by certain doctrinaire people as if it constituted a superior virtue. It is one thing to choose frugality for reasons of a private or spiritual nature, and another to impose shriveled ambitions on everyone. There is a narcissism of spectacular poverty that betrays, repainting poverty in the colors of joie de vivre and smiles, the feeling of disenchantment that seizes certain European nations in the grip of crisis.

Whereas political economy seeks to offer the greatest number a decent life, a new, radical way of thought would like to manufacture poor people on a grand scale. This is proposed, for instance, by Jonathan Crary, an American art critic and academic. To resist the devastating temporality of capitalism, which, according to him, contributes to mass insomnia and stress, he recommends "rejecting the destructive character of the millionaire culture, the toxicity of all the images and fantasies of material wealth. For those of us who have children, this means abandoning all the impossible and desperate hopes that are projected for their professional careers. And conversely, it means offering them the vision of a habitable, shared future."[3] Thus we are supposed to teach children resignation, forbid them to aspire to a prestigious career, to acquire diplomas. We must make people feel guilty about their ambitions and cut off at the root their desire to rise. This argument recalls that of Charles Péguy, who longed for the poverty of the past, when man "was at least guaranteed in poverty. . . . It was a retreat, an asylum. And it was sacred."[4] But the modern world has gone off the rails; it has thrown the masses into poverty. "The ideal state," John Stuart Mill said in the nineteenth century, "is the one in which, no one being poor, no one has the desire to be more wealthy or fears being left behind by the efforts made by others to get ahead."[5] With an ataraxia of the appetites, an atony of desires, human history is supposed to stop and arrive at a stationary point that nothing will disturb. Anyone who tries to rise risks falling still further.

All this forgets that poor people have a justifiable desire to become a little wealthier, and that there is nothing shameful about that.[6] This life can be better, a bed of roses and not a field of thistles, and self-mortification and self-incrimination are pointless. Surrounding the least well-off with a quasi-sacred aura is a way of binding them to their condition by lending it the attractions of Eden. For example, trying to introduce into the penal code a crime of "discrimination against those in a precarious situation," as the National Consultative Commission on Human Rights has done, would be tantamount to creating a new crime of opinion, a new word police.[7] Speaking ill of the excluded would be prosecutable; it would be a further extension of the politically correct that freezes new social categories one after the other. But verbal "respect" is another way of not fighting the phenomenon.

For a whole segment of the moral left wing, condemning the powerful is a way of escaping the duty to reflect on the means of saving millions of people from disease, famine, and insecurity.[8] For these critics insulting wealth takes the place of policy. In their view, it is better to soak the rich than to enrich the poor; as for the latter, they have to be reeducated to accept sacrifice, be taught that it is folly to try to improve their situation. When Pope Francis, visiting South Korea in August 2014, castigated materialism and capitalism, while the Vatican maintains a luxury worthy of a Renaissance palace, he was attacking the wrong target. The frenetic quest for money may be sterile, but it is not materialist. Instead, it is terribly idealist, and that is what makes it dangerous; like all ideas, it is insatiable. To denounce the desire for money as "blindly quantitative" is not to see the real peril: poverty alone is materialist, and it subjects us to the humiliating constraints imposed by need, hunger, and inadequate housing and clothing. It is when it is lacking that money rules our lives and tyrannizes us.

The Paradoxical Grandeur of the Parvenu

What is admirable is how India, China, the Asian powers, Brazil, and some African countries (Nigeria, Ghana, Benin, and South Africa) have emerged from poverty; some of them are even rivaling Europe and the United States in wealth. Thanks to hard work, several billion people have experienced a considerable improvement in their situation. Non-European peoples, who used to be called, condescendingly, the "third world," have escaped their stereotype and become the masters of their fate.

But what is stupefying is the ingenuity and work that allow individuals to succeed even though they come from disadvantaged families (like Narendra Modi, who moved from being a tea-seller to being prime minister of India). That is why for the past two centuries immigrants constituted the great contemporary narrative, the one about the quest for a better life through uprooting, tearing oneself away from one's past (on the condition that the tensions that lead to these population displacements not be omitted, and that legal immigration, which is useful to the receiving country, be distinguished from a massive influx of refugees, which is tolerable if it is temporary, but difficult if it persists). "All of us are immigrants spiritually," Walter Lippmann wrote in 1914, celebrating the determination and courage of new arrivals in America, who were eager to blaze a new path and to escape their original condition.[9]

Not to mention nouveaux riches, internal immigrants who blur the boundaries of the circle of complicity among the powerful. Whence the importance of the particular path taken in these success stories told by people from every nation and every social stratum: the brilliant idea or the superhuman effort that allowed them to escape poverty. The ascension of a child of the slums or ghettos to the pinnacle of society does more to feed the dream of rising in society than do weighty sociological tomes. This irruption functions like a machine for doing away with fatality. Let us not forget, either, the spectacular advances made by certain communities—for example, the Gujaratis in India (63 million) who have succeeded, thanks to a system of guilds and solidarity, in creating a worldwide commercial network, succeeding everywhere they have settled, in Asia, the United States, and Africa, and who already control three-quarters of the diamond industry in Antwerp.[10]

All the great novelists of the nineteenth century—Zola, Trollope, Balzac, Maupassant, Victor Hugo, Henry James—tell the same story: People are no longer at home in their social worlds. Everywhere we find pushing and shoving, the abrupt elevation of coarse adventurers, crooks disguised as gentlemen, Rastignacs in skirts. Two characters, who are legion these days, inspire writers' eloquence: the arriviste and the parvenu. The former is both laughable and touching. By trying a little too hard to show the external signs of success (a country house, a boat, expensive cars), he seeks confirmation of his new status. Excess instead of simplicity, flagrant ostentation instead of distinction—that is what betrays the commoner eager to join the upper class. Today as yesterday, *there are those who have money and those who are money.* The former have gotten rich by bold actions; the latter have the demeanor and the upbringing provided by generations of wealth. They *are* money precisely because they don't talk about it, don't flaunt it, but just live it with all the simplicity of people with good manners. The parvenu, in contrast, is a person who comes from nowhere, whose position remains unsettled so long as he has not converted the grammar of *having* to the grammar of *being.* In his effort to rise in society, he constantly makes blunders in taste, language, and dress. You have to learn to be rich: decades are sometimes required to join the world of "high" society, to become familiar with the ways of the upper crust. The parvenu has the bank account but not the dynastic memory, the understanding, and the codes that have to accompany his high position. He is not part of any bloodline and seeks desperately to have his rank confirmed. In "good society" he sticks out, showing a pronounced taste for the flashy, and is relegated to his obscure origins, like those billionaire sportsmen who bring with them everywhere, even into drawing rooms, the atmosphere of stadiums and locker rooms.

What was peculiar to Europe and North America a century ago now extends to the four corners of the earth. The confusion of rules and labels as multiple as they are imprecise show how hard it is for the dominant classes to separate the wheat from the chaff. This confusion has reached its apex in the current age of globalization. Everywhere, in Asia, Africa, Russia, and the Americas, there are millions of individuals who have succeeded and are longing to be recognized. They have to reinvent, by copying them, politeness, civility, manners, and ways of speaking. Then there is a twofold risk: they might betray their origins or overdo the conventions, looking like they've dressed up in their Sunday clothes, just as servants overdo their masters' etiquette. Whatever they do or say, they lack the nonchalance, the ease, of those to the manner born. But without these plebeians, there would be no social mobility, and without the insidious corruption of codes in which they are engaged, there would be no innovation. Their vulgarity is one of the ways novelty comes into being. There is a phenomenal energy in their awkwardness. By imitating the manners currently in force, they unwittingly invent a new civilization. These usurpers are creators. And they are present throughout the world, as is indicated by the Pakistani author Mohsin Hamid's novel *How to Get Filthy Rich in Rising Asia*, which presents itself as a "self-help book."[11] The genius of literature consists in showing an extreme sensitivity to social nuances, to advancing castes, to interlopers, and to aspirations that are as legitimate as they are ridiculous.

So long as citizens retain, through good times and bad, the hope of increasing their incomes, they can avoid discouragement. What does it matter that the rich are getting richer—it's normal that those who take risks should be well remunerated—provided that others do better as well. If that assurance decreases, the

The Oracle of Omaha

In *L'Argent* (1891), Zola presents the character of a very rich fool, a certain Amadieu, "a fat gentleman with a ruddy, clean-shaven face" who has, "through his stubbornness as a lucky lout" invested all his money in shares of a mining operation in central France that have fallen to the lowest level. When real and considerable veins of ore are discovered, he realizes a sudden profit of fifteen million francs. "And his idiotic investment that would earlier have gotten him interned in an asylum raised him to the rank of the great financial minds." People come from all over to seek his advice. To each question, he replies with a grimace, and the beggar has to interpret his silence. Surrounded by the aura produced by his brilliant stroke of luck, this visionary has chosen the attitude of an oracle: mumbling and silence.

As if reality were imitating art, more or less the same situation is found in the "power lunches" with the billionaire Warren Buffett ("the Oracle of Omaha") organized by the Glide Foundation, a charitable association. In 2014, eating with this famous investor cost the modest sum of 2.34 million dollars (the first lunch, in 2000, went for twenty-five thousand dollars).[12] But there is a major difference from Zola's character: Warren Buffett is a well-known financier, and his tips are worth a fortune. Sitting down with him can be very profitable, and his simple presence is a guarantee of doing better. But isn't an element of magic involved here? Fifteen years ago the *Wall Street Journal* reported that had a stock portfolio managed by a recognized firm of experts also been played by the *Journal*'s editors, at the end of twelve months the yield would be have been about the same.

What good are financial analysts? They rationalize chance, make it appear logical. Many of them understand nothing about the derivatives that they put on the market and use a jargon suitable for impressing suckers. Their mathematical models are a kind of palm reading. Seeing entrepreneurs and major CEOs abdicating all reason long enough to eat a very expensive lunch is always stupefying. The economy is inseparable from oracular pronouncements: the art of saying neither yes nor no, of explaining nothing, of denying nothing, of drowning every statement in a saving vagueness. Saint Augustine saw the Divine Word as an obscure allegory that no one could boast of explicating. Are Warren Buffett's guests also reduced to interpreting their host's tongue-clicks, the sound of his chewing, the hubbub of the restaurant, the tinkling of glasses? Let us pay homage to such a talent. How can we not think of the remark made by Alan Greenspan, the former chairman of the Federal Reserve, at the beginning of this century: "I know you think you understand what you thought I said, but I'm not sure you realize that what you heard is not what I meant."[13]

social chasm becomes intolerable. Some people's advantages appear to the majority to be abominable privileges. The vitality of a democracy is gauged by the number of people from the lower and middle classes who succeed in augmenting their standing in the course of their lives. And in that regard, France, as the victim of its "structural choice of unemployment" (Jean Tirole), has a singular lack of vitality.

Wealth Is Plural

Wealth is an adventure in two stages: first it is acquired, and then it is deserved. It is not enough to condemn it in the name of purity or asceticism. It is not solely the enjoyment of a privilege but also the seat of a responsibility. The ruling classes, Hegel said, have to realize the triumph of Reason through their particular purposes.[14] These "contingent and revocable elites" are the agents of a goal that transcends them and that they vaguely perceive. If history is "a cemetery of aristocracies" (Pareto), that is because many of them died as a result of their obstinacy and behaved in a vapidly selfish way by refusing to consider interests other than their own. The power provided by money should entail a duty, as the Greeks knew, a mixture of care, good will, and justice. It is only at that price that a common world can be established.

Thus it is important to use the word "prosperity" in the plural, and not to connect it solely with income. At every point we must maintain the competition between desirable lifestyles and challenge the uniformity of dominant manners. It is possible to be a vagabond king who is happy to have little, because he enjoys everything, and a naked millionaire who lacks all that matters. Wealth is a victory over all its possible meanings, spiritual, material, financial, aesthetic, and natural, which never cease to confront one another. Since these valuable objects, paintings by old masters, high-end cars, fine furniture, race horses, yachts, and elite schools remain out of reach, recent generations have a redoubtable power: they can make them unfashionable and direct collective desire elsewhere. It is pointless to compete in the domain of luxury, on pain of falling into tackiness; one has to try something different. The miracle of surrealism and of the 1960s was inventing new collective desires, orienting bodies and souls toward new thrills. Creating other rarities, free love, studious leisure, the exchange of ideas and knowledge, walking, the enjoyment of the great works of the mind, the sense of everyday transfiguration—that is great art (this was already the choice made by Rousseau in his *Reveries of a Solitary Walker;* the enemy of aristocratic luxury defined in part by the luxury of our own age, the enjoyment of fundamental things). By taking the view opposite that of the dominant credo, aesthetic insurrections oriented people's gaze toward unprecedented sources of opulence: rediscovering the beauties of contemplation, nature, and the poetry of the streets, and even seeing what other people do not, discovering the sumptuous beneath what has already been seen, the marvelous beneath the commonplace.

In reality, we live only for the superfluous: the simple satisfaction of our needs, paying our bills and feeding and housing ourselves, is a curse. We gladly spend on our desires, but we resist paying for our duties. During the Great Depression, American historians note, some of the most modest households preferred to buy cheese and cigarettes rather than essential food supplies, and a woman in New York nearly starved herself to death so that she could use her welfare check to have her hair set and dyed.[15] An aberrant attitude? No doubt, but it remains that being human always resides in excess and not in simple survival. (Think of King Lear's anguished cry when his daughter suggests that he doesn't *need* all his retainers: "O, reason not the need!")

Make Capitalism Moral?

Wealth has two meanings: it is a privilege reserved for a few or a promise made to all. "Only capitalists can kill capitalism," said Felix Rohatyn, a former commercial banker who helped prevent New York City from having to declare bankruptcy in the 1970s. Let us add that only wise capitalists can save capitalism. What communism could not do, some people's thoughtlessness might succeed in doing: destroying the market economy from the inside. As I wrote in 1990, the market economy is in danger of dying from its victory over the Soviet system now that it is no longer threatened by an implacable enemy.[16] Capitalism will never be reduced to an apology for extortion; even if it is "the night visitor" that invents nothing—neither the market nor consumption, and especially not hierarchies—and finds everything already in place, it is still the amazing machine for creating wealth saluted by Marx, who wanted to abolish it by extending it to the whole world.[17] It remains for capitalism to realize all the possibilities it bears within itself: the notion of legitimate profit, the fruit of labor and initiative, and the promise made to the massive group at the base of society that it will "move beyond the ground floor of life."[18] But it is reaching a degenerative phase by abetting the triumph of a finance detached from any economic wealth and put in the service of a "predatory plutocracy."[19] It is viable only when it leans on democratic systems that ruthlessly expose its weaknesses and scandals.

We have gotten over our illusions regarding the transcendence of the capitalist system, which thrives on announcements of its demise, always postponed. Even the crisis of 2008 did not succeed in killing it. The challenge is to put the power of this amoral apparatus in the service of the common good. The best state,

Kant said, is the one that forces people, who are a priori selfish and hostile, to cooperate in view of their mutual interests.[20] Capitalism and communism were like two twin brothers who supported each other, each challenging and at the same time seeking to eliminate the other. One of them died of exhaustion, and the other needs a new adversary, or lacking that, a tutor who could correct it. It owes its survival to its enemies as much as to its followers, and draws its dynamism from being constantly attacked and thus obliged to reform itself.

We are witnessing its chaotic refoundation after the financial revolution of the 1980s and the crisis of 2008. A number of measures have been proposed in the resulting confusion and clamor: the reevaluation of the role of the welfare state, of the realms of the public and the private; the separation of deposit banks and investment banks; the worldwide prosecution of tax fraud, mechanisms for monitoring stock exchanges, the gradual elimination of tax havens; the regulation of bonuses and golden parachutes; and levying enormous fines on banking establishments that have cheated. An immense corrective labor is currently under way in the world economy, but it is not clear that it will suffice.[21] The same banks that sold billions of dollars' worth of bad securities to taxpayers have agreed, shamelessly, to be bailed out by the latter. We can make restrictive laws, punish offenders, throw them in prison, and increase taxes on the wealthiest, but success would probably require above all a moral revolution which for the time being has not been achieved. The market economy, no longer having any rival, has to reinvent its own regulatory mechanisms. Inventing a new way of using money, civilizing it as much as it civilizes us without losing the energy of its circulation, regulating it in accord with merit and honesty—those are some of the challenges that confront us.

If capitalism destroys the conditions for our adherence to its logic, promising a prosperity and freedom that are not forthcoming, it will lose the classes that have carried it to power. Unless we want to see it sink into an ideology of plundering, we have to criticize it in the name of the promises it has made to us but not kept. It needs a straitjacket, a spiritual policeman who can channel it and put it in the service of the common good. *It is therefore possible that one of the remedies for the current crisis is a return, whether we want it or not, to a certain original asceticism:* going back to the cult of work done well, productive investments, the profit motive contained within the limits of a collective project. There is no need to return to the clergyman's black robe or Victorian puritanism in morals. The conquests of the emancipation of the body and of desire are irreversible, at least in civilized nations. But a certain respect for effort, moderation, decency, and honesty will be necessary to battle the casino economy and the orgy of spending. For the past twenty years, the two mastodons, India and China, have been engaged in an enormous, rapid creation of wealth: the stake now is how these two nations are going to redistribute it. Public power has to protect access to the market for all, to take great care of money as a public good that is as vital as access to healthcare.[22] Helping the most destitute entails opening to them the doors of financial institutions, of efficient networks that allow them to avoid falling into the clutches of usurers.[23]

Communism collapsed without dignity, but the reasons for its emergence, the disparities that it denounced, have not disappeared. Whence the nostalgia it arouses in the countries of the ex-Soviet bloc, because although it did not provide freedom, it did at least provide security. The age when capitalism is accepted is less than ever the age of capitalism calmed. As it is extended, it

Value or Price?

Money is supposed to profane the most sacred things, whatever their quality might be, and confuse price with value. But value has several meanings, moral, religious, and economic, whereas price has only one. Thus it is absurd to oppose them to each other as the true and the false; price is the contingent way in which value manifests itself to us. The price of life, for example, decreases with age, since it is determined by the resources to be expected from a person before his foreseeable demise.[24] A baby is worth infinitely more than a sixty-year-old person, and an American is worth more than an African or an Asian. There is a difference between the subjective feeling of my own existence and the economic evaluation society may make of it. The fact that I am a capital that is constantly diminishing as I grow older in no way reduces my attachment to my existence, which I cherish all the more the shorter it becomes. At the same time that we are scandalized to see that the market sets the statistical value of human life, we are also scandalized by the excessively modest sums paid to beneficiaries when they lose a family member in an accident. The indemnity is never great enough; we cry out that even if millions are paid, they will never bring our dear one back to us. The money is the symbolic equivalent of the deceased, a phantom person: it quantifies an absence. Though it cannot resuscitate the dead, it comforts the survivors.

Individually, we would advise our children or spouse, in the event of our own death, and independently of the sorrow felt, to demand the maximum from insurance companies. Thus we agree to be instrumentalized, reduced to a pure calculation. To think about the price of life is to think about one's death and thus to think about the survivors. "Why continue to live when we could bury you for a hundred dollars?" asked an American advertisement of the 1920s, meaning that our will to live has a financial and psychic cost for which we have to take responsibility, whereas suicide settles our accounts and frees us of all care.[25]

As for things that are free of charge, there are at least two kinds of them. One is part of a hooking strategy: something is given to you for nothing that will later cost you a great deal. "If you're not paying for the product, you are the product," as the slogan says. Digital platforms and music sites are accessible without paying anything because your address will subsequently serve as an exchange currency and transform you into a bull's-eye. Products are no longer sold to a customer, customers are sold to an advertiser. This is also the strategy of the dealer or merchant who gives you a sample of what he will later sell you, once you have become accustomed to it. The free gift transforms you into a potential purchaser. The other kind of thing given free of charge is a political choice; education, public transportation, hospitals, are all services that have a precise cost paid by the collectivity. What is free of charge is always financed. Moreover, what is free of charge quickly loses its value—buses and subways are neglected and vandalized; the healthcare system frees patients of responsibility and makes them into unbearable consumers who have a right to everything.

Speculation is denounced as the origin of all our ills; but it is only the magnification of an event, an idea, or a reputation that is overinflated and suddenly pops like a balloon. There are speculative bubbles in every part of life, including matters of love. Lovers intoxicate each other before they fall back into the prose of everyday life. A terrible phenomenon of demonetization: a public statement or a politician suddenly ceases to have any weight, as if the blood had been drained from a body. We no longer bother to refute them; we ignore them. Life is a continual war of values. We constantly reevaluate people, things, and works, and devalue others. Some stand fast over the centuries, while others collapse and will perhaps one day be raised up again by our descendants. Modernity is the overwhelming experience of values that fluctuate, rise and fall. The Japanese have even given the name *wabi-sabi* to the fact that a damaged object, a cracked vase for example, may acquire the melancholy beauty of a worn thing. What it loses as an item of merchandise it gains in sentimental importance.

Value has been lost, the nostalgic tell us. But it has always already been lost; it has never existed other than as an absence, in the form of a regulative idea that has to be defended in every generation. It is what should happen, not what is given. More than greed or corruption, what kills our most cherished values—freedom, resistance, the critical spirit—is cowardice, the spirit of capitulation. When someone dear to us is in danger, when the homeland is invaded, our families threatened, then we enter into a different order, that of transcendence, of sacrifice. What is priceless is what is more dear to us than anything else, what we are ready to die for.

will be necessary to become accustomed to subversive actions that are all the more bitter because it is only a question of a better sharing of the pie. Capitalism will be attacked not because it is bad but because it is the only system on the field and the hope that a substitute for its reign will emerge no longer exists.

TEN

The Hand That Takes, the Hand
That Gives Back

This Mirabeau is capable of doing anything for money, even something good.

RIVAROL

ON November 15, 2009, the website Mailorama, trying to score a marketing coup, announced that it was going to hand out forty thousand euros in small bills at the foot of the Eiffel Tower. When the organizers saw the crowd, nearly seven thousand people, they got scared and canceled the event, swearing to pay the whole sum to a charity. The crowd, composed chiefly of young people from the working class suburbs, rioted and attacked policemen, roughed up a photographer, and began vandalizing this fashionable part of the capital city. Nothing illustrates better the inflammable value of the gift than this anecdote in which thoughtlessness competes with provocation. Announcing "free" money and then retracting is like taking manna from starving mouths. It makes us think of those celebrations under the Old Regime in which, on the occasion of a birth, a coronation, or a royal marriage, handfuls of coins, even louis d'or, were thrown to the people, along with the remains of a banquet— turkey, sausage, loaves of bread and brioches—just to hear the poor wretches cry "Long live the king!" and be assured of their obedience.[1]

The Collection and Alms

In the Catholic and Anglican world, the collection taken up during the mass is a particular moment. Everyone digs into his pocket, concerned to do his duty, and is aware that a failure to do so would be an admission of stinginess. What is peculiar to this ritual is that only small amounts are required. There are two kinds of baskets for holding the money: open and half-closed. In the former, coins clink as they fall in and get lost in the mass, in a mixture of colors and sizes. The collector makes the metal jingle, just as the beggar does his bowl, to remind parishioners of their obligations. We can imagine the sacristan or the choirboys counting it up afterward, coin by coin, and being dismayed by how little has been gathered in. The other kind of basket, which is more elegant, is brought out on great occasions, a marriage, a burial, a first communion. With a pretty, openwork design and covered with a white cloth, its function is to hold the bills prisoner for a moment in the cloth to testify to the donor's prodigality. It gives rise to a discreet rivalry among the faithful; they cannot give less than their neighbors. The generous person can take pride in the amount of his contribution, and the penny-pincher will be glad to bury his in the middle of the multicolored wad. The total amount is modestly hidden from people's eyes by the folds of the cloth, and no one can tell how much was given on that day.

Everything changes with the beggar's open palm. In large cities begging is a kind of daily tax levied on the goodness of our hearts, but it is also a market divided up by networks that take possession of locations and sidewalks (in this task, the Roma of central Europe deploy—in Paris, for example—a remarkable organizational sense). Posted at street corners, at the foot of buildings, moving through the cars in the subway, the homeless person regularly sounds his laments. He excuses himself for bothering us and appeals to our hearts. And if he were the only one! But a cohort of other beggars follow the first one, and are just as worthy of attention. Each one has to make himself the small entrepreneur of his own poverty, catch people's attention with a short spiel recited between two subway stations or on the terraces of cafés. He has to get his message across without tiring us, and not overdo things: being too relaxed is as deleterious as being overly dramatic. There is a way of hamming it up, because the poor wretch has to act out his poverty in order to make it exist. Will we respond to the eloquence of distress?

So we are approached several times a day by all kinds of people whose sight overcomes us. Why give to this one and not that one, who is just as poor? Some of them revolt us, others move us—an intonation of the voice, a worrisome thinness. We can resist a malodorous, ragged person or a belligerent one, but not those with unfathomable sufferings. Those eyes that glare at us, asking: What are you doing for us? How can you go about your business when we're dying alongside you?

We begin by being indignant at the social system that allows such a decline. What is the government doing about this? We end up giving the beggar some small change, only too aware of how inadequate this gesture is. It would take more than a euro to save these poor wretches. We give not only to allow them to buy a sandwich or a cup of coffee but also to ward off bad luck. We could someday find ourselves on the other side of the mirror, if fate turned against us. These are propitiatory coins that we slip into the beggar's palm so that his bad luck won't reach us. In charity, we are also buying Providence, in the sense in which Saint Augustine said that giving alms was an investment made in heaven by the wealthy, who console themselves for a small loss by the prospect of great profits.[2]

We sometimes wish, to our shame, that all these beggars would be cleared off the streets, as they were during the Renaissance, when the *sans-aveu* (homeless people, considered potentially dangerous) were inventoried in order to incarcerate them and force them to work, on pain of worse punishments, such as branding with a hot iron, mutilation, and whipping.[3] There was a time when poverty was exotic, the curse of distant countries or past centuries. Now it is returning, under the impact of the economic crisis and migrations, to our streets and our neighborhoods, creating veritable *Cours des miracles* (areas where unemployed migrants from rural areas congregated in premodern Paris). In the end, the gap between us and these excluded groups is not so great, and it is precisely this proximity that frightens us. Our generosity is subjected to the rule of the sporadic: it is discretionary and capricious. Waves of emotion are followed by periods of hardening. We carry out a kind of psychological partition; we move amid these disadvantaged groups without seeing them until finally our heart breaks on seeing a human wreck lying on the pavement. Rabbi Israël Salanter (1810–1883) wrote: "Others' material needs are my spiritual needs." We have roofs over our heads, we have jobs, while these poor wretches sleep on the street. For a modest outlay, we can relieve their suffering. But no matter what we do, it will never be enough. For charity is tricky: if it is mechanical, it can degrade the donor and the beneficiary alike. Didn't the philosopher Jacques Ellul advise giving money the better to profane it, to perpetrate, through this act, "an attack on Satan"?[4] Such an order testifies to narcissistic contempt and not to compassion. The worst affront occurs when a beggar to whom we have given nothing thanks us effusively. That is politeness that verges on insult. He kills us in the guise of affability.

The Tip and the Offering

"Keep the change." These little coins or bills, left behind in a discretionary manner, on the table in a restaurant, with a taxi driver or a delivery man, signify that the waiter's diligence or the driver's amiability deserve a reward over and above the stated price. It is a person-to-person homage, beyond commercial concern, and perfectly legitimate—for example, waiters in the United States, who are very attentive to diners, because the tip constitutes most of their remuneration, which is otherwise extremely small. In many countries, a restaurant bill comes in a small black leather case, as if it were a bit of bad news; it is the "painful bit" whose shock has to be attenuated and whose discretion must be guaranteed. Some workers, ushers in theaters for instance, live only off theatergoers' tips; as a result, the latter lose their optional character and become part of the price of the ticket. Giving nothing would be intolerably boorish.

Here as elsewhere, there is the risk of crushing others by the lavishness of the gift: for example, by indiscriminately tipping every member of a hotel's staff, from the chamber maids to the head porter, to leave a wonderful memory. Or, like a mysterious customer in San Francisco in 2014, leaving on the bar sums from five hundred to two thousand dollars after a lunch or a simple beer. In this we can see a scatterbrain's act, a desire to be loved, or a way of taunting other customers. Or again, the whims of the heiress to the L'Oréal fortune, Mme. Bettencourt, who handed out the interest on her interests, estimated at a million euros a day, to anyone who was lucky enough to please her: for example, a million to her chauffeur to walk her dog after her death, or a check for five hundred thousand euros made out to a girl of nineteen to whom she took a liking. And again, according to the state prosecutor, a billion euros to François-Marie Banier, who amused her, or five million more, for his retirement, to Patrice de Maistre, her wealth manager, who was already paid two million a year. Apart from the moral reprobation attached to this kind of behavior, in the name of what can it be penalized? As the Gates Foundation website explains: "From those to whom much has been given, much will be demanded."

To put it another way: to get rich is also to become indebted to those who have less. These generous gifts are not innocent: they create a bond of dependence, make those they benefit into vassals (in German, *Gift* means both "poison" and, now archaic, "gift"). The poets, dramatists, fabulists, musicians, and painters pensioned by the kings and the court in Old Regime France were not entirely free either in what they wrote or where they took their inspiration. It was the invention of copyright (in England with the Copyright Act of 1709, also known as the "Statute of Anne," in France with Beaumarchais in 1777) and the creation of the market and public opinion that allowed artists to live off their work, without having to answer to their protectors. A gift becomes domination when it seals an impossible reciprocity: how can you pay back a person who showers gold on you because he likes your looks? To dazzle and to subject: that is the effect of an excessively sumptuous gift.

From this point of view, Christmas is at once the apogee of the mercantile orgy and an anxiety-producing liturgy to confirm connection. This holiday can weld families together or break them apart. Behind the fairyland of ribbons, multicolored wrappings, and slightly forced cries of joy a subtle dramaturgy is at work. One must be both original and attentive, avoiding giving the same thing each year, a form of amnesia peculiar to the absent-minded and the indifferent. Some people are in no hurry to open their presents, knowing full well that it is the gift itself, in its epiphany, its motives, that is full of an overwhelming promise. There is a vast spectrum between the niggardly gift that signals your lack of importance, and the overly beautiful gift, whose munificence is annihilating. What should we say about those who sell their presents online or airheads who give you what you gave them a few months earlier? Or about those who offer only half-hearted thanks, considering your gift to be something they were owed? One can decide to stop celebrating Christmas or birthdays, except for children, in order to escape the headache of buying presents and the labyrinth of sensitivities. The weary task of receiving and distributing gifts, of following the slightest rituals of social life, makes us dream of suspending exchanges for a time. But this abstention feels like a defeat. Living in society encloses you in a network of gifts and countergifts that is not easy to escape. Some presents burden us with their uselessness, taking up residence like incongruous guests who ruin our lives. Others take months to find their place and then reveal themselves to be indispensable. Anyone who grants me a favor for no reason arouses my distrust. What does this fine gesture conceal?

Giving should be taught like table manners and politeness. A gift has nothing to do with its price; it consists entirely in the intention and beauty of the act of giving it. No matter how humble it may be, it is like an emissary from the giver and bears his imprint on it. There are people endowed with a talent for being lavish advisedly, who can shop the stores and boutiques to dig up the object that will please a precise person, showing delicacy and refinement. All gifts do not have the same value; some are simple formalities, others, more difficult, involve the whole person and are reserved for family and close friends. A good present is a factor of intensification; it gives new life to relationships in danger of growing stale. Whence the malaise we feel when we give objects that are too personal to people we don't know well, and gifts that are too impersonal to close friends who will be offended by them.

Here is a perverse form of generosity: constantly reminding someone of the generous things you have done for him, with the goal of keeping him in your debt. However, nothing is forgotten faster than a favor: a dinner invitation, a vacation paid for, a service provided are all things that memory erases. Then recollection gives way to the disagreeable feeling that a debt has been contracted, and can turn into resentment. Wisdom consists in knowing how to offer our friends delights, while at the same time thanking them for accepting our gifts. The politics of good deeds should be as radical as it is simple: no payback is to be expected for a generous act. The best recompense for a gift is the gift itself, the pleasure of giving pleasure.

The Damnation of Abundance

Every robber baron of finance or of industry, every Mafia godfather or mob boss, dreams of someday being good. The hand that takes wants also to become the hand that gives back. There comes a time, as the American steel magnate Andrew Carnegie (1835–1919) clearly saw, when immense wealth becomes a curse, an infirmity, if it is not put in the service of others: "The man who dies leaving behind him millions of available wealth, which was his to administer during life, will pass away 'unwept, unhonored, and unsung.' . . . Of such as these the public verdict will then be: 'The man who dies thus rich dies disgraced.'"⁵ The judgment is terrible and might be endorsed by a revolutionary socialist. If nothing or the minimum must be left to heirs, if the state must tax property at a rate of almost 100 percent, according to Carnegie that is because wealth is a collective product that is in the hands of certain people only by accident. The latter are only its skillful administrators, and not its owners; they must return it to its true owners. You have to pay back to society what it has allowed you to earn, restitute your surpluses to those who have a right to them, except drunkards and lazy people. Charity is an investment and not alms. There is no question of helping the incapable; one has to help those who want to help themselves.⁶

In the name of that ideal, the boss has the right to cut back his employees' salaries, and to impose hellish production schedules on them to increase his company's profits. A singular turnaround. An enthusiastic supporter of an implacable generosity, Andrew Carnegie advocates a kind of privative communism for the use of the best, a Bolshevism of the elite in the service of the destitute. The current suffering of wage earners will be recompensed by the happiness of future generations. Carnegie deplores his moments of weakness and would like to have even more money so that he could assign it to the domains he considers indispensable (he himself, in addition to the libraries, foundations, and various institutes that he created, donated almost eight thousand organs to churches in the United States and elsewhere, a sign of a personal motivation).⁷ Knowing that one is going to do good later on makes it possible to pressure workers now. Philanthropy is the continuation of business by other means.

This is at the antipodes of another of Zola's characters, the Princess of Oviedo, the widow of a crook who wants to redeem her late husband's ill-gotten gains by devoting them to the poor, spending his money down to the last penny. At Neuilly, she builds a veritable palace intended for orphans, a splendid structure in marble and fine woodwork. She wants to have the poor children sleep on silk sheets, offer them princely foods, and accord them "the delights of the triumphant." Although she is robbed blind by entrepreneurs, suppliers, and valets, she is seeking solely to erase her husband's financial thefts. She wants to be the queen of alms down to the last traces of the stain, to the point that the money from his gambling is "drunk by poverty like a poisoned water that has to disappear." That is the ambiguity of her project; she does not do good from love of the poor but from hatred of the criminals: "The accursed spring would be dried up, she had not given herself any other mission."[8]

We know the warning voiced by Frederick T. Gates, a Baptist preacher recruited by the founder of Standard Oil, John D. Rockefeller, in the late nineteenth century to advise him in his charitable activities: "Your fortune is rolling, rolling like an avalanche. You have to distribute it faster than it grows. Otherwise it will crush you, you and your children and the children of your children."[9] An ancient theme already found among the Romans, who practiced "euergetism," donations in the form of bread and circuses provided to the common people to maintain social cohesion: patricians, senators, decurions, and magistrates gave the people sumptuous festivals, battles between thuggish soldiers or gladiators, and banquets, but also temples, aqueducts, and amphitheaters.[10] There was ferocious competition between donors eager to show themselves to be more magnificent than their neighbors, trying to outbid their neighbors and combining their gifts with clientelism. Their prodigality maintained civic peace and at the same time increased their prestige.

Wealth is sometimes experienced as a curse: for example, by Søren Kierkegaard's father, a poor shepherd in Jutland in Denmark at the end of the eighteenth century. At the age of twelve, he cursed God for having reserved such a cruel fate for him. Shortly afterward, he was called to Copenhagen by an uncle who ran a hosiery shop and took him on as his apprentice. Against all expectations, this was the beginning of a brilliant and rapid fortune that allowed him to retire from business at the age of forty. But he was guilty of having one day revolted against his Creator, of having "sinned against hope," and he saw in his success a subtle form of damnation, an aggravation of his offense.[11] God had punished him by granting him every favor. He conveyed this guilt to his son, who became the philosopher of sin and anguish. Closer to us, Zell Kravinsky, an American real estate magnate who began life with one thousand dollars, turned over almost all his assets to medical research organizations and donated one of his kidneys to a poor African American. In an interview, he even considered sacrificing his second kidney if that would save a life. A moral extremism that borders on oblation: take everything I have even if that should kill me. An astonishing success is brandished the better to disqualify it; the worldly journey from acquiring wealth to divestment is accomplished.

Thus there are people who know the misfortune of succeeding too well and on whom sweet things fall like so many calamities. Economic favor turns into metaphysical bad luck—with the result that Holland's richest cities in its Golden Age long existed side by side with a clergy hostile to money itself: a strange coexistence of the Golden Calf and its official disapprobation. In 1581, for example, an ordinance deprived bankers of communion; they were likened to pawnbrokers, actors, jugglers, acrobats, quacks, and brothel keepers.[12] Was this an old-fashioned puritanical reflex or an intuition of a risk worse than penury: being clogged up by excess? "People are saddened by poverty and get tired of well-being," Machiavelli wrote. A terrible prospect: desire succumbing to the melancholy of surfeit. The cornucopia can become a threat of force-feeding, a danger of suffocation. Thus there is something in money that destroys money. Whence the necessity of protecting it against itself. How else can we explain the seductive attraction of bankruptcy felt by some traders? It is better to destroy everything, so as to be able to start all over, even if it means taking millions of your fellow citizens down with you. People can be the instruments of their own ruin in success as well as in failure. *Richesse oblige ou afflige.*

Generosity as an Exploit

Old money liked to remain in the background; new money loves the spotlight, especially to show its magnanimity. Virtue is now public. As if people aspired to wealth solely in order to transform it into largesse. We must be glad, of course, that a drive to altruism still exists in this world. Let us forget the clichés regarding the indifference of our individualistic age and the misdeeds of consumerism. Society would be unbearable without this multitude of small gestures of mutual aid and friendship that lead people to help each other in everyday life, without waiting for government help. There is nothing shocking about the fact that celebrities or rich people devote part of their time to the poor as a way of thanking fortune for the blessings it has showered on them. *Charity done out of vanity is better than vanity without charity.* Ostentatious competition in generosity is better than apathy in sated egoism. It is encouraging that business firms are also becoming foundations that decide to act where public powers are deficient and that they work with local associations to dig wells, conduct vaccination campaigns, fight AIDS, malaria, and rare diseases. The market is in no way the enemy of charity, even if it cannot overlap with it in every respect. A reckless speculator like George Soros, who was once prepared to destroy the pound sterling, can in the course of ten years be transformed into a friend of freedom and do excellent work in various nongovernmental organizations that he finances in central Europe. Hubris in greed, hubris in charity. What does it matter what the motivation is—repentance, a coming to awareness, weariness with one's milieu? *In a gift, all that matters is the intention, not the result. In philanthropy, all that matters is the result and not the intentions.* It is more intelligent to urge the privileged to show their solidarity than to overwhelm them with reproaches. Defaming donors in furious pamphlets is a satisfaction as hollow as it is frivolous.

Consider the Giving Pledge, launched in 2010 by Bill Gates and Warren Buffett, which urges billionaires throughout the world to give half their fortunes to humanitarian causes. This charitable multinational, which is oriented toward the development of tools for promoting public health, was endowed with 43.5 billion dollars in 2015. (Warren Buffett gave 99 percent of his fortune, the remaining 1 percent still representing an astronomical sum for each of us.) In this ambition there is vainglory, a desire to impress people by the large sums involved. Bill Gates is truly the hero of spectacular giving combined with great modesty in his bearing. His act is a kind of feat and positions him as an exceptional figure: who will be able to compete with such amounts? The philanthropist chooses his cause and the way he will treat it, the better to control it. In addition, as in the humanitarian domain, there is the law of media buzz which demands that he trumpet his exploits. We are far from the anonymity of giving recommended by Judaism and Christianity. "Beware of practicing your piety before men in order to be seen by them," says the New Testament (Matthew 6:1). Patrons and benefactors will take pride in seeing their names on university buildings, libraries, hospitals, and museums.

"The generosity of millionaires," Balzac said, "can be compared only with their eagerness for profit. As soon as a whim or a passion is involved, money is no longer anything for the rich; in fact, it is harder for them to have whims than to have gold."[13]

Some showbiz celebrities hire agents to handle their charitable actions, in order to reconcile magnanimity with publicity: an excellent way of restoring a flagging reputation or to display, in a long career, the heart's capital gains. What is a star, these days? A Mother Teresa who plays soccer, sings on the stage, or makes films. All these people dream of only one thing: becoming saints, knights of virtue, and winning ardent goodwill through their commitment to the starving and the weak. Each charitable organization has its star ambassador. Like medieval princes, these public figures, who are completely obsessed with appearances, have to encourage, by setting an example, "an ample circulation of necessary generous acts" (Georges Duby). The continual stream of their good will guarantees them an eminent status. Thus we enter into the third age of extravagant generosity: The first was that of the sovereign who distributes his largesse to the people the way the sun spreads its benefits.[14] The second, in the monotheistic religions, recommends charity in the name of compassion and justice (the Jewish *tzedakah*, the Muslim *sadaqah*). The third age, the new philanthropy, is generosity managed like a multinational corporation, in the name of efficiency.

However, such generous acts, though praiseworthy, cannot take the place of the state or make taxes obsolete. Even an anthropology of oblation cannot replace the patient work of an administration or government that takes charge of the countless details of a nation. What citizen would want to make a donation to pay for sewers, roadwork, or public transportation in his country? For such a gift, there is no return on investment, only a sad necessity. To give, a particular emotion is required, a revolting situation, a communion with our fellow human beings. In this regard Peter Sloterdijk's proposal that the Roman tradition of euergetism be revived—that is, that taxes be abolished and replaced by the generous giving of the best people, is as exciting as it is problematic. "The angry poor have had two centuries to show whether they were capable of improving the world. The results have been sometimes devastating, sometimes ambivalent. A counterproposal: let the rich show whether they can do any better."[15]

This morality of goodwill is agreeable, even if it rather reminds us of the catechism of our childhoods. It is true that we have to reconsider taxation and the sledgehammer effect it can have on the most enterprising. But to go so far as to advocate its abolition is to move into the irrational. Taxation makes us passive citizens who have the unpleasant feeling that we are being bled in every which way. Charity, on the other hand, is a voluntary tax that allows us to decide freely where our money goes by monitoring the use that is made of it. It is as if each taxpayer knew how the finance ministry allocated his contribution, down to the last euro. An intelligent fiscal reform should take into account not only the amount of the levies but also exactly what they are to be used for: a way of reminding drivers, passengers, and patients of the cost of a bridge, a railway line, a day in the hospital, or an MRI. This would be proof that their tax payments have not been in vain, that they have been both their instigators and their beneficiaries.

In reality, three actors, both competing and complementary, face each other in the field of charity: the new philanthropists, the classic humanitarian association, and public institutions. It is essential to connect these three authorities that correct and challenge one another, by distinguishing between short- and middle-term urgency. If contemporary philanthropists call themselves social entrepreneurs and choose their problem and the way they intend to resolve it, that is because they want to distinguish themselves from the great ladies of earlier times who gave charity balls for high society. Everything changes when the logic of the checkbook is left behind and people agree to visit the site to talk with the natives and to make bonds of friendship with them. To remain effective, charity has to have tasks on its own scale; it wants to remain a face-to-face altruism. People exist for us only through situations in which we can meet them. Solidarity is a personal involvement or it is merely an idea that is as generous as it is vague.

Let us add that in the United States "venture philanthropy," which introduces the methods of risk-capital into the domain of solidarity, is driven above all by distrust of the federal government, whereas in France, it is the republican state that sees itself as the builder of social solidarities, as responsible for national cohesion (France has more than two thousand foundations). The demands for accounting are the result of seeing the failures of public power and the waste of funds by bureaucracies; the goal is to introduce the "religion of balance sheets" into the management of donations.[16] Mixing the logic of profit with the exercise of volunteerism, giving the expert priority over the elected official, is a way of proclaiming: "We are already the best in our domain; we can also win the battle against pollution, poverty, and disease. Our capitalist success makes us more competent actors than governmental agencies." Apprentice benefactors try to resolve the problem bit by bit with the audacity of an entrepreneur attacking a new market.

"This Colossal Idyll of the Good" (Zola)

Enjoying a budget three times larger than that of the World Health Organization, Bill and Melinda Gates have a redoubtable power with regard to impoverished governments. These "impatient optimists" believe in their will's omnipotence to do away with misfortune. They want to change the rules of the game, at the risk of establishing a private monopoly and taking control of world health as a whole. In a certain way, these giants of the good display the same libertarian credo, the same distrust of apparatuses and political parties as do nongovernmental organizations. They embody our last dreams of direct democracy, upsetting administrative rigidities and organizing a new international activism devoted to dealing with emergencies. Thus two systems are emerging: that of official charity, which proceeds from the frigid monster of the state or the UN, and that of ardent charity, which proceeds from the initiative of tycoons. But the logic of philanthropy—the will "to do good better" (Philipp Egger)—cannot be substituted for genuine politics. Foundations, besides the fact that they have also been contaminated by the bureaucratic cancer, sometimes conceal partisan or religious ambitions, platforms for tax evasion or money laundering that have been duly repainted in the colors of generosity and kindness. In the Muslim world, they sometimes serve as fronts for terrorist groups. In the United States, they were slow to recognize the rights of women and minorities, missing out on a historic movement.[17] All the ills of states, notably the difficulty they have in calling themselves in question, recur in the very people who claimed to be moving beyond these dead ends. Not to mention the danger of clientelism, which was already present in ancient Rome when the princes showered gifts on the common people to ensure their loyalty, and distributed benefices and favors to their clients to ensure their support.[18] This was pointed out by Montesquieu: "The worst Roman emperors were the ones who gave the most, Caligula, Claudius, Otho, Vitellius, Commodus, Heliogabalus, and Caracalla."[19] Indispensable in their domain, these counterpowers participate, alongside nongovernmental organizations, in this aspiration to democracy that is roiling modern societies. But they in no way make already existing institutions obsolete; they supplement them.

If the future of the rich resides in intelligent sharing of their fortunes, their generosity, for its part, continues to be governed by infatuations. Even if they deploy worldwide ambitions, their sympathy is often limited to their own cities or countries. Journalists are aware that one death at home is more moving than ten thousand abroad. The former is a tragedy, the latter a statistic. As a humanitarian enterprise, new-look philanthropy collides with a well-known phenomenon: the vagaries of the heart. In a certain sense, we always decide which victims we are going to help; we alone judge which aspect of a situation is intolerable. Some calamities are attractive to the media and others hardly deserve mention. Depending on current events, some victims are more desirable than others, at least for a time, before they themselves are eclipsed by new sufferers. The logic is less that of urgency than that of preference. The limit of both philanthropy and charity is that it acts from outside on poor people whom it has, in a way, chosen, whereas history involves us in crises or tragedies that we cannot escape. That is the law of versatile brotherhoods: there will always be poor, starving, and ill people whom we will like more than others. The only ones who concern us are those whom we have chosen or that move us. Philanthropy, like humanitarian aid, is "à la carte."

Finally, there is a danger of showing a tyranny of generosity in order to buy the gratitude of whole peoples, to become, as it were, the owners of their sufferings. The scandal of charity is the dissymmetry of the relation between donor and beneficiary; the latter can only receive without responding. To love him for that reason alone is to exercise on him not our nobility of soul but our desire for power. Being dependent on the goodwill of a third party for our survival is the most humiliating situation of all. There is a kind of charity that emancipates, and there is another that debases people, drives them deeper into their infirmity.[20] One is a charity of elimination that seeks to destroy itself through its action; the other is a charity of commiseration and is moved by its own sorrow and the world's misfortune. For example, the Habitat for Humanity foundation, organized by Jimmy and Rosalynn Carter and others, seeks to promote the former: based on partnership, it requires the peoples targeted to cooperate in their rehabilitation. Thus the morality of the offering is replaced by a morality of the contract. A society of complete compassion that established a one-way passage from the well-off to the others would be unbearable. *The goal of the philanthropist should be to disappear as such.* Except when he needs the poor wretches to do good. Then the relationship is reversed—it is no longer the unfortunate who are calling for help; it is the benefactors who are looking for a tragedy they can use to aggrandize themselves. They are transformed into friends of poverty rather than friends of the poor: the latter bleed only to allow them to come to care for them and to acquire a thoughtless prestige. There is a kind of cannibalism in this concern that is hungry for outsiders in order to raise one's own status.

To this self-abnegation corresponds the forgetfulness, and sometimes the resentment, of those whom we aid. Being helped subjects people to the debtor's complex. "I have no enemies, I haven't done anyone favors," Jules Renard said. On the theme of the heartless person, Jean Renoir made a delightful film, *Boudu sauvé des eaux* (1932), with Michel Simon. A bum, pulled out of the Seine by a bookseller, insults his savior, wrecks his apartment, and steals his wife before taking a powder. The benefactor, Aristotle noted, loves his debtor, who is his work and who has cost him something, whereas the recipient has received the alms in a passive way. "All men love more what they have won by labour; e.g. those who have made their money love it more than those who have inherited it."[21] Whence the interest of the anonymous gift made by the welfare state, which is less degrading than a direct donation made by a private individual, since the recipient is not indebted to anyone. Just as the debtor ends up hating his creditor, the beneficiary often shows little gratitude to his benefactor (whereas the disciple does not hide what he owes to his teachers). Let the generous expect nothing from the unfortunate people they help; their devotion itself must be enough. The fact that so many individuals or peoples in difficult situations refuse to allow themselves to be treated as victims means that they don't want the world's pity. Let us not hope that they will thank us. We owe them assistance, whatever happens. Our reward may come when, having become free and masters of their fate, people who used to be afflicted will be able in their turn to help those who are suffering tomorrow.

Should We Pay Our Debts?

Mathilde Loisel, the ravishing wife of a clerk at the Ministry of Education, who married beneath her rank, is invited to a great party at the ministry. To uphold her position in society, she borrows a diamond necklace from one of her friends. She parades about all evening, admired and adulated, but when she gets home, she notices that she has lost the necklace. Not daring to tell the friend who lent it to her, she finds an identical one, which her husband pays for by going deeply into debt, and for the following ten years they lead "the horrible life of the needy." When she finally runs into her friend "still young and beautiful," she tells her the truth. "Oh, my poor Mathilde!" the friend cries. "Mine wasn't real! It was worth five hundred francs at the most!"[22] This short story by Maupassant teaches us a fundamental truth: in life, one must not be mistaken about debts.

The orgy followed by remorse: that is the usual fable of borrowing. Some transactions contribute to the ruin of both the lender and the borrower, and resemble the Danaïds' sieve. Each dreams of taking without giving back, borrowing without paying, lending without paying out. The credit card or the debit card: the marvelous evaporation of money without a bad conscience. But the 2008 crisis proved that the system had reached its limits, that a household with a small income could not have the moon without finding itself in the street. Then comes the time of expiation: during public ceremonies at Debtors Anonymous, for example, the accursed credit cards that have led us into sin are destroyed—this is called a "plastectomy"—run through blenders, blown up with fireworks, or pierced with bows and arrows.[23] In the United States, chapter 9 of the Bankruptcy Code allows municipalities as well as private enterprises to be declared insolvent and sheltered from their creditors long enough to restructure their debts. There follows an elaborate negotiation that may last for years (as in the case of Detroit). The essential point is to be able to begin over from zero and to consider the failure not as a sanction but as a stage on the way to success. The right to declare bankruptcy is as fundamental as the pursuit of happiness and freedom.[24]

Wisdom sometimes demands that we cancel a debt. Leviticus called for debts to be forgiven every fifty years, on the occasion of the Jubilee, the day when everyone returned to his own property, when slaves were freed and financial obligations canceled. All through European history, the great concern of borrowers, princes and kings, was to delay the repayment of their debts, or even to erase them, if need be by blaming them on indelicate creditors. A disproportionate debt load can kill a nation, put it in an irremediable state of dependency; Greece and Argentina offer examples of this. There comes a time when countries have to be allowed to catch their breath, even the most prosperous. We suspect that none of the great countries of Europe, any more than the United States, will every repay what it owes, because these countries borrow just to pay the interest on their debts. It is better to clear the slate and start over on a new basis.

We know the people's ingratitude with regard to soldiers who have died for their countries. It is perhaps the condition of existence: we can't spend every day thanking our predecessors without finding ourselves unable to move forward. Our heritage wavers between the erasure of the past, on the one hand, and its crushing preponderance on the other. Europe, for example, is bowed down under a burden of sins that it calls the duty to remember and that often goes hand in hand with forgetting its tradition. Long before Nietzsche, Bossuet emphasized how much the tragic death of Christ to redeem our sins constituted a nonreimbursable debit. Every day we crucify him by our "torrents of iniquities," every day we have to beat our breasts.[25] His passion weighs on us forever. We owe everything to God, to whom we cannot give anything back. Debts are not made to be repaid but to be recognized and transmitted, and are not the same at birth and at death. The only word that we should utter each morning, in gratitude for the gift that has been given us, is: Thanks! Thanks for the mad grace that was the gift of life. The day when the debt is extinct is also the day of the extinction of existence, when we can no longer offer anything or return anything to others and become, through death, the prey of the living.

Conclusion: An Acknowledged Schizophrenia

For the life of the mind, a modest affluence suffices.

FRIEDRICH NIETZSCHE

THE wisdom of money consists in the combination of three virtues—freedom, security, and being free of care—balanced by three duties: probity, proportion, and sharing. The delights it authorizes cannot be separated from the obligations it entails. Liberation from material necessity is only one of the conditions of freedom; it is not summed up in it. But the problem with money is that it doesn't stay where it is. Thus there is an inevitable schizophrenia with respect to it: an indispensable fluid, it can at any time become a little demon that will not leave us in peace. It is truly the Platonic *pharmakon*, remedy and poison at the same time.

Whence the discomfort it provokes. With it we are always at "the beginning of wisdom" (Proverbs 4:7), or rather there is no wisdom concerning it except in situation. Seeking a better salary is the right of the disadvantaged. Whether one can later say "that is enough" is a personal matter, on condition that we agree regarding the word "enough." It is up to each individual to decide, in his heart of hearts, which pitfalls he wants to avoid, whether he wants to change his life or improve it, to make financial success a mystique or a springboard. Money frees us when it allows us to decrease the venal part of life. Then it becomes a bridge that allows us to traverse difficult times without mishap, a narrow ridge path running between various precipices called Avarice, Pettiness, Crime, Humiliation, Fraud, Greed, Arrogance, and Envy like a modern version of the road to the Celestial City in Bunyan's *Pilgrim's Progress.*

Wisdom consists in desacralizing money, not loving it or hating it more than is reasonable. It remains a friend so long as we don't transform it into an enemy, by our own fault. Let us not allow ourselves to be forced to make the appalling choice between a deserving poverty and a corrupt abundance. Virtue and prosperity can cohabit well. There is a life outside financial ruminations, but the latter have never prevented dazzling artistic achievements or the blossoming of sublime values. In itself, money is such a marvelous invention, and the advantages it offers are so obvious, that it has become a fundamental human right. Its only crime is its unequal distribution, the extreme concentration that prevents it from flowing when it should remain an ardent river, a liquid substance that sows its miracles as it spreads—an irrigation rather than a coagulation. That is why reason commands those who have a lot of money to put their surplus in the service of those who have little or none. Civilizing money means democratizing it, redistributing it everywhere as a treasure that potentially belongs to everyone. We have to rehabilitate, in a single movement, the desire for lucre and the ethics of giving; greed and generosity; the two extremes: abuse and moderation.

In conclusion, two remarks: money is a recompense as well as a grace. We are not its owners but its usufructuaries. Fortune, a capricious goddess, has blessed us with her benefits. Let us enjoy them; she can take them away from us at any time. Finally, it is good that money should maintain the dream of its own abolition—the works that announce its imminent death are beyond counting. But we have to acknowledge its follies, which are the flipside of its innumerable benefits. Like sexuality, it is the object of a double utopia: either domesticate it or set out in this drunken boat at the risk of multiplying the dangers. Prohibition or permissiveness: everyone would like to restrain it while at the same time allowing it to prosper. Thus it is useful for a nation, a developed society, to include it in its hand as a fine risk. Let us not hope for a reconciliation, but rather accept the rift of an endless combat. With the Golden Calf, we remain torn: the instrument of transfiguration is also the instrument of decline. It is a utopia that functions in the two senses of abomination and marvel.

The essential thing is that the dice are always cast anew, that today's winners will soon be replaced by yesterday's losers. In the circulation of fortunes, it is society itself that is circulating, guaranteeing the mobility of its members, illustrating by financial fluidity the values of equality that it declares. Social classes, elites, and leaders must emerge and disappear, moving like tectonic plates, and reject immobilization. *The transitory nature of all things:* that is the lesson taught by money, which falls to us and then flees us, favoring some, only to later abandon them in an alternation of ruins and resurrections. That was what the apostle Matthew meant, adopting the Stoics' teaching, when he recommended that we remain poor in our hearts (Matthew 5:3). The gifts of life leave us as promptly as they come. As on a gaming table, the dice roll, sometimes in our favor, sometimes to our detriment. Fortune is only a metaphor for life, so beautiful, so fragile. We have to accept that everything that has been accorded us can be taken back—and nonetheless draw from it an immense feeling of gratitude. That is the ultimate wisdom.

Notes
Index

Notes

INTRODUCTION

1. Michel Aglietta and André Orléan, *La monnaie: Entre violence et confiance* (Paris: Odile Jacob, 2002), 124.

1. THE DEVIL'S DUNG

Denouncing "the unrestrained ambition of money that commands," on July 9, 2015, in Bolivia, Pope Francis accused money of spreading the odor of the "Devil's dung." The expression is that of fifth-century Father of the Church, Basil of Caesarea. The far-left monthly *Le Monde diplomatique* saluted this papal initiative in its September 2015 issue as "an anti-capitalist discourse from the South."

1. Ilana Reiss-Schimmel, *La psychanalyse et l'argent* (Paris: Odile Jacob, 1993), 29.

2. A summary of this play can be found in François Rachline, *D'où vient l'argent?* (Paris: Panama, 2006), 71–74.

3. Plato, *Laws*, 919 b–c, in *The Collected Dialogues of Plato*, ed. E. Hamilton and H. Cairns (Princeton, NJ: Princeton University Press, 1961), 1471 (919 c).

4. "L'argent peut-il tout acheter?," *Marianne*, August 15–21, 2014.

5. In *La gratuité, c'est le vol* (a title borrowed from Denis Olivennes), Richard Malka correctly notes: "In this way a situation unprecedented in the history of humanity would be created: three or four private actors would be likely eventually to gain control over knowledge worldwide, on the pretext of offering it free of charge at first." *La gratuité, c'est le vol: 2015: La fin du droit d'auteur* (Paris: SNE, 2015), 18.

6. Émile Zola, "L'argent dans la littérature," *Le Messager de l'Europe*, March 1880.

7. Aristotle, *Nicomachean Ethics*, Bk. 5, § 3, in *The Complete Works of Aristotle: The Revised Oxford Translation*, vol. 2, ed. Jonathan Barnes (Princeton, NJ: Princeton University Press, 1984).

8. Ibid., Bk. 5, § 4. For Aristotle, there is a good and a bad chrematistics, the good belonging to the domain of *oikonomia*.

9. Aristotle, *Politics*, Bk. 1, § 5, in Barnes, *The Complete Works of Aristotle*, vol. 2.

10. Aristotle, *Nicomachean Ethics*, Bk. 7, § 4.

11. Ibid., Bk. 8.

12. Surah 18:46: "Wealth and children are an ornament of life of the world." Mohammed Marmaduk Pikthall, trans., *The Glorious Koran* (New York: Mentor, 1953).

13. Jacques Attali, *Les Juifs, le monde et l'argent* (Paris: Livre de Poche, 2003), 119–120.

14. André Pézard, *Dante sous la pluie de feu* (Paris: Vrin, 1950), quoted in Jacques Le Goff, *La Bourse et la vie* (Paris: Pluriel, 2011), 64.

15. Aristotle, *Politics*, Bk. 1, § 10, in Barnes, *The Complete Works of Aristotle*, vol. 2.

16. In Islamic countries, the prohibition on usury persists and is extended to lending at interest. In Egypt it gave rise, in the 1960s, to Islamic finance: the creditor does not lend money but instead purchases the good desired by the client, who then buys it from him on the installment plan. Financial products must remain "sharia compatible." *Challenges*, October 2015.

17. On this subject, see Le Goff's excellent synthesis in *La Bourse et la vie*, 37–38.

18. See Alfred W. Crosby, *The Measure of Reality: Quantification and Western Society, 1250–1600* (Cambridge: Cambridge University Press, 1997), 70.

19. Le Goff, *La Bourse et la vie*, 37–43.

20. Ibid., 46.

21. Marc-Alain Ouaknin, "Entre la terre et l'exil," in *L'Argent: Pour une rehabilitation morale*, ed. Antoine Spire (Paris: Autrement, 1992), 194–195.

22. Attali, *Les Juifs, le monde et l'argent*, 86–87.

23. Matthew 25:14–30, Luke 19:12–27.

24. Claude Lelièvre, *Mediapart*, January 6, 2016.

25. Le Goff, *La Bourse et la vie*, 86.

26. Augustine, *Confessions*, Bk. 9, trans. R. S. Pine-Coffin (London: Penguin, 1961), 204.

27. Blaise Pascal, *Pensées*, trans. A. J. Krailsheimer (London: Penguin, 1995), 123.

28. Marc Shell, "L'art en tant qu'argent en tant qu'art," in *Comment penser l'argent?*, ed. Roger-Pol Droit (Paris: Le Monde, 1992), 111–112, 114.

29. Joris-Karl Huysmans, *Sainte Lydwine de Schiedam* (1901; repr. Paris: Éditions À rebours, 2002), 218.

30. On this subject, see Jacques Le Goff's standard study, *La naissance du Purgatoire* (Paris: Folio-Gallimard, 1991).

31. Quote from Jacques Le Goff, *The Birth of Purgatory*, trans. Arthur Goldhammer (Chicago: University of Chicago Press, 1986), 74.

32. Jacques Chiffoleau, *Crise de la croyance: Histoire de la France religieuse*, vol. 2 (Paris: Seuil, 1988), 138, 144.

33. Ibid., p. 142.

34. The historian of ideas Alfred W. Crosby traces this phenomenon in Europe back to the period between 1275 and 1325, when the first mechanical clocks and the first cannons were manufactured. See *The Measure of Reality*, 18–19.

35. Joël Schmidt, "Sans ostentation," in Spire, *L'Argent*, 73.

36. Philippe Simonnot, *Le sexe et l'économie* (Paris: JC Lattès, 1985), 89–91.

37. An excellent synthesis on this subject is found in Pascal Morand, *Les religions et le luxe* (Paris: IFM, 2012).

38. For a description of the Shah Jahan's peacock throne, which was surmounted by a canopy supported by twelve emerald pillars, see Morand, *Les religions et le luxe*, 134–135.

39. Malek Chebel, *Dictionnaire amoureux de l'Islam* (Paris: Plon, 2004), 347, quoted in Morand, *Les religions et le luxe*, 123.

40. These were the terms in which he castigated, in November 2013, the "idolatry of money" in a *verbum domini* entitled *Evangelii gaudium* (The Joy of the Gospel).
41. According to what the new administrator of the Vatican Commercial Bank, Jean-Baptiste Franssu, a Frenchman assigned the task of reforming the institution, was told (July 10, 2014).
42. Davide Casati, "Robin Hood or Money Launderer?," *International New York Times*, October 18, 2014.
43. In recent years, the Vatican's total revenues have come close to its total operating budget of nearly $700 million. Major sources of revenue have been, for the city-state, $130 million from museums, and for the Holy See, $70 million in Vatican Bank profits. Shawn Tully, "This Pope Means Business," *Fortune*, Aug. 14, 2014, 66–78.
44. Quoted in Philippe Raynaud, *La politesse des Lumières: Les lois, les moeurs, les manières* (Paris: Gallimard, 2013), 228–229.
45. The first refutation of Weber goes back to Werner Sombart, in *Der Bourgeois* (1913), in which he shows that the rationalization of life has its source in Scholastic thought and that the gamut of bourgeois virtues was already present as early as the fifteenth century in the Florentine humanist Alberti (Book II, Section II, Chap. XVI). See also Max Weber, *The Protestant Ethic and the Spirit of Capitalism*, trans. T. Parsons (New York: Charles Scribner's Sons, 1958). Weber's thesis gave rise to a major misunderstanding that seems to have dictated reality and history and led a posteriori to a break between northern and southern Europe (which the Greek crisis proved). A strange adventure for a text, to end up imposing a direction on history more than it interpreted it.
46. Le Goff, *La Bourse et la vie*, 119.
47. Herbert Lüthy, *Le passé présent* (Paris: Éditions du Rocher, 1965), 63. Translated by Salvator Attanasio as *From Calvin to Rousseau: Tradition and Modernity in Socio-political Thought from the Reformation to the French Revolution* (New York: Basic Books, 1970).
48. *Certitudo salutis*. Quote from Max Weber, *Protestantism and the Spirit of Capitalism*, trans. T. Parsons (New York: Scribner's, 1958), p. 141.

49. Martin Luther, "La liberté du chrétien," in *Les grands écrits réformateurs*, 230–231.

50. Blaise Cendrars, *L'or* (Paris: Folio-Gallimard, 1973). Translated by Nina Rootes as *Gold: The Marvellous History of General John Augustus Sutter* (London: P. Owen), 1982.

51. Quoted in Crosby, *The Measure of Reality*, 228, 132.

52. Don Rosa, *The Life and Times of Scrooge McDuck* (Timonium, MD: Gemstone Publishing, 2007).

53. Seneca, *Letters to Lucilius*, trans. R. M. Gummere (Cambridge, MA: Loeb Classical Library, 1917), Letter 21.

2. ON THE EMINENT DIGNITY OF THE POOR?

1. Jacques-Bénigne Bossuet, *Sermon sur la mort et autres sermons* (Paris: Garnier-Flammarion, 1970), 183.

2. Jacques-Bénigne Bossuet, *Sermons et oraisons funèbres* (Paris: Seuil, 1998), 31–32.

3. Saint Augustine, *The City of God*, trans. M. Dods (New York: Random House, 1950), 1:10.

4. Bossuet, *Sermon sur la mort et autres sermons*, 70.

5. Ibid., Sap. VI-7.

6. Herbert Lüthy, *Le passé présent* (Paris: Éditions du Rocher, 1965), 63. Translated by Salvator Attanasio as *From Calvin to Rousseau: Tradition and Modernity in Socio-political Thought from the Reformation to the French Revolution* (New York: Basic Books, 1970).

7. Roger Stauffeneger, "Réforme, richesse et pauvreté," *Revue d'histoire de l'Église de France*, no. 149 (1966): 47–58.

8. Damien de Blic and Jeanne Lazarus, eds., *Contre l'argent fou*, Les Rebelles vol. 6 (Paris: Le Monde, 2012), 27.

9. Ibid., 181–184.

10. Niall Ferguson, *The Ascent of Money: A Financial History of the World* (London: Penguin, 2009), 107.

11. Leon Trotsky, *The Revolution Betrayed*, trans. Max Eastman (Mineola, NY: Dover, 2004), 50.

12. Ferguson, *Ascent of Money*, 246.

13. Michel Aglietta and André Orléan, *La monnaie: Entre violence et confiance* (Paris: Odile Jacob, 2002), 100.

3. FRANCE, OR THE TABOO ON MONEY

1. Jean de La Bruyère, "Des biens de fortune," *Les caractères*, 5:58.
2. Jean-Jacques Rousseau, *Confessions* (Paris: Folio-Gallimard, 2009), 1:35.
3. Voltaire, *Dictionnaire philosophique*, s.v. "Luxe" (Paris: Garnier-Flammarion, 1964).
4. Jacques Roux, "Les riches, c'est-à-dire les méchants," in *Contre l'argent fou*, Les Rebelles vol. 6, ed. Damien de Blic and Jeanne Lazarus (Paris: Le Monde, 2012), 12 ff.
5. Léon Bloy, "Le sang du pauvre" (1909), in ibid., 131.
6. Léon Bloy, "Les amis de Job," in ibid., p. 131.
7. Léon Bloy, "Le sang du pauvre," in ibid., p. 127.
8. Jacques Julliard, *L'argent, Dieu et le diable: Péguy, Bernanos, Claudel face au monde moderne* (Paris: Flammarion, 2008), 122, 155.
9. Charles Péguy, "Note conjointe sur M. Descartes" (1914), *Œuvres en prose completes*, La Pléiade, vol. 1 (Paris: Gallimard, 1987), 291, quoted in Julliard, *L'argent, Dieu et le diable*, 159.
10. Charles Péguy, "Marcel, premier dialogue de la cité harmonieuse," *Œuvres en prose complètes*, quoted in Julliard, *L'argent, Dieu et le diable*, 161.
11. On this subject, see the illuminating commentary in Emmanuel Levinas, *Difficile liberté* (Paris: Livre de Poche, 1984), 177–178.
12. Quoted in Julliard, *L'argent, Dieu et le diable*, 175. Julliard comments with understanding on Claudel's views regarding money.
13. Françoise Bettencourt-Meyers, January 29, 2015.
14. "Fifty-two percent of the French think that today one cannot arrive at the summit without being corrupt." Yann Algan et Pierre Cahuc, *La société de défiance* (Paris: Cepremap, Éditions Rue d'Ulm, 2007), 9.
15. Serge Latouche, *Le pari de la décroissance* (Paris: Pluriel, 2010), 195–196.

16. "If, after the so-called subprime crisis of 2007–2008 a certain number of traders, bankers, and rating agents had been hung from meat hooks, we might have avoided for a time the Greek crisis and the brutal pressures of the American Tea Party." Laurence Duchêne and Pierre Zaoui, *L'abstraction matérielle* (Paris: La Découverte, 2012), 127–128.

17. Jean-Claude Guillebaud, in *Le Nouvel Observateur* for October 25, 2012, regarding Gaël Giraud's book *L'illusion financière* (Paris: L'Atelier, 2012).

18. Jean-Luc Mélenchon, *Qu'ils s'en aillent tous!* (Paris: Flammarion, 2010).

19. Philippe Torreton, "Alors Gérard, t'as les boules?," *Libération*, December 17, 2012.

20. Jean-Claude Guillebaud, *Télé Obs*, May 2, 2015. The weekly magazine *Marianne,* in its issue for July 31–August 6, 2015, had this headline: "The obscene: They are indecent, amoral, offensive . . ." The reference was to the king of Saudi Arabia, who was guilty of having privatized a beach on the Côte d'Azur; to Jacques Séguéla, who had stigmatized the poorest people; to the model Inès de La Fressange, who had trampled on the rules of urban planning by having unauthorized work done on her vacation home in southern France; to Patrick Drahi, who was buying up media outlets, et al.

21. The richest 20 percent of French households paid 75 percent of the nation's taxes for the preceding two years. The number of those subject to the ISF [*impôt de solidarité sur la fortune,* a tax on the wealthy] is 331,000 and constantly growing. In 2014, the ISF brought in 5.19 billion euros. *Le Monde,* October 10, 2014.

22. The socialist leader Julien Dray, the vice-president of the regional council in Île de France, in *Le Monde* for December 16, 2014: "I've had enough of that left that wants to run people's lives and make them happy without their help, I've had enough of that left of prohibitions, and even that left of the envious. When I'm on the left, when I see someone passing by in a nice car, my goal is not to take

it away from him. I don't hate the rich. My dream is that everyone might be rich. We're not going to share poverty."

23. Pierre Rabhi, *Vers la sobriété heureuse* (Arles: Actes Sud, 2010), 31, 47.
24. "À vous de juger," a show hosted by Arlette Chabot, France 2, June 8, 2006.
25. Algan and Cahuc, *La société de défiance*, 15.
26. Laurent Mauduit, *L'étrange capitulation* (Paris: Gawsewitch, 2013).
27. François Hollande reacted very strongly to this accusation: "I experienced this attack on the poor, on the destitute, as a blow struck against my whole life. . . . In all my public service, in all my terms of office, I have thought only of helping, of representing those who are suffering. . . . I do not want it to be possible to say or write that I make fun of the pain of the poor, because that is a lie that wounds me. . . . I have met people in the worst difficulties, used up by life. They had trouble taking care of their teeth. That is a sign of pure poverty. . . . My maternal grandfather, [was] a humble tailor from Savoy. . . . My paternal grandfather was a schoolteacher who came from a family of poor peasants in northern France. . . . And you think I could despise the milieu in which I have my roots, my reason for living?" *Le Nouvel Observateur*, September 10, 2014.
28. Dominique Jamet, *Marianne*, August 4, 2012.
29. Albert Londres, *La Chine en folie* (1922; repr. Paris: Serpent à Plumes, 2001).
30. Regarding the difference between a graduated tax and a punitive tax: "A fiscal system is optimal when the gains in social justice produced by an increase in fiscal pressure balance the losses in economic efficiency." Bertrand Jacquillat, *Fiscalité: Pourquoi et comment un pays sans riches est un pays pauvre* (Paris: Fondapol, 2012), 11.
31. I suggested this hypothesis in *La tentation de l'innocence* (Paris: Grasset, 1995).
32. "The system revolves around the banks. . . . In order for everything to collapse, you go into your bank and take out your money," Cantona said.
33. Alain Badiou, "Le rouge et le tricolore," *Le Monde*, January 27, 2015.

34. According to a study published in October 2012 in the *Journal of Consumer Research*. See also Pierre Barthélémy, "Le billet craquant vaut plus que le mou," *Le Monde*, December 24, 2012.
35. The FBI used a picture of a Spanish politician as a model for a photo-fit of Osama Bin Laden.
36. Marc Shell, "L'art en tant qu'argent en tant qu'art," in *Comment penser l'argent?*, ed. Roger-Pol Droit (Paris: Le Monde, 1992), 109.

4. AMERICA, OR SPIRITUAL MONEY

1. Viviana A. Zelizer, *The Social Meaning of Money: Pin Money, Paychecks, Poor Relief, and Other Currencies* (Princeton, NJ: Princeton University Press, 1997), 17. Jean-Joseph Goux asserts that in the United States the abandonment of the gold standard was seen as tantamount to relegating God to the second rank and increasing the state's grip on citizens. Monetary atheism paved the way for political statism. Jean-Joseph Goux, *Les monnayeurs du langage* (Paris: Galilée, 1984), 188–190.
2. *Le Monde*, November 8, 1988, quoted in Bernard Maris, "L'argent du riche et l'argent du pauvre," in *Comment penser l'argent?*, ed. Roger-Pol Droit, 335.
3. On the construction of the United States dollar, see Malek Abbou's excellent book, *Fondements métaphysiques du dollar* (Paris: Fage, 2012).
4. Marie Cuillerai, *Le capitalisme vertueux: Mondialisation et confiance* (Paris: Payot, 2002), 111–112.
5. "The governments of the countries associated in the adventure of the euro did not seize this historic opportunity to make the introduction of the fiduciary currency the first day of a developing federal sovereignty. The political discourses were very distant from solidarity of the event." Michel Aglietta and André Orléan, *La monnaie: Entre violence et confiance* (Paris: Odile Jacob, 2002), 312.
6. Ilana Reiss-Schimmel, *La psychanalyse et l'argent* (Paris: Odile Jacob, 1993), 95–96.

7. In the United States, the richest 1 percent of the population controls almost 33 percent of the country's wealth. This is the group whose income has increased the most since World War II, while the middle classes have seen their incomes stagnate or fall. See Robert Frank, *Richistan: A Journey through the American Wealth Boom and the Lives of the New Rich* (New York: Crown, 2007), 242.

8. Interview in 1905, in Peter Collier and David Horowitz, *The Rockefellers: An American Dynasty* (New York: Holt, Rinehart and Winston, 1976), 48.

9. Raymonde Carroll, "Une histoire de singes et de malentendus," *Communications*, no. 50 (1989): 197.

10. Robert Sobel, "Coolidge and American Business," Calvin Coolidge Presidential Foundation, 1988, https//coolidgefoundation.org /resources/essays-papers-addresses-35/.

11. The expression "robber barons," which first appeared in the *Atlantic Monthly* in 1871, refers to the captains of industry who ruthlessly exploited workers, bribed officials, controlled the national resources, and destroyed competition. President Theodore Roosevelt called them "malefactors of great wealth" and took action to put an end to their monopoly.

12. Frank, *Richistan*, 118.

13. "There are instances of millionaires' sons unspoiled by wealth, who, being rich, still perform great services in the community. Such are the very salt of the earth, as valuable as, unfortunately, they are rare." Andrew Carnegie, "The Gospel of Wealth," *North American Review*, no. 391 (June 1889), quoted in his *The "Gospel of Wealth" and other Writings* (London: Penguin, 2006), 6.

14. Alexis de Tocqueville, *De la démocratie en Amérique*, vol. 2 (Paris: Garnier-Flammarion, 1993), 181 ff.

15. "Everyone, when a discovery is announced, immediately cries: will there be money to be made? It is to satisfy this dominant inclination that I have to dwell at length on everything that concerns profit." Charles Fourier, *Le nouveau monde amoureux* (Paris: Presses du réel, 2013), 166.

16. In the USA, the wealthiest 1 percent receive 22.5 percent of the revenue. The richest 1 percent receive 10 percent of the GNP, as compared to 2 percent twenty years ago, which means that their income is now a hundred times more than the average (Thomas Piketty).

17. Played by Catherine Frot in *Marguerite*, a film by Xavier Giannoli, 2015.

5. MONEY, THE RULER OF THE WORLD?

1. Émile Zola, *Money*, trans. Valerie Minogue (Oxford: Oxford World Classics, 2014), 238.

2. Alfred W. Crosby, *The Measure of Reality: Quantification and Western Society, 1250–1600* (Cambridge: Cambridge University Press, 1997).

3. Honoré de Balzac, *Melmoth réconcilié* (1835), in *La maison Nucingen* (Paris: Folio-Gallimard, 1989).

4. Honoré de Balzac, *La maison Nucingen* (1837).

5. See the unsurpassable study by Albert Hirschman, *The Passions and the Interests* (Princeton, NJ: Princeton University Press, 1997).

6. Regarding grades: Roland Bénabou and Jean Tirole, quoted in Daniel Cohen, *Homo economicus: Prophète (égaré) des temps nouveaux* (Paris: Albin Michel, 2012), 51. Regarding books: Michael Sandel, *What Money Can't Buy: The Moral Limits of Markets*, repr. ed. (New York: Farrar, Straus and Giroux, 2013). Regarding education in India: Laurence Fontaine, *Le marché: Histoire et usages d'une conquête sociale* (Paris: Gallimard, 2014), 227.

7. Regarding China: Fontaine, *Le marché*, 161. Regarding Germany: Pascal Bruckner, *Has Marriage for Love Failed?*, trans. Steven Rendall (Cambridge: Polity, 2013).

8. For example, *Le viager*, a film by Pierre Tchernia, scenario by René Goscinny, 1972.

9. Sandel, *What Money Can't Buy*, 155.

10. Ibid., 111.

11. Regarding rewards for grades and reading: Sandel, *What Money Can't Buy*, 34. Regarding payments for attending school and its

effects: Roland Bénabou and Jean Tirole, quoted in Daniel Cohen, *Homo economicus*, 51–52.

12. Maya Beauvallet, *Les stratégies absurdes* (Paris: Seuil, 2009), quoted in Daniel Cohen, *Homo economicus*, 50–51. The same example is mentioned in Sandel, *What Money Can't Buy*, 64.

13. Ibid., 266 sqq.

14. Benjamin Franklin, *Poor Richard's Almanack* (1737), no. 131.

15. Benjamin Franklin, letter to Benjamin Vaughn, from France, July 26, 1784.

16. On "Bowie bonds" or "celebrity bonds," see Wikipedia, s.v., "celebrity bond."

17. Richard Posner and Elisabeth Landes, "The Economics of the Baby Shortage," 7 *Journal of Legal Studies* 323 (1978).

18. In Isaac Kramnick, *Bolingbroke and His Circle: The Politics of Nostalgia in the Age of Walpole* (Cambridge, MA: Harvard University Press, 1968), 73, quoted in Hirschman, *The Passions and the Interests*.

19. Quoted in Hirschman, *The Passions and the Interests*.

20. Examples given by Georg Simmel, *Philosophie de l'argent*, trans. Sabine Cornille and Philippe Ivernel (Paris: PUF, 1999), 471.

21. "They think only of making money, to the point that it might almost be said that they are consumed like a flame by the desire for possession." Dante, quoted in Werner Sombart, *Le bourgeois*.

22. Simon Schama's magisterial work *An Embarrassment of Riches: An Interpretation of Dutch Culture in the Golden Age* (New York: Knopf, 1987), 347.

23. Laurence Fontaine, "La 'bulle' des tulipes ou les jeux de la distinction, du pouvoir et du hasard dans la formation des prix," *Le marché*, 288 ff.

24. Serfdom was abolished in 1861 in Russia, in 1959 in Tibet, and in 1960 in Nepal. Indentured servants were manual laborers hired in the colonial period who were bound to their masters until the money they had borrowed was repaid. In the nineteenth century, Mexico allowed contracts of servitude for debts to run for ninety-nine years.

This kind of contract still exists for foreign workers, especially in the Persian Gulf states, which practice a form of persistent serfdom.

25. The poignant testimony of a Yazidi girl kidnapped and sold by ISIS, reported by Thierry Oberlé in *Esclave de Daech* (Paris: Fayard, 2015).

26. Robert Musil, *Der Mann ohne Eigenschaften* in Musil, *Gesammelte Werke,* ed. Adolf Frise (Hamburg: Rowhohlt, n.d.), 2:519.

27. Emmanuel Levinas, *Difficile liberté* (Paris: Livre de Poche, 1984), 209.

28. Immanuel Kant, *Foundations of the Metaphysics of Morals,* trans. L. W. Beck (Indianapolis: Bobbs-Merrill, 1959), 53.

29. Caroline Oudin-Bastide and Philippe Steiner, *Calcul et morale: Coûts de l'esclavage et valeur de l'émancipation* (Paris: Albin Michel, 2015), chap. 1.

30. Crosby, *La mesure de la réalité,* 26–27.

31. Ibid., 200 ff.

32. Paul Ricoeur, "L'argent: D'un soupçon à l'autre," in Spire, *L'argent,* 68.

33. Viviana A. Zelizer, *The Social Meaning of Money: Pin Money, Paychecks, Poor Relief, and Other Currencies* (Princeton, NJ: Princeton University Press, 1997).

34. Ibid.

35. In an article published in 1994 Michael Stewart of the London School of Economics shows how among Hungarian gypsies money is a factor of sociability that reconciles glory, play, and pride in success. "La passion de l'argent, les ambiguïtés de la circulation monétaire chez les Tsiganes hongrois," *Terrains,* no. 23 (October 1994): 45 ff.

36. Thomas Piketty's conception of Islamist terrorism as a "social and equitable development" testifies to this blindness: "It's obvious: terrorism feeds on the inegalitarian Middle East powder keg that we have in large measure helped to create." *Le Monde,* November 22–23, 2015. Marxist, liberal, or social-democratic, this way of

seeing things, which is incapable of grasping the religious factor, remains narrowly reductive.

37. On this subject, Hirschman's *The Passions and the Interests* remains unsurpassed.

38. Charles Péguy, *L'Argent* (1913; repr: Paris: Gallimard, 1932).

39. Victor Hugo, *Choses vues, 1870–1885*, vol. 2 (Paris: Folio-Gallimard, 1997), 272, 398, quoted in Jean-Joseph Goux, *Les monnayeurs du langage* (Paris: Galilée, 1984) 133–134.

40. Paul Valéry, *Mauvaises pensées et autres* (Paris: Gallimard, 1942), quoted in Goux, *Les monnayeurs du langage,* 41.

41. Quoted by Serge Koster, "D'Harpagon à Shylock," in Spire, *L'argent,* 33.

42. See Jean-Joseph Goux, *Les monnayeurs du langage,* 156–158, and his illuminating commentary.

6. DOES OPULENCE MAKE PEOPLE UNHAPPY?

1. Stanley Kubrick, *The Killing,* 1956. An analogous theme—the money scattered in a swimming pool—is found in Henri Verneuil's film *Mélodie en sous-sol* (1963), with Alain Delon and Jean Gabin.

2. Simone de Beauvoir, *La cérémonie des adieux* (Paris: Folio-Gallimard, 1974), 153.

3. François Rachline, *D'où vient l'argent?* (Paris: Panama, 2006), 110–112.

4. See Damien de Blic and Jeanne Lazarus, *Sociologie de l'argent* (Paris: La Découverte, 2007), 60–62.

5. Robert Frank, *La course au luxe* (Geneva: Markus Haller, 2010), 79 ff.

6. Richard Easterlin, "Does Economic Growth Improve the Human Lot?," *Nations and Households in Economic Growth: Essays in Honor of Moses Abramovitz,* ed. Paul A. David and Melvin W. Reder (New York: Academic Press, 1974).

7. Jean Gadrey, *Adieu à la croissance: Bien vivre dans un monde solidaire* (Paris: Les Petits Matins / Alternatives économiques, 2010), quoted in Laurence Duchêne and Pierre Zaoui, *L'Abstraction matérielle* (Paris: La Découverte, 2012), 183.

8. Robert and Edward Skidelsky, *How Much Is Enough?: Money and the Good Life* (London: Allen Lane, 2012), 104.

9. David G. Myers, *The American Paradox: Spirited Hunger in an Age of Plenty* (New Haven, CT: Yale University Press, 2000).

10. Especially since a number of investigations, running against the grain of these received ideas, affirm that the richer one is, the happier. Thus Ruut Veenhoven and Floris Vergunst, of the University of Rotterdam, have based their studies on the "World Database of Happiness" and have compiled information on sixty-seven countries. Similarly, Daniel W. Sacks, Betsey Stevenson, and Justin Wolfers, working for the German institute IZA, have also concluded that the level of satisfaction is higher in countries where the per capita income is higher. See Marie de Vergès, *Le Monde*, February 26, 2013.

11. Daniel Cohen, *Homo economicus* (Paris: Albin Michel, 2012).

12. I refer the reader here to my book *Perpetual Euphoria: On the Duty to be Happy*, trans. Steven Rendall (Princeton: Princeton University Press, 2010), in which I dismantle the myth of obligatory happiness.

13. Frank, *La course au luxe*.

14. "At the age of 70, people recover the happiness of a young person of 30. At 80, they have recovered (on average) the joy of being 18. How can we understand this surprising result? . . . Old age frees us from a burden, that of accumulating useless things, and returns intrinsic goods to their place." Cohen, *Homo economicus*, 27.

15. Such as ibid., 198–199 ff.

16. "Les anti-économistes ont la parole," *Le Nouvel Observateur*, October 23, 2014.

17. Canetti as quoted in Niall Ferguson, *The Ascent of Money: A Financial History of the World* (London, Penguin, 2009), 105.

18. Regarding frauds of the past thirty years: Jacques de Saint-Victor, *Un pouvoir invisible: Les mafias et la société démocratique* (Paris: Gallimard, 2012), 346.

19. Jay McInerney, *Brightness Falls* (New York: Vintage, 1993).

20. Robert Goolrick, *The Fall of Princes* (New York: Algonquin, 2015).

21. Kevin Roose, *Young Money: Inside the Hidden World of Wall Street's Post-Crash Recruits* (New York: Grand Central Publishing, 2014), ix.

22. A French stock trader working for the bank Société Générale who was convicted in 2008 of forgery and unauthorized use of the bank's computers that resulted in losses estimated at 4.9 billion Euros.

23. See Robert Frank's excellent *Richistan: A Journey through the American Wealth Boom and the Lives of the New Rich* (New York: Crown, 2007), chap. 10.

24. Chrysippus, as quoted in Cicéron, *Le bonheur*, IVe et Ve Tusculanes.

25. Diogenes Laertius, *Lives of Eminent Philosophers*, chap. 5, § 24. Quoted in Frank, *Richistan*, 209.

26. Frank, *Richistan*, 50; Seneca, *Letters to Lucilius*, trans. R. M. Gummere (Cambridge, MA: Loeb Classical Library, 1917).

27. Seneca, *Letters to Lucilius*.

28. Léon Bloy, *Le salut par les Juifs* (Paris: Mercure de France, 1892), 192.

29. Bernanos as quoted in Jacques Julliard, *L'argent, Dieu et le diable*, 185.

30. Jacques Attali, *Les Juifs, le monde et l'argent*, 295.

7. HAS SORDID CALCULATION KILLED SUBLIME LOVE?

1. Taken from www.demotivateur.fr. The article is said to have appeared in a financial magazine in the United States. *Se non è vero, è ben trovato.*

2. On complementary currencies issued by private individuals and applied to local collectivities or regions, see Paul Jorion's iconoclastic blog and his *L'Argent: Mode d'emploi* (Paris: Fayard, 2009), 274 ff.

3. Honoré de Balzac, *La cousine Bette* (Paris: Folio-Gallimard, 1972), 172–173.

4. Ibid., 331: "I don't love you, Valérie," Crevel said. "I love you like a million." "That's not enough!" she replied, jumping on Crevel's knees and throwing her arms around his neck as if it were a coat-

peg. "I want to be loved like ten million, like all the gold on earth and more than that."

5. Georg Simmel, *Philosophie de l'argent*, 483–484. Simmel explains drolly that the amount of the sum may make up for the baseness of principle, and that such a sum is an homage indirectly paid to the husband.

6. Pierre Klossowski, *La monnaie vivante*, with a letter preface by Michel Foucault (1970; repr. Rivages, 1997).

7. Ibid., 16.

8. Robert Musil, *L'homme sans qualités*, 180. See also Jean-Joseph Goux, *Les monnayeurs du langage* (Paris: Galilée, 1984), 159 ff.

9. Leaping into the breach opened by Gary Becker, who sees the family as a unit of the "production of utilities," a considerable part of the feminist movement would like to introduce the salary relationship into the domestic space and make the husband pay for services provided by their wives in the areas of housekeeping, education, and sex. See Philippe Simonnot, *Le sexe et l'économie* (Paris: JC Lattès, 1985), 157. The American activist Lauren Chief Elk asks that men pay women for all the "emotional work" they have provided to men free of charge since time immemorial in order to do "gender justice." Behind the gift there is an immense resentment.

10. A few dates: in 1881, married women were allowed to open a savings account without their husband's permission; in 1907, they could do what they wished with their salary; in 1965 they could hold a job without their husband's authorization; and in 1985 spouses managed their assets on equal terms, according to Intern@nettes.fr.

11. Viviana A. Zelizer, *The Social Meaning of Money: Pin Money, Paychecks, Poor Relief, and Other Currencies* (Princeton, NJ: Princeton University Press, 1997).

12. Damien de Blic and Jeanne Lazarus, *Sociologie de l'argent* (Paris: La Découverte, 2007), 82–83.

13. Gilles Lipovetsky, *La troisième femme* (Paris: Gallimard, 1997), 306.

14. De Blic and Lazarus, *Sociologie de l'argent*, 81–83, and Zelizer, *Social Meaning of Money*.

15. Denis Moreau, *Pour la vie ? Court traité du mariage et des séparations* (Paris: Seuil, 2014), 88.

16. Seneca, *Letters to Lucilius*, trans. R. M. Gummere (Cambridge, MA: Loeb Classical Library, 1917), Letter 18:8.

17. Arthur Schopenhauer, *Aphorismes sur la sagesse dans la vie*, trans. J.-A. Cantacuzène (Paris: PUF, 1994), 34.

18. Alexis de Tocqueville, *De la démocratie en Amérique*, vol. 2 (Paris: Garnier-Flammarion, 1993), 182.

19. Cicero, Tusculan Disputations, Bk. 5, "Les infirmités physiques empêchent-elles le bonheur?" and "Objection: Le sage est-il heureux dans les supplices," 112–113.

20. On these philosophical deaths after Socrates, see the excellent book by Paul Veyne, *Sénèque: Une introduction* (Paris: Tallandier, 2007), 262.

21. Jane Austen quoted in Marie-Laure Massei-Chamayou, *La représentation de l'argent dans les romans de Jane Austen: L'être et l'avoir* (Paris: L'Harmattan, 2012).

22. Marie-Laure Massei-Chamayou, "Jane Austen et l'argent: Entre manque et subversion," in *Les écrivains et l'argent*, ed. Olivier Larizza (Paris: Orizons, 2012), 98–99.

23. Massei-Chamayou, *La réprésentation de l'argent dans les romans de Jane Austen*, 101.

24. Regarding philanderers, see Søren Kierkegaard, *The Seducer's Diary*, trans. H. V. Hong (Princeton: Princeton University Press, 1997). This work seems rather ironic when one knows that the author remained a virgin all his life.

25. Jane Austen, *Emma* (1815).

26. Stefan Zweig, *The World of Yesterday*, trans. Anthea Bell, chap. 1.

27. Gary Becker, *A Treatise on the Family* (Cambridge, MA: Harvard University Press, 1993).

28. Ibid., 289.

29. Honoré de Balzac, *La maison Nucingen* (Paris: Folio-Gallimard, 1989), 178–179.

30. Guy de Maupassant, *Bel-Ami* (Paris: Folio-Gallimard, 2011), 174.

31. Here I refer to two excellent works on the question of sexuality and money: Philippe Simonnot, *Le sexe et l'économie* (Paris: JC Lattès, 1985), and Serge Koster's more literary *Le sexe et l'argent* (Paris: Léo Scheer, 2009).

32. Honoré de Balzac, *Splendeurs et misères des courtisanes* (Paris: Pocket, 1991), 254.

33. *Elle*, January 2, 2015.

34. Koster, *Le sexe et l'argent*, 62–63.

35. Françoise Gil, *Prostitution: Fantasmes et réalités* (Paris: ESF, 2012).

36. On the five different types of relations entertained by the "taxi girls" in Chicago in the 1920s: dances in exchange for payment, dances free of charge, a regular customer for a few months, a plural relationship with three or four men, one of whom pays the rent, another the grocer, the third pays for clothes, etc., and finally an all-night stay. But none of these distinctions sufficed to put them in the category of prostitutes. Zelizer, *Social Meaning of Money*.

37. "Telle trouve à se vendre qui n'eût pas trouvé à se donner."

38. Dostoevsky, *Notes from the Underground and The Gambler*, trans. J. Kentish (Oxford: Oxford University Press), 138.

8. SHOULD BOURGEOIS VALUES BE REHABILITATED?

1. Damien de Blic and Jeanne Lazarus, *Sociologie de l'argent*, 105. The anecdote is taken from Norbert Elias, *The Court Society*, trans. E. Jephcott (New York, Pantheon, 1983).

2. Lucien Jerphagnon, *Connais-toi toi-même* (Paris: Albin Michel, 2012), 98.

3. Benjamin Franklin, *The Works of Benjamin Franklin* (Milwaukee: A. Whittemore, 1856), 81.

4. Daniel Bell, *The Cultural Contradictions of Capitalism* (New York: Basic Books, 1996), 72.

5. Pierre-Michel Menger, *Portrait de l'artiste en travailleur* (Paris: Seuil, 2003).

6. Measures to prevent these excesses have been proposed: paying back bonuses in the event of losses, as Citigroup has done, refusing

to pay the fifteen million dollars in exceptional bonuses to its CEO Vikram Pandit, or fighting against predatory funds that destroy industrial strategies and keep money from being invested in long-term projects. "The financiers' interests are diametrically opposite those of workers and employees, because the less they pay for labor and raw materials the higher their profits will be." Laurence Fontaine, *Le marché: Histoire et usages d'une conquête sociale* (Paris: Gallimard, 2014), 266 ff. In France, the heads of the EDC (Entrepreneurs et Dirigeants Chrétiens) union decreased their gross salaries by 20 percent after the economic crisis in solidarity with their employees.

7. Robert Frank thinks that only one-third of the richest Americans owe their fortunes to an inheritance. *Richistan: A Journey through the American Wealth Boom and the Lives of the New Rich* (New York: Crown, 2007), 107.

8. Nietzsche, *Thus Spoke Zarathustra*, trans. A. Del Caro (Cambridge: Cambridge University Press, 2006), 219.

9. Quoted in Albert Hirschman, *The Passions and the Interests: Political Arguments for Capitalism before Its Triumph* (Princeton, NJ: Princeton University Press, 1997).

10. Andrew Carnegie, quoted in Marc Abélès, *Les nouveaux riches: Un ethnologue dans la Silicon Valley* (Paris: Odile Jacob, 2002), 75–76. Andrew Carnegie, *The "Gospel of Wealth" and Other Writings* (London: Penguin Classics, 2006), 12.

11. *Le Monde*, April 27, 2013.

12. The pseudonyms of two French artists, the photographer Pierre Commoy and the painter Gilles Blanchard, whose work is often described as kitsch.

13. Karl Marx, *The Economic and Philosophic Manuscripts of 1844 and the Communist Manifesto*, trans. M. Milligan (New York: Prometheus, 1988). See also, Luc Boltanski and Eve Chiapello, "À l'épreuve de la critique artiste," *Le nouvel esprit du capitalisme* (Paris: Gallimard, 1999), 501 ff.

14. Daniel Bell, *The Cultural Contradictions of Capitalism* (New York: Basic Books, 1996), 81.

15. Luc Ferry, *L'innovation destructrice* (Paris: Plon, 2014), 104. See also Ferry's *L'invention de la vie de bohème* (Paris: Cercle d'art, 2012) and Pierre-Michel Menger's very pertinent *Portrait de l'artiste en travailleur.*

16. It has been calculated that the criminal underworld siphons off almost one hundred billion euros annually from the Italian economy. David Wolman, *The End of Money: Counterfeiters, Techies, Dreamers—and the Coming Cashless Society* (New York: Di Capo, 2012).

17. Jacques de Saint-Victor, *Un pouvoir invisible: Les mafias et la société démocratique* (Paris: Gallimard, 2012), 256.

18. Jacques de Saint Victor (ibid., 341) adopts the hypothesis according to which there is a close relationship between the capitalist ethos and the Mafioso ethos, both of which are based on the culture of risk and competitive destruction.

19. John Maynard Keynes, First Annual Report of the Arts Council (1945–1946). Quoted in Zygmunt Bauman, *Les riches font-ils le bonheur de tous?* (Paris: Armand Colin, 2014), 54.

20. See David Wolman's eloquent plea in *The End of Money,* and Jean-Claude Carrière, *L'Argent, sa vie, sa mort* (Paris: Odile Jacob, 2014), in which the author, who makes Money speak in the first person, foresees its imminent death.

21. John Maynard Keynes, "Economic Possibilities for our Grandchildren" (1930), in *Revisiting Keynes: Economic Possibilities for our Grandchildren,* ed. L. Pecchi and G. Piga (Cambridge, MA: MIT Press, 2010), 157.

22. Robert Musil, *Essais* (Paris: Seuil, 1978), 296.

23. Edith Wharton, *The House of Mirth* (1905; repr. New York: Norton, 1990).

24. According to a study carried out by Wealth-X and UBS, there will be 3,800 billionaires in the world by 2020. For the most part,

modern millionaires have not inherited their wealth; 81 percent of them have built their own fortunes. According to Oxfam, in 2016 the accumulated assets of the richest 1 percent will be greater than those of the remaining 99 percent of humanity. This 1 percent nonetheless represents 73 million individuals, including 2,325 billionaires. The richest 10 percent of Chinese control 75 percent of their country's total assets.

25. Quoted in Andrew Ross Sorkin, "Robert Diamond's Next Life," *New York Times*, May 5, 2013.

26. Frank, *Richistan*, 35.

27. Annie Cohen-Solal, in Pascal Morand, *Les religions et le luxe* (Paris: IFM, 202), 67.

28. Robert Frank, *La course au luxe* (Geneva: Markus Haller, 2010), 25.

29. Frank, *Richistan*, chap. 7.

30. Frank, *La course au luxe*.

31. Philippe Ariès, *Essais sur l'histoire de la mort en Occident du Moyen Age à nos jours* (Paris: Points-Seuil, 1977), 83.

32. Quoted in Norman O. Brown, *Life against Death: The Psychoanalytical Meaning of History*, 2nd ed. (1950; repr. Middletown, CT: Wesleyan University Press, 1985), 287.

33. Aristotle, *Nicomachean Ethics*, Bk. 4, chap. 1, 1120a.

34. "La nouvelle puissance des riches," *L'Express*, July 23–29, 2014.

35. In addition to her donations of several million dollars to hospitals and charitable organizations, Leona Helmsley, who died in 2007, bequeathed twelve million dollars to her dog Trouble, to ensure that he had a comfortable old age (the amount was later reduced to two million dollars). Her legacy was described by the magazine *Fortune* as one of the 101 stupidest moments of the year.

36. In February 2015 the rating agency Standard & Poor's was sentenced to pay a fine of 1.5 billion dollars for having set up "a system intended to deceive investors" and for having presented toxic products as secure investments.

37. Max Weber, *The Protestant Ethic and the Spirit of Capitalism*, 201, n. 1.

38. Guy de Maupassant, *Bel-Ami*, 356.

39. Laurence Fontaine, *Le marché: Histoire et usages d'une conquête sociale* (Paris: Gallimard, 2014), 303.

9. GETTING RICH IS NOT A CRIME

1. Jean Delumeau, *La peur en Occident,* (Paris: Fayard, 1978), 533 ff.
2. Regarding financial transactions, Niall Ferguson, *The Ascent of Money: A Financial History of the World* (London: Penguin, 2009). For the discussion on the ambivalences of property ownership and the importance of work for women, also see ibid. Setting up government institutions as in developed nations is one of the solutions proposed by Abhijit Banerjee and Esther Duflo in *Repenser la pauvreté* (Paris: Seuil, 2012).
3. Jonathan Crary, interview in *Libération,* June 21–22, 2014.
4. Charles Péguy, *L'argent* (1913; repr: Paris: Gallimard, 1932).
5. John Stuart Mill, *Principles of Political Economy* (1886), quoted in Robert Skidelsky and Edward Skidelsky, *How Much Is Enough?: Money and the Good Life* (London: Allen Lane, 2012), 54.
6. Yvonne Quilès, "Le rêve des pauvres," in *L'argent: Pour une rehabilitation morale,* ed. Antoine Spire (Paris: Autrement, 1992), 167 ff.
7. This is advocated by Christine Lazerges, the president of the Commission, and by ATD Quart Monde. Jean-Christophe Sarrot, Bruno Tardieu, and Marie-France Zimmer, *En finir avec les idées fausses sur les pauvres et la pauvreté* (Paris: ATD Quart Monde/L'Atelier, 2015), 214.
8. According to the United Nations, over the last three decades, the proportion of the world population living in extreme poverty— that is, on less than $1.25 a day—has decreased from 47 percent in 1990 to 22 percent in 2010. The UN hopes, through its Millennium Development Goals, to completely eradicate extreme poverty by 2030. This is a global program involving all the factors of poverty, health, food supplies, agricultural and industrial production, consumption, and financial management.
9. Walter Lippmann, *Drift and Mastery* (New York: Mitchell Kennerley, 1914), xvi, quoted in Richard Sennett, *The Corrosion of*

Character: The Personal Consequences of Work in the New Capitalism (New York : Norton, 1998), 119.

10. "The Gujarati Way: Secrets of the World's Best Business People," *Economist*, December 19, 2015.

11. Mohsin Hamid, *How to Get Filthy Rich in Rising Asia* (London: Riverhead, 2013), 4.

12. Jen Weiczner, "This Is How Much It Costs to Eat Lunch with Warren Buffett," *Fortune*, June 1, 2015.

13. Remark attributed to Alan Greenspan by Rupert Cornwell, "Alan Greenspan: The Buck Starts Here," *Independent*, April 27, 2003, quoting an unspecified Capitol Hill hearing. On other attributions, see https://en.wikiquote.org/wiki/Alan_Greenspan#Misattributed.

14. G. F. W. Hegel, *La Raison dans l'Histoire*, (Paris: Union générale d'éditions, 1965), 113.

15. Examples quoted in Viviana A. Zelizer, *The Social Meaning of Money: Pin Money, Paychecks, Poor Relief, and Other Currencies* (Princeton, NJ: Princeton University Press, 1997).

16. Pascal Bruckner, *La mélancolie démocratique*, (Paris: Seuil, 1990).

17. Fernand Braudel, *La dynamique du capitalisme* (Paris: Flammarion, 1988), 70–71.

18. Ibid., 64.

19. Skidelsky and Skidelsky, *How Much Is Enough?*, 181.

20. Immanuel Kant, "Perpetual Peace," in *Kant: Political Writings*, trans. H. S. Reiss (Cambridge: Cambridge University Press), 112.

21. A few examples among many others: in 2015, tax fraud became a criminal offense in Switzerland, and banking secrecy will be ended by 2017, when the automatic exchange of banking data among states will go into effect. The French economist Gabriel Zucman, in *La richesse cachée des nations* (Paris: Seuil, 2013) proposes to establish a worldwide financial registry analogous to the land registry, listing all the stocks and bonds in circulation with the names of their beneficiaries.

22. Michel Aglietta and André Orléan, *La monnnaie: Entre violence et confiance* (Paris: Odile Jacob, 2002).

23. Ferguson, *Ascent of Money,* 39–40.
24. See for example Denis Kessler, "Quelle est la valeur économique de la vie humaine," in *Comment penser l'argent?,* ed. Roger-Pol Droit, 310 ff.
25. Ibid., 321.

10. THE HAND THAT TAKES, THE HAND THAT GIVES BACK

1. Jean Starobinski, *Largesse* (Paris: Gallimard, 2007), 181–182.
2. Augustine, *The City of God,* trans. M. Dods (New York: Random House 1949), chap. 10.
3. Jean Delumeau, *La peur en Occident* (Paris: Fayard, 1978), 534–537.
4. Jacques Ellul, *L'homme et l'argent* (Paris: Presses bibliques universitaires, 1978), 144, quoted in Ilana Reiss-Schimmel, *La psychanalyse et l'argent* (Paris: Odile Jacob, 1993), 10.
5. Andrew Carnegie, *The "Gospel of Wealth" and Other Writings* (London: Penguin Classics, 2006), 12.
6. Ibid., 10, 11.
7. Marc Abélès, *Les nouveaux riches: Un ethnologue dans la Silicon Valley* (Paris: Odile Jacob, 2002), 77–78. When he died, Carnegie left his family only fifteen million dollars, hardly 5 percent of his fortune.
8. Emile Zola, *L'argent,* 68–69, 131.
9. In John Ensor Harr and Peter J. Johnson, *The Rockefeller Century* (New York: Charles Scribner's Sons, 1988), 51–52.
10. Paul Veyne's *Le pain et le cirque* (Paris: Seuil, 1976) is the standard work on this subject. Translated by B. Pearce, *Bread and Circuses: Historical Sociology and Political Pluralism* (London: Penguin/Allen Lane, 1990).
11. The story is told in Georges Gusdorf, *Kierkegaard* (Paris: Seghers, 1963), 29–30.
12. Simon Schama, *The Embarrassment of Riches: An Interpretation of Dutch Culture in the Golden Age* (New York: Knopf, 1987), 347, 330. This edict was not abolished until 1658.
13. Honoré de Balzac, *Splendeurs et misères des courtisanes,* 172.

14. On this subject, see Jean Starobinski's definitive book, *Largesse*.
15. Peter Sloterdijk, *Repenser l'impôt* (Paris: Maren Sell, 2012), 278, 239–240.
16. Abélès, *Les nouveaux riches*, 35.
17. Alexandre Lambelet, *La philanthropie* (Paris: Presses de Sciences Po, 2014), 81–82.
18. Pierre Grimal, preface to *La vie heureuse*, by Seneca (Paris: Gallimard, 1996), 26.
19. Montesquieu, *De l'esprit des lois* (Paris: Garnier-Flammarion, 1993), 5:18.
20. As early as the fifteenth century in Perugia and Siena, the Franciscan and Recollect monks invented pawnshops to counter questionable charity and lethal usury by providing a kind of virtuous loans for the least well-off. The first pawnshop in France was established by Théophraste Renaudot in 1837.
21. Aristotle, *Nicomachean Ethics*, Bk. 9, chap. 7, *The Complete Works of Aristotle: The Revised Oxford Translation*, vol. 2, ed. Jonathan Barnes (Princeton, NJ: Princeton University Press, 1984), 1168a.
22. Guy de Maupassant, *La parure* (1884; repr. Paris: Livre de Poche, 1995).
23. David Wolman, *The End of Money: Counterfeiters, Techies, Dreamers—and the Coming Cashless Society* (New York: Di Capo, 2012), 86.
24. Niall Ferguson, *The Ascent of Money: A Financial History of the World* (London: Penguin, 2009), 64–65.
25. Jacques-Bénigne Bossuet, "Sermon sur la passion de Notre-Seigneur," in *Sermon sur la mort et autres sermons* (Garnier-Flammarion, 1970), 152 ff.

Index

accounting, 20, 98, 166
activities that can be bought, 82–83
admiration, 126–127
adversity (difficult times), 117–124, 234–235. *See also* suffering
advertising, 74, 83, 169
Africa, 196, 197, 199, 207
aging, 4, 128, 138, 207, 253n14. *See also* retirement
Alberti, Leon Battista, 25, 242n45
Amazon, 100, 185
ambition, 195
America (United States): capitalism and, 190; credit and debt and, 113–115, 232; debt and, 232; feminism and, 255n9; food and, 130; foundations and, 227–228; France vs., 41–42; generosity and, 189; gold standard and, 247n1; Great Depression and, 203; Gujaratis and, 197; inherited fortunes and, 258n7; marriage and, 142, 149; money as master and, 75; parvenus and, 199; philanthropy and, 226; poverty vs. wealth and, 193, 194; Protestantism/capitalism and, 24, 34–35; richest 1 percent of, 248n7, 249n16; sex and, 141, 156; sex vs. money and, 64–65; social bonds and, 88; spiritual money and, 60–75; success and, 46; tips and, 215; value of Americans, 207;

violence and, 102; virtue and money and, 54–55; wealth and, 71. *See also* Dodd-Frank Act (U.S.); Scrooge McDuck *and other Americans;* Tea Party; U.S. Supreme Court; Wall Street
American Revolution, 125–126
Amsterdam, 94–95. *See also* Holland
Anglicanism, 212
anticapitalism, 92–93
anti-Semitism, 131–133
Antwerp (Belgium), 197
Apple, 100
Arendt, Hannah, 175
L'Argent, sa vie, sa mort (Carrière), 259n20
Argentina, 232
Aristophanes, 10, 94, 141, 194
Aristotle, 12–13, 14–15, 73, 118, 184, 193, 230
artistic/literary trades, 52, 105–107, 170–175, 176, 178, 216. *See also* patrons; royalties
asceticism, 120
Asia, 196, 197, 199
Au bonheur des dames (Zola), 142
Augustine of Hippo, 14–15, 17, 26, 32, 81–82, 201, 213
Aurelius, Marcus, 144
Austen, Jane, 80, 148–149, 150
Austria, 58. *See also* Steiner, Rudolf *and other Austrians*

Index

Bach, J. S., 23
Badiou, Alain, 56, 92
Balibar, Étienne, 92
Balzac, Honoré de: bourgeois values
and, 166; on charity, 224; debt and,
80; financialization of world and,
81; on fortunes / crime, 43; on
marriage, 149–150; on parvenus,
198; on power, 186–187; on
prostitution, 159; on selling
love / sex, 137, 156–157, 254n4
Banerjee, Abhijit, 261n2
bank data, 253n10
bank notes (currency), 56–59, 60,
61–62, 137, 177. *See also* coins
Bankruptcy Code (US), 232
banks and bankers: Holland and,
221–222; Jews as, 132; language of,
168; organized crime and, 175;
regulation and, 205; Swish, 172.
See also Barclay's Bank *and other
banks;* finance; repentant trader
Barclay's Bank, 179
Barks, Carl, 28
Basil of Caesarea, 239
Bataille, Georges, 187
Baudelaire, Charles, 178
Bavarian Council Republic, 137
Beaumarchais, 11, 216
beauty: art and, 173; consumption
and, 179; culture and, 134; of
giving, 217; good life and, 134; love
and, 136, 138; money and, 29, 68,
189; poverty and, 48; quantification
and, 97–98; religion and, 22, 23; of
worn things, 209
Beauvoir, Simone de, 109
Beck, Ulrich, 62–63

Becker, Gary, 16, 149, 255n9
beggars, 34, 212–215. *See also*
mendicants
Bel-Ami (Maupassant), 138, 156
Belfort, Jordan, 120–121
Belle de jour (Kessel), 159
Besancenot, Olivier, 92
Bettencourt, Mme., 215–216
Bettencourt-Meyers, Françoise, 45
Bhutan, 118
billionaires, 259n24
"Bin Ladens," 58, 247n36
Blanchard, Gilles, 173, 258n12
Bloch, Marc, 50
Bloy, Léon, 44, 131, 133
Bohemia, 106
Bolingbroke, Henry St. John, 93
Bolsheviks, 37, 54, 95, 137, 219
Bonaventure, 28
Bonfire of the Vanities, 82
boredom (monotony), 52, 116, 134,
183, 188
Bossuet, Jacques-Bénigne, 31, 233
Boudu sauvé des eaux (film), 230
Le bourgeois (Sombart), 242n45
bourgeois values, 165–170, 172–189,
181, 186, 187
Brakni, Rachida, 56
brands, 87
Branson, Richard, 172
Braudel, Fernand, 25, 187
Brazil, 196
Breaking Bad (TV series), 104
Brecht, Bertolt, 101
Britain, 62, 75. *See also* Europe
Buddenbrooks (Mann), 187
Buffett, Warren, 185, 200, 201, 223
Bulgaria, 24

overview, 110–111; poverty and, 192; quantification and, 96; real estate loans, 20; regulation and, 188–189; repayment and, 231–236; virtuous, 264n20. *See also* interest; usury
Crédit Lyonnais bank, 56
crime. *See* values (morality) (virtue) (crime)
crisis of 2007–2008, 245n16
Crosby, Alfred W., 241n34
culture: America and, 71; bank notes and, 62; bourgeois values and, 167; France and, 52–56, 59, 71; the market and, 87; meaning of life and, 68; wealth and, 170. *See also* artistic/literary trades; civilization

Dalí, Salvador, 173
Dante, 14, 94, 250n21
death, 33–34, 91, 130, 207–208, 233. *See also* heirs
death instinct, 183
debt. *See* credit and debt
De Gaulle, Charles, 45, 49
democracy: capitalism and, 204; charity and, 227–228; civilizing money and, 235; contradiction of, 129–130; gambling and, 161–162; lack of money and, 129–130; middle classes and, 193; money and, 86; parvenus and, 201–202; prostitution and, 157. *See also* equality; France *and other democracies;* freedom
Deng Xiaoping, 53
dental care, 51
Depardieu, Gérard, 47
desire for money: corruption vs., 53; Dante on, 250n21; denunciation of, 196; in itself, 40; overview, 2–3; satiety and, 127–128; well-being and, 130
desires: anarchy of, 158; capitalism and, 89; conservatism/liberalism and, 88–89; credit and, 110; detachment and, 129–130, 133–134, 144–146; instantaneous satisfaction of, 115; marriage and, 140; narcissism and, 181; 1960s and, 175, 203; poverty and, 53; redirection of, 203; 2008 crisis and, 114–115; wealth and, 130. *See also* desire for money; love and sex
destiny, 112, 160
detachment, 129–130, 133–134
"The Diamond as Big as the Ritz" (Fitzgerald), 152
diamond industry, 197
Diamond Jr., Robert, 179
Dickens, Charles, 190
dignity, 12, 31–40, 73, 97, 98, 157–158
discreet servant complex, 73–74
discrimination, 195–196
dispensations, 20
diversity, 45–46
Dodd-Frank Act (U.S.), 123
Dostoevsky, Fyodor, 109, 114, 160
double-entry bookkeeping, 98. *See also* accounting
Drahi, Patrick, 245n20
Dray, Julien, 245n22
drug cartels, 104
Duby, Georges, 224
Duchêne, Laurence, 245n16
Duflo, Esther, 261n2

Index

Parsees, 26, 29
parvenus, 196–199, 201–202
Pascal, Blaise, 18, 160, 166
passions, 2–3
patrons, 11, 187, 189, 216
pawnshops, 264n20
peacock throne, 241n38
Péguy, Charles, 44, 195
Penia, 10
Le père Goriot (Balzac), 43
Persian Gulf states, 251n24
philanthropy. *See* charity and
generosity; patrons
philosophers. *See* Plato; sophists;
other philosophers and schools
physicians, 51
Pierre and Gilles, 173, 258n12
Piketty, Thomas, 251n36
Pilgrim's Progress (Bunyan), 17–18, 235
Pinçon-Charlot, Michel and
Monique, 49
Plato, 10–11, 97, 171, 234. *See also*
Socrates
Plutus (Aristophanes), 10
political correctness, 196
politics, 63, 74, 102
Pol Pot, 95
Poor Richard's Almanac (Franklin), 85
poverty: advertising and, 83;
American God and, 66; attitudes
toward, 114; Bossuet on, 33;
Calvinism and, 34–35; desire for
wealth and, 53; dignity and, 31–40;
four stages of, 190–194; Franklin
on, 66; governments and, 212–215;
Hollande on, 51, 246n27; Machia-
velli on, 222; of others, 126; praise
of, 194; race and, 66; simulated,

144–146; suffering and, 196; world
percentages, 261n8. *See also* charity
and generosity (philanthropy);
detachment; poverty vs. wealth
poverty vs. riches: crime vs. virtue
and, 190. *See also* inequality
poverty vs. wealth: America and, 70;
charity and, 229–230; communism
and, 191; envy and, 124–127; France
and, 69; gap between, 192;
happiness and, 115–116; labor and,
116, 193–194; lack of money and,
129–130; marriage and, 143, 146,
151–153; middle classes and, 193;
overview, 10–14; power and,
178–181; religions and, 22–23,
190–191, 193; social ascent and,
169–170; taxes and, 184–187; virtue
and, 235; well-being and, 194. *See
also* envy; labor; parvenus; poverty;
values (morality); wealth
power, 93–98, 100, 178–181, 186–187,
196, 229
predestination (fatalism) (fate),
25–26, 145, 151, 161, 197, 235
Preobrazhensky, Yevgeni, 38
price, 97, 207–209
pride, 145
prisons, 20
profits, 92, 102, 206, 219, 248n15,
258n6. *See also* entrepreneurial
spirit; speculation; trader, repentant
prostitution, 157–159, 162, 257n36
Protestantism, 23, 25, 29–30, 34, 66,
69, 72, 74–75. *See also* Calvinism;
Lutheranism; puritanism;
Reformation
Proudhon, Pierre-Joseph, 43, 71

trader, repentant, 120–123
traders, 46. *See also* finance; stock
   market
transparency, 55
Trierweiler, Valérie, 51
Trollope, Anthony, 198
Trotsky, Leon, 38
tulip mania, 95, 188–189
2008 crisis: American anger and, 46;
   beggars and, 214; capitalism and,
   204–205; corruption and, 123,
   254n22; debt and, 231–232; desires
   and, 114–115; economists on, 118, 188;
   Greek crisis / Tea Party and, 245n16

UN, 227
United States. *See* America
universal minimum income, 116–117
U.S. Supreme Court, 91
usury, 15, 33, 140, 183, 206, 264n20
Utopia (More), 37

Valéry, Paul, 105
value (monetary). *See* price
value (worthiness), 154. *See also* dignity
values (morality) (virtue) (crime):
   America and, 54–55; Aristotle on,
   13; bourgeois, 165–189, 173–174, 186;
   capitalism and, 89–93, 98–99,
   204–205, 210; commercialization
   and, 83, 103–104; Franklin and,
   84–85; Italy and, 259; love and sex
   and, 90, 94; organized, 173–175;
   overview, 89–93; poverty vs. wealth
   and, 235; profits and, 206; public,
   222–223. *See also* corruption;
   dignity; gangsters; love and sex;
   Mafia; poverty vs. wealth; taboos

Vanderbilt, Cornelius, 179–180
Vatican, 19, 23–24, 196, 241n41,
   241n43
Veenhoven, Ruut, 253n10
Venezuela, 174
vengeance, 96
Vergunst, Floris, 253n10
Verneuil, Henri, 252n1
Viansson-Ponté, Pierre, 52
Villon, François, 128
violence, 96, 102
Virgil, 27
Virgin Mary, 58
virtue. *See* values (morality) (virtue)
   (crime)
Une voix sur Israël (Claudel), 44–45
Voltaire, 42–43, 56, 187

Wallerstein, Immanuel, 92, 93
Wall Street, 69, 188
Warhol, Andy, 61
wars, 100, 102
wealth: America and, 41–42, 69,
   71; culture and, 170; as curse,
   218–222; disaster and, 188–189;
   duties of, 202–206; Europe and,
   72; France and, 48, 72, 245n22;
   Franklin on, 85; management of,
   12–13; narcissism and, 178–181;
   petrification and, 181; social
   conventions and, 199; unbounded,
   13. *See also* charity and generosity
   (philanthropy); chrematistics;
   fortune (riches); greed; heirs;
   1 percent; poverty vs. wealth
Weber, Max, 25, 167, 170, 186, 242n45
welfare state, 205
well-being, 130, 222

West, Kanye, 1
Wharton, Edith, 81, 149, 179
"Whore of Babylon," 20–21
Wilson, Woodrow, 60
wisdom of money, 4–5, 40, 85, 129,
 232, 234–236
Wittgenstein, Ludwig, 68
Wolfe, Tom, 82
Wolfers, Justin, 253n10
The Wolf of Wall Street (film), 121
Wolman, David, 259n20
Wolsey, Thomas, 126
women, 99. *See also* love and sex;
 marriage
wonder, 134
Wurst, Conchita, 173

Yazidi girl, 251n25
Yiquian, Liu, 173

Zaoui, Pierre, 245n16
Zelizer, Viviana A., 99
Zizek, Slavoj, 92
Zola, Émile: on buying love / sex,
 79, 137, 138; on charity, 219–220,
 228–230; on envy, 124–125; on
 exploitation, 35; on marriage,
 142; on odor of money, 54; on
 parvenus, 198; on proletarians,
 190; on rich fool, 200; on
 royalties, 12
Zucman, Gabriel, 262n21
Zweig, Stefan, 58